TOMORROWMIND

TOMORROWMIND

Thriving at Work with
Resilience, Creativity,
and Connection—Now and
in an Uncertain Future

Gabriella Rosen Kellerman
and Martin Seligman

ATRIA BOOKS
New York London Toronto Sydney New Delhi

For Jesse
Gabriella Rosen Kellerman

In Memory of Aaron Temkin Beck (1921–2021)
Mentor, Friend, and Model
Martin Seligman

CONTENTS

TOMORROWMIND

Introduction

Long before he became "the human error," before computers had even entered the picture, plan A, for Graeme Payne, was the army.

Graeme grew up middle class in Christchurch, New Zealand, in the 1970s, the oldest of three. As a boy he'd relished structured activities that required him to master new skills. Rugby, an early passion, remains a pillar of family activity for Graeme and his own sons today.

In high school, Graeme joined the Army Cadets, where he quickly rose up the ranks, his discipline drawing the admiration of peers. He also nurtured a love for tinkering and building. When Ferrymead, a local historic park, received the gift of a massive anti-aircraft gun, he recruited friends to help restore it. The gleaming gun complete, Graeme used the effort's success to launch the founding of a military museum.

Not every idea met with success. A renegade foray into bagpiping ended . . . swiftly.

Graeme's father was an accountant, and so it was unsurprising when Graeme demonstrated a propensity for numbers. Thinking back, he recalls that it wasn't the math that interested him most about accounting. It was the learning. Every audit process began with discovery, the need to quickly and thoroughly understand the inner workings of a business—the flow of activities, the systems of production. Only then could you get down to numbers. Deep learning was what he loved and took to naturally. The spreadsheets, he didn't mind.

For years Graeme had planned to enlist after high school. Right before he left, however, he caught wind of a university scholarship offered by the accounting firm Arthur Young (known today as Ernst and Young). On a whim, he applied—and won. He accepted the scholarship while joining the army reserves to earn his basic training units.

"I've always embraced change," he says, reflecting on this formative, sudden pivot. "What the heck? What have you got to lose?"

Change was already coming, like it or not, for him and many other New Zealanders. After decades of agricultural boom, on the backs of which New Zealand enjoyed one of the world's highest standards of living, its long-standing wool, meat, and dairy economy had begun to wane. In its place, alongside manufacturing, the newer services sector was on the rise. Today, services account for 60% of the GDP in Canterbury, the region surrounding Christchurch.

Big changes were coming to the field of accounting, too. When Graeme started as a financial auditor for Arthur Young in Christchurch, there was a single IBM PC serving the whole office. Within a few years, each person had a so-called luggable at their desk. Older partners viewed the newfangled gadgets with suspicion, as gimmicks rather than time-savers. They preferred their "word processors"—not the electronic kind, but human beings, typically women, who would type up recorded voice memos.

Graeme, by contrast, embraced new technology. He took pleasure in understanding how the machines worked, using their programs to build graphs, lightening his workload with software that could perform calculations faster and more reliably than he could on his lined yellow pads. He spent hours teaching himself the basics of computing from books.

"I was an early adopter," he says, a half smile emerging. "I even had the Apple Newton."

Ever the leader, Graeme did his best to help others around him adapt. He and a colleague produced an instructional video on how to use a PC, which they mailed to the homes of partners for viewing on their personal VCRs. In time, Arthur Young came to value Graeme's proficiency. They asked him to create a computer training program for all of New Zealand. He did, and for the most part it worked, though some older partners continued to struggle. Graeme recalls one who, well into the email era, would have his assistant print out then read aloud each email message as it arrived.

Even for Graeme, the pace of change could be hard to keep up with. But he understood what was at stake: the very future of the firm. Outside the walls of Arthur Young, computers were rapidly transforming the businesses of its corporate clients. Auditing now meant understanding how this new technology was being incorporated into practices like data storage, payroll, and analytics. The credit industry, for example, had for a century relied on paper records: first notebooks, then storehouses full of file cards. The 1960s brought a shift to electronic records. By the 1970s and '80s, everything was on a mainframe, housed in a data center. In those days, keeping the records safe meant restricting access to these centers. A guard at the door, say, or a heavy-duty padlock.

Enter the internet.

Seemingly overnight, the world of security was turned on its head. Hackers created computer viruses that tore across unprotected networks, wreaking havoc. The threat to global industry was immediate and existential, and an entirely new sector sprung up to meet it: information security. In 1995, Citibank hired Steve Katz as chief information security officer, believed to be the first CISO—pronounced *SEE-so*—in history.

Graeme saw potential in the chaos. This new information security Wild West needed tools, and he had ideas. During a stint in Auckland, Graeme built a product called "Advisor" that could flexibly analyze different types of computer systems. At a meeting in Singapore, a like-minded US partner quickly grasped the product's value and invited Graeme to the United States to work on it. Curious, open-minded, and hungry, Graeme moved eight thousand miles first to Cleveland and then to Atlanta, to open Ernst and Young's inaugural security consulting practice. He was not yet an expert in the field—but then, no one was. The tides were shifting too quickly, the problems too new for old wisdom. A wave of opportunity was cresting. Graeme grabbed his surfboard and rode.

Today the CISO is a standard position at any major corporation. Forty-one percent of corporate boards see cybersecurity experience as a key qualification for overall directorship. By 2024, the cybersecurity market will reach $300 billion. A worldwide shortage of cybersecurity professionals means 2.9 million positions sit unfilled, while financial losses due to cyberattacks are growing 62% annually, a loss of *$1 trillion* in 2020 alone.

By 2011, Graeme was ready for a new kind of change.

Now he *was* an expert in his field. He'd been traveling the world as a security consultant for fifteen years, and life as a road warrior was beginning to grind him down. His two boys at home in Atlanta needed more guidance in their many (structured, skill-based) activities.

When the offer came to join Equifax as vice president for IT risk and compliance, he jumped. Here was exactly the type of stable, in-house role he was craving. Though the firm was mature, there was still plenty of building and fixing to be done. By 2017, Equifax held records of one billion consumers, one hundred million small and medium businesses, one hundred million employees, $20 trillion in property data, and $20 trillion in wealth data. That August, during an address at the University of Georgia, CEO Richard Smith put it this way: "If you think of the largest library in the world—the Library of Congress—well, Equifax handles twelve hundred times that amount of data every day."

With numbers that large, things went wrong. Often.

In March 2015, for example, Katie Manning, a resident of Portland, Maine, arrived home from work to find her mailbox bursting with letters from Equifax—three hundred in all. Each was addressed personally to her but contained the complete credit history, social security number, and bank account information of a stranger.

Equifax asked Graeme to investigate. He soon learned that Katie wasn't the only one; other people had received hundreds or even thousands of letters containing strangers' private data. Because the reports were on paper, Equifax dispatched teams to retrieve them in person. One recipient in Washington, DC, became paranoid and refused to answer the door. Instead he had the team meet him at night on a public street. At the appointed hour, the Equifax agents had to flash their headlights three times, like spies in a thriller. Only then did the man hand over the reports.

Vulnerabilities and bad actors were always changing, and breaches were more common than Graeme would have liked. With each incident, Graeme's team's goal was to understand, correct, and learn. No one, to his recollection, was laid off.

―――――――

In July 2017, Graeme spent the weekend of his fifty-fourth birthday with his wife and boys, outdoors in the scorching Georgia sun. That Sunday he came home to a series of missed calls from his own CISO, Susan Mauldin.

The news was not good. A security breach had targeted a piece of software Graeme managed. The full extent of the breach was as yet unknown, but it was all-hands-on-deck.

Graeme's title at this time was chief information officer for Global Corporate Platforms. Under his purview was the ACIS Portal, a software system used to log records of consumers who wanted to dispute credit reports, report identify theft, initiate a security freeze, or request a copy of their records. A piece of software known as Apache Struts connected ACIS to the database.

Four months before the breach was discovered, 429 Equifax employees, including Graeme, had received email notice of a vulnerability in Apache Struts. The appropriate teams had investigated and applied a patch they believed would suffice.

They were wrong. Hackers broke in and stole data for 148 million US consumers and fifteen million British consumers, including names, social security numbers, home addresses, and driver's license numbers. It has been called the most expensive data breach in history.

Amid the public fallout, several senior employees were let go or sent out for early retirement.

On Monday, October 2, 2017, at a meeting with HR that he thought was about something else entirely, Graeme was fired.

The next day, former CEO Richard Smith testified before Congress. He blamed the breach on a combination of "technological failure" and "human error," attributing the latter to a single individual. Senator Al Franken jokingly dubbed this person "Gus": "Why is the security of 145 million Americans' personal information all in the hands of one guy? Why is it all up to Gus?"

Graeme, suddenly unemployed and watching the congressional session live on TV at home, knew they were talking about him. He was Gus. Soon enough his real name was leaked, along with an epithet: "the human error."

The dubiousness of pinning a systemic breakdown on one person was clear enough, even to Congress. As stated in one congressional report, "A senior Equifax official was terminated for failing to forward an email, an action he was not directed to do, the day before former CEO Richard Smith testified in front of Congress. This type of public relations–motivated maneuver seems gratuitous against the backdrop of all the facts."

Modest dissemination of this more reasonable counternarrative did little to undo what had rapidly become the accepted reality: Graeme Payne stood for everything that had gone wrong.

The bitter irony was that, up until then, through the lens of our current world of work, Graeme had done everything *right* in his career.

He had identified opportunity early. His curiosity, appetite for learning, and agility allowed him to quickly establish expertise in a booming new field. Time after time, he drew motivation and energy from the meaning he found in mastering new skills and building creative products. Through careful prospection, he took calculated risks, then pushed forward through challenge after challenge.

In short: Graeme Payne had a Tomorrowmind.

And somehow, even so, in 2017 Graeme found himself at the edge of an abyss.

Getting fired feels terrible. It harms our psychological well-being and physical health in a million ways. Pile on top of that the extremely public nature of Graeme's firing, and it's no wonder that he struggled mightily. In those months, Graeme felt deeply the fear that would have in fact deterred most of us at so many points earlier in his journey.

"When the congressional report was released and my name was published all over the internet, I really thought that that was the end of my professional career," Graeme says. "I started to wonder about my future job prospects. How would my association with Equifax be viewed by prospective employers?"

For many senior Equifax leaders, that *was* the end. CISO Susan Mauldin hasn't been heard from publicly since her post-breach resignation. CEO Richard Smith and CIO Dave Webb have likewise faded from view. In 2018, the company laid off a whole new slate of employees—hundreds more people forced to start over, now with a stain on their résumé.

Faced with that, how many of us would feel paralyzed? How many of us would want to give up?

Graeme Payne chose another way.

From the depths of his despair, he began reaching out to friends and former colleagues. He'd helped a lot of people over the years, and they were eager to reciprocate. "I was encouraged by friends and colleagues to look at this in a more positive light. They told me that I really had a lot to offer to others, having been through one of the largest data breaches in history."

The same skill set that had led Graeme to the heights of his career—his resilience, his cognitive agility, his prospection, his creativity, the meaning he found in gaining new skills—now brought him back from the edge. He'd always run toward challenge and the opportunity to gain mastery amid chaos. Drawing courage from his strengths and his social network, he began piecing his career back together, brick by brick.

What once looked like an unmitigated personal catastrophe has today transformed into a successful new chapter in cybersecurity consulting. Graeme's friends were correct. Companies want to learn from someone who knows firsthand what to do and what not to do. Graeme advises corporate boards and senior executives on cybersecurity readiness. He continues to build new capabilities and offerings to help his consultancy grow into new marketplaces. "Some of our best lessons in life come from our mistakes," Graeme advises. Today he wears the label of "the human error" with ironic pride.

The two of us, Marty and Gabriella, came together around the time Graeme lost his job at Equifax. The dramatic challenges posed by our new world of work—the rapid pace of technological change; the overnight disruption of entire industries by new upstarts; the rise of uncertainty and volatility in every global market—had already come to consume our interests. We have both devoted our careers to improving psychological well-being and felt alarmed by people's inability to rise to these mounting challenges. And this was all years before the COVID-19 pandemic, which in 2020 spun a rising storm into a full-on tornado. Roughly half the US workforce struggles with burnout. Seventy-six percent see workplace stress negatively impacting their personal relationships. Excessive stress at work accounts for $190 billion in healthcare costs each year, plus hundreds of thousands of unnecessary deaths. At work, where we spend the majority of our waking hours on this planet, we are too unhappy, too tired, and too sick.

A great deal of ink has been spilled on the topic of how the so-called future of work will change business. But how will it change *us*? And how can we make sure we come out on top? We've now partnered with hundreds of companies, employing millions of workers around the globe to face these questions.

This book will share our answers. We begin by grounding our understanding of today's challenges in the past. This is not the first time that our species has had to adapt to a new world of work. As we'll see in chapter 1, our brains evolved over millions of years in relationship to a specific type of work, the type our ancestors knew best: hunting, fishing, and gathering. Foraging is still the work our brains are best adapted for. The forager's brain is well suited to a five-hour workday, to communal life, to the creative exploration of new terrain, and to an ever-present connection to nature. By about 10,000 BCE, however, that same brain had invented technologies and structures that produced our very first labor transformation, from foraging to farming. This was an immensely painful transition given the mismatch between our forager capabilities and this new life of a farmer.

Each subsequent labor transformation—first to agriculture, then industrialization, and then, today, to our technology-driven world of work—has come at a wrenching human cost. In some cases that cost has been so great that historians and anthropologists still struggle to explain how it happened. Why, as a species, would we have shifted to such alien forms of work? Forms of work that run so contrary to our native abilities that pursuing them causes human hardship? Greater collective productivity and technological sophistication have been the societal reward. But that reward has come on the backs of billions of long-suffering individuals who never reaped its benefits.

Today's transformation, a future alive and present all around us, threatens our well-being in its own unexpected new ways. As chapter 2 details, the sheer pace of change means we are now already changing or losing jobs twice as fast as at the height of industrialization. By one estimate, eight hundred million global workers will see their jobs replaced by automation by 2030. As many as 80% of us will see our wages reduced due to automation in this same period.

We know how this will play out. In the year after job displacement, death rates increase by 50–100%. Unemployment alone raises our risk of heart attack by 35%, and, along with job instability, raises the rate of nearly every major category of psychological distress—depression, anxiety, and substance abuse.

Now factor in the risks driven by the new nature of work itself. Start with the socially isolating aspects. Gone are the days of twenty-year-long colleagueship, of stable, in-person work communities that would support us throughout our careers. Average job tenure is about 2.8 years for workers aged twenty-five to thirty-four. Peers come and go, as do we, creating a historic and unnaturally fast rate of turnover in our working groups. An estimated 25–30% of the US workforce will be working remotely in the years to come. The prevalence of loneliness has doubled in the last twenty years, increasing our rates of depression, heart disease, and of all-cause mortality.

Add to that the volatility and uncertainty that we must navigate—individually and as organizations—even under the best of circumstances. Companies find their business models disrupted overnight; the ankle-biting competitor is suddenly the industry leader. Teams learn that the product they'd spent months building is now obsolete, the group fractured into a half dozen pieces, each recycled into entirely new initiatives around the globe. Sixty-one percent of full-time employees say the stress of the modern workplace has made them sick; this tumult accounts for about 120,000 excess deaths per year in the US, and up to one million in China.

And yet.

We are not doomed.

We know this from the stories of remarkable people like Graeme. Graeme is remarkable, truly, in his ability to navigate the riptides of change so deftly, and to help those around him in the process, but he is not singular. There are other Graemes out there as well, possessing Tomorrowminds we can learn from.

And we know this now, too, and quite well, from decades of research into the science of psychological well-being and thriving.

The two of us have dedicated our lives to this science, as clinicians and as innovators. For Marty, the journey began in the 1960s at the University of Pennsylvania. His research over three decades established the conditions under which people either thrive or falter under great stress. Much to Marty's frustration, academic psychology was not yet ready to follow these studies to their logical conclusions. Yes, his findings were applied to depression treatment—call that the psychopathology lens. But their implications were even more important for how to live a more resilient, more fulfilling existence—and how to avoid those negative outcomes to begin with. By the 1990s, as we'll see in chapter 3, Marty was leading the charge for a new field of study, called positive psychology. As president of the American Psychological Association and founder of Penn's Positive Psychology Center, Marty has spent the last thirty years demonstrating that flourishing is within reach; and that in fact our potential for growth is enormous, so long as we are willing to take this science and its core principles to heart.

Gabriella, a medical doctor by training, spent the first ten years of her career in fMRI brain research, psychiatry, and public health. Like Marty, she aspired to do more than reduce psychopathology; she wanted to help large populations thrive. In 2008, she identified an opportunity to innovate more radically through behavioral health technology, a career change that had her, like so many of the individuals profiled in this book, starting over from scratch. In 2014, Gabriella pioneered one of the first tech-enabled behavioral health offerings on the market, a product that would serve millions of workers at all levels. She has since led or advised product and innovation at a wide range of companies, including as chief product officer at BetterUp, a company focused on fostering employee flourishing through virtual coaching, AI technology, and behavioral science.

In 2017, BetterUp CEO Alexi Robichaux asked Gabriella to start BetterUp Labs, a research organization focused on workplace thriving skills. The Lab partners with academics around the world and makes use of BetterUp's global development platform to measure and promote flourishing at work. Marty's lifelong work on optimism, positive emotion, social connection, and well-being made him a natural collaborator.

Important allies in this research have been forward-thinking leaders of large companies who need their people to be as productive as possible, and who understand what workers are up against: increasing psychological pressures amid an ever-accelerating pace of change. The most innovative corporate leaders have an appetite for experimentation, an orientation toward data and science, and a belief that there is a better way. These leaders will, we hope, find much helpful guidance in this book. They have also been, in many cases, direct partners in the research described here, helping to develop the knowledge base itself.

You might be a manager, an individual contributor, or a top executive. You may work the front lines of customer service in a call center, in a school or hospital, or on a manufacturing team behind the scenes. Regardless of your role, you have probably picked up this book because you understand that this topsy-turvy workplace is here to stay. You, like Graeme, have felt the urgent weight of change, and you know that it will come at you again and again, and keep on coming.

We cannot stop change. But we don't need to fall victim to it. We hope that this book will become your dog-eared, reread, personally annotated guide to flourishing as a fully human being in a world of work that's increasingly controlled by machines. We hope this knowledge will help you sprout the wings to fly higher than you ever could have imagined. The skills described here won't be developed overnight. They will take thought, practice, and commitment. In time they will function as superpowers to guide you steadily over swirling waters, to help you preserve balance and focus through a centered, empowered lens on the world. We call this thriving. This is the lived experience of work that we all deserve, and which we can all achieve.

Consider the case of Graeme—the pivots, the highs and lows, from cadet to accountant to IT to information security guru. You may well know someone like Graeme in your own life, someone who's been through it all, career-wise, and somehow manages to land on their feet or even come out on top. These people are real. They are human, just like any of us. What makes it possible for some of us to surf these turbulent tides while so many others drown?

Our Lab's studies of thriving at work, including data from hundreds of thousands of workers in all industries around the world, have identified five psychological powers as most critical for workplace thriving in the twenty-first century:

1. Resilience and cognitive agility (**R**): The bedrock of thriving through change
2. Meaning and mattering (**M**): The motivation to propel us forward
3. Rapid rapport to build social support (**S**): The connection we need to flourish
4. Prospection (**P**): The meta-skill positioning us ahead of change
5. Creativity and innovation (**I**): Our uniquely human gift, restored to workplace prominence today after its assembly-line decline

A handy (if out of order) acronym you can use to remember these five is PRISM. Taken together, they are the five components of a Tomorrowmind—the mindset that allows us to anticipate change, plan appropriately, respond to setbacks, and achieve our full potential.

This book will describe each power in detail, including why it matters to thriving in the future of work, and how you can develop it. We weave together our own novel research with the existing literature to give you the most complete, up-to-date understanding of each skill.

How to Read This Book

So far, we've described the contents of chapters 1–3, all of which set the stage for an in-depth exploration of each of the PRISM powers. If those powers are what interest you most, feel free to skip ahead to chapter 4, which leads off with resilience.

Psychological resilience lets us bounce back from defeat without harm. At its best, resilience looks like antifragility: the ability to grow stronger from challenge. Recall Graeme's response to the rapid evolution of his clients' computer tools. For older partners, this new development was a threat, whereas Graeme saw an opportunity to learn new skills and use them to his advantage to open new markets. Resilience is closely related to cognitive agility—our ability to flex in and out of new ideas adeptly, balancing opportunistic scouting with focused effort. These skills form the bedrock of a psychologically healthy approach to the volatility of our new world of work. Thanks to decades of scientific research, including our own, we know that these skills can be cultivated and taught.

Resilience describes *how* we bounce back from change. Chapter 5 takes us into the *why*. Reinventing ourselves in role after role, as we will all need to do, requires great effort. The motivation for reinvention will come from our sense of meaning and purpose. How do we stay connected to our professional "why" in a world of constantly changing "whats"? Graeme leaned hard into his why as a builder and creator of value for many years. In his darkest hour, he saw the opportunity to turn his ghastly experience into a positive by applying his hard-won learnings in service of new clients. Understanding meaning and purpose has led us to the newer concept of mattering, which offers a more concrete and actionable framework. We all want to matter, and with the right tools, we can cultivate this sense, both as individuals and as organizations.

It was also in his darkest hours that Graeme discovered how critical social support is to professional success. But what does it mean to cultivate relationships successfully in our lonely, ever-shuffling, often remote workplace lives? Chapters 6 and 7 introduce rapid rapport, a social skill that we will all need to become expert at. As teams form and dissolve and reconstitute, spanning continents and languages and cultures and diverse skills, we need to quickly build trusting and meaningful relationships with our new coworkers, for the good of our well-being and for the quality of our work. On the one hand, such rapid relationship building is not natural to our ancient brains. On the other, we know a great deal from psychology and neuroscience about shortcuts that make this achievable.

In chapter 8 we arrive at prospection: our ability to imagine and plan for the future. Prospection is *the* meta-skill for today's workers. In an era of rapid change, we need every bit of edge we can get in anticipating what is to come. Skilled prospection confers advantages in our careers and in our well-being. We'll examine what prospection is and how it works and offer tools to help us become better prospectors.

A specific form of prospection being demanded more and more of the workforce is creativity. Gone are the days of "creative departments." Chapter 9 dissects what it means to live in an era where *everyone* is expected to be a creative. We'll get deep into the brain science of creativity and break down what we know about how individuals, teams, and organizations can foster greater innovation. We'll also widen the lens on creativity to show how it can take different forms. Recall how much of Graeme's success came not only from embracing change but also from evolving new solutions to help customers. Graeme does not think of himself as a creative, per se, but as a builder who loves to learn. That mindset is available to all of us.

Our final chapter turns to the organization itself. In collaborating with leading companies over the last ten years, we have learned quite a lot about what makes some corporations successful at building employee thriving while others flop. There are clear historical and structural reasons why so many businesses default to the same inadequate solutions again and again. We propose a creative reimagining of those structures in favor of a holistic system better suited to the challenges of the future.

There is no shortage of books to be found on how and why work is changing. This book addresses, through the lens of behavioral science, why those changes are so hard for us, and how we can rise to the occasion. History is replete with lessons on the high human cost of labor transformations. The last several decades of positive psychology and neuroscience give us a unique advantage, one unavailable to our ancestors. While our brains have changed little since they first evolved, their collective scientific efforts offer us a new operating manual for how to use the same ancient neural matter to support our modern goals.

We begin at the beginning, of work and the brain itself.

CHAPTER ONE

Our Brains at Work

In the beginning, change came slowly. And it came, primarily, through the weather. Early human species faced ice ages alternating with interglacial warming at intervals of one or more millennia. Sea levels rose and fell dramatically, rendering large swaths of land sporadically habitable. The cycle was slow enough that early humans could afford to adapt the old-fashioned way: by evolving through natural selection. European Neanderthals, for example, facing chilly climates, developed shorter forearms and lower legs. Shorter limbs meant less surface area, so Neanderthals could more easily keep warm.

Something like seventy thousand years ago, however, something happened that irreversibly changed the game. The brains of one particular group of humans—*sapiens*, our ancestors—underwent profound alterations, including enlargement and rounding of the parietal and cerebellar regions. These regions contribute to planning, long-term memory, language, tool use, and self-awareness. The newly complex intelligence of *Homo sapiens* let us respond to environmental challenges in exponentially smarter, faster ways. Nothing on earth has been the same since.

Case in point: Unlike their Neanderthal neighbors in the same climates, *sapiens* still possessed the longer arms and legs of those living in the tropics. How did we keep our long limbs from freezing? Rather than wait thousands of years to evolve new body parts, *sapiens* solved the problem in a way only we could: through technology.

Outerwear, as evidenced by eyed needles, kept us warm. Fire could be produced at will, as demonstrated by rotary markings on perforated stone, a rudimentary motor used to create friction and then fire. Remains of snares and fishing traps speak to more energy-efficient forms of hunting. Our bigger, more globular brains let us work smarter, in cozy clothes with neat traps and a fire crackling nearby.

Best of all, these technological innovations didn't need to be constantly reinvented. Instead, *sapiens* could communicate about them in great detail, thanks to our single most important tool: language. Complex syntactic language enabled each generation to build on the knowledge of the one before. Modern human language allowed for the exchange of abstractions, for shared imagination, for collective meaning-making and invention. It need not only describe the here and now; language could speak to all the possibilities of the future.

Beneath these breakthroughs—linguistic; industrial; domestic— lay a common set of cognitive skills uniquely ours. Generating and understanding long sentences, plotting out snares, and fashioning coats from rawhide all require working memory, planning in steps, and the ability to mentally transcend the here and now. These advantages allowed *sapiens* to "win," overcoming the harsh conditions that snuffed out every other early human species.

You're alive to read this thanks to your amazing brain—a three-pound, pale pink, convoluted football of flesh, processing these words under a helmet of calcium—and to all those amazing brains that came before.

The Secret to Foraging Success: Adaptability, Generalism, and Creativity

For 95% of our history, *Homo sapiens* relied on hunting, gathering, and fishing to survive. This is the "work"—the regular set of activities needed to support oneself—that our brains evolved to do. It's a hunter-gatherer's brain you still have today, and a hunter-gatherer's brain we will need to use to succeed in our drastically different world of work.

Three key characteristics of the hunter-gatherer mind are generalism, adaptability, and creativity. Our forager ancestors were, first and foremost, *generalists*. Everyone had to know how to avoid snakes, how to tell nutritious berries from poisonous ones, how to anticipate predators, how to bait a hook, how to track prey. We lived in small, interdependent tribes, protecting one another by banding together with high levels of trust. Though we think that women did more of the gathering, and men more of the hunting and fishing, the roles were likely more fluid than not, as tribes had to shift strategies in response to fluctuating resources. Anyone who's ever been self-employed will get it: some days you're a marketer, some days an administrator, other days a customer service agent. You need to know how to do it *all*.

All of which kept work interesting, as did the fact that life was nomadic. Hunting or fishing or gathering in each new setting made for new discoveries. Each location required *adaptation*—to the climate; to the length of the day; to the terrain—while offering opportunities to develop new skills. We believe that foragers spent only three to five hours each day working. This shortened "workday" would have allowed plenty of time for learning, not to mention leisure and socializing and exploration.

In turn, leisurely exploration facilitated *creativity* and *innovation*. Our ancestors harnessed their powerful brains to yield outsized results for both individuals and the species. While Neanderthal archaeology shows little in the way of technological or cultural progress, the art and technology of *Homo sapiens* developed at a staggering clip. Weapons became more and more complex, composed of a greater number of parts. Sophisticated boats allowed us to travel as far as Australia, settling lands inaccessible to other species. Simple cave drawings blossomed into mythical creatures, rendered in ivory and ceramic.

As foragers, we were in fact so innovative that we innovated ourselves right out of that way of life. We did this in part by inventing food storage, which saved us the effort of having to continually roam the land in search of our next meal. True to *sapiens* form, once we'd invented food storage, we iterated over and over again, getting better and better. Storage techniques evolved rapidly, from the use of animal hide to kiln-fired pottery to cooling units. By 10,000 BCE, hunting and gathering had yielded to a monumentally different form of work: farming.

For several hundred thousand years, creativity, adaptability, and generalism served our species brilliantly. The next era of labor would give rise to a whole new set of problems, demanding that we swiftly repurpose the same cognitive machinery.

Agricultural Labor: When Work Became a Job

As ordinary as farming now seems to us, it's hard to overstate what a radical shift agriculture represents—arguably the most momentous labor leap in all of homonid history. Hunting, gathering, and fishing reap nature's bounty. Farming and herding require humans to *alter* nature itself. Foraging and farming are such dramatically different ways of life—with foraging carrying so many benefits to the individual, and farming so few—that archaeologists struggle to explain why we switched.

As best we can tell, agriculture arose around 10,000 BCE in the Levant, the area of Western Asia currently occupied by Turkey, Lebanon, Israel, Jordan, and Syria. Once again the weather paved the way, this time in the form of global warming. Prior to this period, ice ages had meant drought, with fresh water locked up in the polar caps and the massive sheets of ice covering Europe, Asia, and North America. Carbon dioxide had been sequestered in the frigid oceans, so even the plants struggled. Huge dust clouds blew over the world.

Although there had been warmer periods, they had been too brief and too variable to allow for farming.

At the end of the last ice age, global warming brought increased rainfall, a rise in sea level, and a large boost in the available carbon dioxide. Forests shrank, and grassy areas, with edible wild grains, expanded. Our ancestors initially harvested these wild grains, then selected those that could be domesticated.

Together with food storage, early learnings on animal and plant domestication meant formerly nomadic tribes could stay in one place for extended periods of time. Hunting and gathering coexisted with agriculture—even today there are a handful of foraging cultures still left—but as technology grew more sophisticated, settlements more elaborate, and trade between geographies more fluid, agricultural societies came to dominate the planet. Life became sedentary, populations mushroomed, and we settled into a new way of working.

What united foragers and farmers was a connection to the land. Both were at the mercy of the weather, which they used spirits and gods to understand.

The similarities ended there.

While hunters and gatherers followed nature's lead, wandering to find the resources available, agriculturalists bent nature to their needs. Farmers removed naturally occurring species and replaced them with domesticated plants. Pastoralists, too, imposed their will on evolution, breeding for docile animals, beasts of burden or beasts to eat.

Subduing nature required planning on an unprecedented scale. Foragers took what was available. They often didn't need to think further ahead than lunch on Thursday, because there was little they'd do differently if they did. Farmers, by comparison, needed to account for all the ways nature could foil them. The time horizon ranged from days (scripting the order of crop-picking) to months (timing the different harvests) to years (breeding the right plants or animals) to decades (storing up against famine).

It's no accident that the most significant architectural landmarks of agricultural societies are granaries—giant, long-term storage units for grain. Granaries are collective savings accounts. Early farmers worked together to build and then to fill them. Consider the mindset of such a laborer: *We may need this food if our fields fail. I may not be alive then, but my kids will be. Either way, I'll be happy to know that these reserves exist.*

The ability to think about the future is called *prospection*, and it's part of what made agriculture possible. This degree of future-mindedness is unique to *Homo sapiens*, the product of partnership between our extremely powerful parietal and frontal lobes. Foragers displayed prospection in, for example, the development of animal and food storage mechanisms. But it was agricultural *sapiens* that fully embraced prospection, and planning in particular, as their best defense against nature's caprice. Even today, analyses of real-time thoughts show that 74% of our prospective thinking is devoted to planning.

This immensely powerful capability, however, has a shadow side.

Foragers certainly knew *fear*, primarily in response to immediate danger: Leopard! Flash flood! Our fight-or-flight response evolved to protect us from these present-tense, highly specific threats.

By contrast, farmers would have been accustomed to *worry*. In their efforts to control nature, agricultural societies learned a lot, and quickly, about all the ways it could go wrong. Drought could wipe out a crop. Plagues could decimate your cattle—or your family. The health of early farmers was notoriously poor, due to the combination of poor nutrition and contagion from neighbors and animals. Rising population density aggravated these problems. Ancient settlements didn't know how to handle refuse and human waste, and disease spread readily.

Prolonged worry over distant and nebulous events is what we call anxiety. Unchecked, anxiety can be disastrous for individuals and societies alike. Anxiety disorders in individuals can produce such a debilitating emotional state that one is unable to work at all. At the collective level, severe anxiety can produce harmful decision-making patterns.

In anxiety we have our first example of the consequences of the mismatch between the type of work our brains evolved to do on the one hand—foraging—and the very different world of work our species created for itself. *Said differently, starting with the Agricultural Revolution, our brains were no longer designed for our work.* To succeed, we needed to lean on parts of our psychological heritage that still made sense, and to cope with those parts that put us at risk for poor outcomes.

The ability to adapt, psychologically and behaviorally, to new challenges without suffering worse consequences is known as resilience. Foragers would have needed resilience in the face of natural setbacks like an avalanche or a fire. Farmers would have had to display resilience to cope daily not only with the challenges of nature but also with the mismatch between their internal psychology and their new world of work.

Though too much anxiety is paralyzing, small doses can be beneficial for performance. Psychological resilience, as we will see in chapter 4, allows us to talk back to our worry and leverage it. Successful farmers and herders would have needed cognitive command of their anxiety, using it to help them plan without letting it run away with itself.

Another significant mismatch produced by the shift to agriculture is between our generalist forager brains and the specialization demanded by farming. Foragers needed knowledge of a broad set of skills because their environment was in constant flux. For agriculturalists—stuck in one place, engaged in the same activity for years at a stretch—it paid to acquire special expertise. If you're born into a tribe that herds goats in the foothills of the Northeastern Levant, you'd better know your subject. Farmers might focus on one species of grain or one aspect of production, like milling flour.

A gruesome illustration of specialization and its attendant monotony comes from skeletal remains found in Xinglongwa, China. Young females from this culture suffered deformed knees from a lifetime of kneeling at the grinding stone. Day after day, hour after hour, they crouched, repeating the same task as their bodies grew warped. Around the globe, studies of the skeletons of agricultural *sapiens* show all sorts of new deformities unknown to foragers, including herniated spinal discs and arthritis. Our bodies, like our brains, did not evolve to farm.

Agriculture also distorted our social structure, enabling a few successful individuals to amass enormous amounts of wealth. While agricultural societies did not begin as tyrannical regimes, most evolved to become them. Despots enforced extreme social stratification, including human slavery. Slavery was rarer among hunter-gatherers, as its widespread institution depends on social stratification, population density, and economic surplus. The consequences continue today: Worldwide, as of 2019, an estimated forty million people were subject to forced labor, including some ten million children.

By almost every metric, the move to agriculture seems like a puzzling choice. As a species, we traded engaging work and leisure time for longer hours, monotony, slavery for many, and worse nutrition for all. There must have been some who rebelled, persisting in the antiquated work of hunting. But those opportunities dwindled over time. By 100 CE, just one to two million foragers remained, compared with 250 million farmers. The vast masses were poor, with large segments detached from their labor and probably bored stiff.

Working with Machines: Industrialization and Its Discontents

We foraged for two hundred thousand years. We farmed for ten thousand or so. The next most dramatic change in our world of work took place just three hundred years ago: the Industrial Revolution.

Surviving records offer us firsthand accounts of what industrial work felt like. Among them is the 1832 testimony of a twenty-two-year-old factory worker, Matthew Crabtree, called before the British Parliament during an investigation into child labor conditions. Parliamentarian Michael Sadler championed the inquiry, bringing no fewer than eighty-nine witnesses to testify to the special committee. Here is Crabtree being interviewed by Sadler himself, an interview so vivid we quote it at length:

> Michael Sadler: At what age did you first go to work in [a factory]?
> Matthew Crabtree: Eight . . .
> MS: Will you state the hours of labour at the period when you first went to the factory, in ordinary times?
> MC: From six in the morning to eight at night . . .
> MS: When trade was brisk what were your hours?
> MC: From five in the morning to nine in the evening . . .
> MS: Will you state the effect that those long hours had upon the state of your health and feelings?
> MC: I was, when working those long hours, commonly very much fatigued at night, when I left my work; so much so that I sometimes should have slept as I walked if I had not stumbled and started awake again; and so sick often that I could not eat, and what I did eat I vomited.
> MS: In what situation were you in that mill?
> MC: I was a piecener.

MS: The duty of the piecener is to take the cardings from one part of the machinery, and to place them on another?

MC: Yes . . .

MS: Do you not think, from your own experience, that the speed of the machinery is so calculated as to demand the utmost exertions of a child supposing the hours were moderate?

MC: It is as much as they could do . . . and toward the close of the day, when they come to be more fatigued, they cannot keep up with it very well, and the consequence is that they are beaten to spur them on . . . The machine turns off a regular quantity of cardings, and of course they must keep as regularly to their work the whole of the day; they must keep with the machine, and therefore however humane the [overseer] may be, as he must keep up with the machine or be found fault with, he spurs the children to keep up also by various means, but that which he commonly resorts to is to strap them when they become drowsy.

MS: And if you had been too late you were under the apprehension of being cruelly beaten?

MC: I generally was beaten when I happened to be too late; and when I got up in the morning the apprehension of that was so great, that I used to run, and cry all the way as I went to the mill.

MS: Then it is your impression from what you have seen, and from your own experience, that those long hours of labour have the effect of rendering young persons who are subject to them exceedingly unhappy?

MC: Yes . . .

MS: You seem to say that this beating is absolutely necessary, in order to keep the children up to their work; is it universal throughout all factories?

MC: I have been in several other factories, and I have witnessed the same cruelty in them all.

Crabtree's testimony—widely publicized by activists on the one hand and condemned by industrialist sympathizers on the other—demonstrates both what work had become, and also what our species was making of these changes.

We learn, for example, that the pace of labor is now enforced by machines. Industrial workers keep up not with seasons, nor with roaming herds, but with man-made engines. Human agency is irrelevant to this type of factory work. Mechanistic precision and consistency are paramount. When one pair of hands falters, it diminishes the productivity of hundreds of others. Unlike individual farmers, factory workers didn't need to plan ahead. The machines and their architects took care of that. As a result, prospection fell out of use as a core labor skill.

From Crabtree's testimony we learn, too, of the reduction of labor to highly specific, highly repetitive tasks, like piecening—putting parts made by one machine onto another. The move toward specialization that began with agriculture has now reached its most extreme form: total segmentation of effort. Tedious though agricultural life might have been, boredom would have reached unprecedented levels as factory workers spent hours repeating the same series of movements day in and day out, with no connection to the natural world, and with only the most tenuous bond to the product of their labor. Factory work took all the already dehumanizing parts of farming and made them worse.

As during the shift from foraging to farming, our species had become the victim of its own success. All the magnificent cognitive complexity of the human brain had been put to work designing the machines—at which point the creative process ground to a halt. Ironically, for those left to operate the machines, almost none of that complexity was needed on the job itself. Only *Homo sapiens* could have dreamed up the cotton gin, but it's quite possible a Neanderthal could have operated it.

Once the industrial tide began to turn, there was no stopping it. People had to follow the jobs. Farming itself grew increasingly mechanized, and agricultural work dried up—slowly at first, and then dramatically. From 1900 to 1940, 40% of the US labor force was displaced from farming to factory settings. Workers left the countryside and flooded cities to fill spots on the assembly line.

Psychological resilience, already important to farmers, became even more essential in this setting, with workers enduring long hours in harsh conditions while uprooted from family. So was social support. Newly urban workers had no community to speak of outside the factory. They had to build from the ground up. Novel social groupings emerged with the explicit goal of mitigating financial turbulence. Friendly societies have been called the most characteristic English working-class institution of this era, providing financial and social services to their members. In 1761, the Fenwick Weavers Society, for example, possibly the first modern cooperative, formed to support weavers in need, and to ensure fair wages for all. Larger-scale labor unions, and eventually entire political parties, would soon coalesce around these goals. But at their inception, these small, local societies aimed to boost resilience for those struggling to adapt. It was thanks to one such society that, as a new immigrant, Gabriella's grandfather found his first job in Brooklyn . . . and also met his wife-to-be.

———————————

There were many who did not make it. Our brains were not built to cope with factory life; they were built to cope with predators and storms and tribal arguments. Our bodies were not built to be pieceners; they were built to wander and gather and hunt and chitchat. It's not surprising that we suffered as a result. This was, however, the first era from which we have records of the individual and societal cost of that mismatch.

We've already heard Michael Sadler's concern about this psychological cost: *"Then it is your impression . . . that those long hours of labour have the effect of rendering young persons who are subject to them exceedingly unhappy?"* he asks, in a characteristically leading fashion. Sadler's agenda was to highlight not only the physical but also the emotional damage caused by factory life.

The connection between work and well-being was impossible to miss in this industrialized world, one that pushed workers to their physical brink, while neglecting their many intellectual gifts. Using brains evolved for the leisurely, discovery-based forager's workday of three to five hours, eight-year-olds in 1800 were expected to cope with fourteen- to sixteen-hour repetitive manufacturing shifts. (Today 160 million children globally are still put to work, half of them in hazardous conditions.)

As a result, many industrial workers came to suffer from mental health disorders. The labels in those days were different: the terms were "neurasthenia" and "hysteria" rather than anxiety, depression, and chronic fatigue. Neurasthenia, in particular, coined in 1869 by American neurologist George Beard as an "exhaustion of the nerves," became a wildly popular diagnosis over the ensuing decades. Neurasthenic patients were described as energetically depleted by the modern pace of life. While it was sometimes considered a disorder of the wealthy, records show extension to the working class. By 1906, neurasthenia accounted for 11% of diagnoses at Queen Square Hospital in London. On the other side of the pond, in 1911, a New York City clinic documented an alarmingly high prevalence of neurasthenia among its garment factory worker population.

Echoes of this suffering remain today. In 2018, labor researcher Martin Obschonka and his team analyzed personality and well-being data from across England and Wales. They compared geographic areas that had once been heavily industrialized—coal mining regions, for example, or regions involved in steam-powered manufacturing—with less industrialized areas. The modern inhabitants of formerly heavily industrialized areas show greater neuroticism, lower life satisfaction, and lower conscientiousness—decades on, long after the industry itself had vanished. Obschonka and team then successfully replicated this analysis in the United States, demonstrating that all these years later, the psychological havoc wrought by the Industrial Revolution continues to haunt our society today.

Factory workers coped with the stress of their new lives in many ways, some healthier than others. Most notoriously, self-medication with alcohol became widespread. New methods of distillation enabled mass production of alcohol, making it cheaper, stronger, and easier to get than ever before, particularly for the urban working class. For lonely, isolated employees working long hours far from home, booze made for a cheap and loyal friend.

In 1844, the young Friedrich Engels described the scourge of drunkenness he observed among local factory workers in the Manchester mill his family owned. He cited reports of thirty thousand drunks on the streets of Glasgow, with 10% of the city's homes serving as bars; and of fourfold increases in the numbers of gallons of alcohol consumed in England from 1823 to 1840. Of the Manchester drinking scene, he wrote:

> On Saturday evenings . . . when the whole working class pours from its own poor quarters into the main thoroughfares, intemperance may be seen in all its brutality. I have rarely come out of Manchester on such an evening without meeting numbers of people staggering and seeing others lying in the gutter. . . . When one has seen the extent of intemperance among the

workers in England . . . the deterioration in external conditions,
the frightful shattering of mental and physical health, the ruin
of all domestic relations that follow may readily be imagined.

Engels intended to expose, rather than improve, the capitalist system.
Later that year, he would meet Karl Marx for the second time, in Paris.
That meeting marked the beginning of the collaboration that would
become *The Communist Manifesto.* For Marx and Engels, the ills of the
modern world of work, so detrimental to the human spirit, were best
addressed by overthrowing capitalism altogether. If the labor system had
caused these human ills, that system itself would have to go.

Others tried to help from within. Chicago businessman Robert
Law was one of the first individual American employers we know
of who intervened. In 1863, he started small, taking in one of his
employees struggling with alcoholism to live with him while he
sobered up. When this de facto rehabilitation program succeeded,
Law opened one of the earliest sober living facilities in history. Out of
this tradition, employee assistance programs (EAP) began to emerge.
By the 1920s, progressive employers like Eastman Kodak offered such
programs to all employees fighting addiction.

Some scholars regard these moves with skepticism, arguing that
they stemmed from a desire to head off rising socialist sentiments.
Another explanation lies in the more immediate interests of the factory
owners, who had begun to understand that perpetually drunk workers
are bad for business. This realization dovetailed with a new obsession
with *productivity* then taking root. An engineer named Frederick
Taylor, the world's first efficiency guru, popularized the notion that
businesses succeed by maximizing worker output. A sober workforce
was a productive one.

From this peculiar confluence of motives—beneficent, self-
interested—we arrive at the structured paternalism of the modern
workplace and its human resource (HR) function. Today, 97% of

large employers offer an EAP to their employees through HR to provide support for all varieties of mental health concerns, far beyond addiction. Companies are *expected* to offer help to those suffering from physical and emotional ailments. The EAP's legacy is both benevolent and capitalist. It is also remedial, with major downsides. In chapter 10 we return to the EAP model and its shortcomings, and offer an alternative approach for HR that conforms better to the principles of behavioral science.

Our vision is not merely about mitigating harm. The best industrialist-era employers could do was help their employees get sober. It was a start. This time around, at the dawn of a new seismic shift in work, we have the opportunity to prevent harm, yes, but more important, to cultivate greatness, innovation, and well-being. Uniquely human skills like prospection and creativity are now, after hundreds if not thousands of years, once again essential. The brilliance of this moment lies in the potential we have to test the limits of these *sapiens* superpowers. If agriculture and then industrialization dehumanized work, the era ahead has the potential to rehumanize it in new and inspiring ways.

Getting there requires clarity about what the near future will require of us. It also requires that we recognize and leverage our unique historical advantage—namely, modern behavioral science, knowledge of how to strengthen the skills we will need to not merely survive but thrive.

For most of us, today's work looks nothing like the berry-picking, tree-clambering, fish-trapping labors our brains evolved for. In that sense, we may rightfully feel scared of the uncomfortable mismatches ahead. But it is also thanks to those immensely powerful forager brains that we can prepare for what is coming—what is, in so many ways, already here.

CHAPTER TWO

The Twin Trials
Automation and the Whitewater World of Work

L ike his father before him, and his son after him, Michigander Robert
VanOrden worked with cars. By day, Robert ran heating and cooling
at General Motors Detroit-Hamtramck Assembly plant. In his spare
time, he and Robert VanOrden Jr. tinkered with fixers, flipping them
for a small profit.

As a factory worker, VanOrden was one of the beneficiaries of a
controversial 1980s decision by Hamtramck's local government. The
town had used eminent domain laws to appropriate three hundred
acres of land from its Poletown neighborhood for GM's factory. Many
had been opposed, skeptical of the promised rewards. Over the
years, community members had cycled in and out of employment
at the plant, relying on it for their income. Even still, the wound of
appropriation never quite healed.

In November 2018, a second controversial decision came, this time
not from the town but from General Motors itself. CEO Mary Barra,
daughter of a GM factory worker, and a GM employee since the age
of eighteen, made the call to shutter the Hamtramck facility.

"GM wants to stay in front of changing market conditions and
customer preferences for its long-term success," Barra explained in a

statement. "What we're doing is transforming this company. This industry is changing very rapidly when you look at propulsion, autonomous driving, and ride sharing. We want to be in front of it while the company is strong and the economy is strong . . . We can take down our capital expenditures, while investing in electric and autonomous vehicles."

Barra is an electrical engineer by training and had herself once managed the Hamtramck plant. Barra's talent had caught the attention of her predecessor, Dan Akerson, while she was serving as vice president of human resources, a post that would have put her up close and personal with the changing talent requirements at the hundred-year-old firm. Her 2013 appointment to CEO had been heralded by the *Wall Street Journal* as a breakthrough for women. Barra has since become known for her commitment to improving GM's quality and brand. She used the occasion of the difficult decision to close Hamtramck to inform the markets that just as the cars themselves were evolving, so, too, the profile of the GM worker needed to change: "We need to make sure we have the right skill set not only for GM today, but for the future, so you will see us adding new people to the company even as we let people go."

GM Cruise, the self-driving automotive company located in San Francisco, was among those that would continue hiring, while Hamtramck and others put thousands out of work.

Hamtramck city officials estimated that the layoffs would cause nearly $1 million in loss to Hamtramck's annual budget, and $115,000 from the city's school aid fund. For longtime residents, the plant's closure substantiated a festering distrust. Columnist John Gallagher gave voice to this resentment: "As William Faulkner once said, the past isn't dead, it isn't even past. So now, nearly forty years after Detroit agreed to wipe out a neighborhood to create an auto plant, don't be surprised if the wounds still bleed, the memories remain strong, and the questions do not go away."

Robert was among those who lost his job, finding himself at risk of foreclosure. The news came as a shock.

"I was devastated," he said at the time. "I sat on my porch for hours, pondering life and what I would do. I'm a smart guy and I don't drink or do drugs. So I focused and said, 'Here I am, at my age, and I'll have to rebuild myself from ground zero.'"

In this, our modern world of work, rebuilding from zero has become a way of life.

We start a career, pivot hard as the market and technology change, then do it all over again. COVID-19 brought this into stark relief for many unaware that the so-called future of work had actually arrived. For millions of workers, though, this reality long predated the pandemic.

About seven years ago, our colleague, futurist and former chief scientist at Xerox John Seely Brown—who goes by JSB—and his writing partner Ann Pendleton-Jullian began describing this as the "whitewater world of work." JSB is a legend in Silicon Valley, known for his BMW motorcycles, his incisive questions, and his 1980s–1990s leadership of the Xerox PARC team that invented the laser printer and the graphical user interface (GUI). The GUI formed the basis for the computer's "desktop" interactions of menus, folders, and mouse.

JSB has also got a way with metaphor: "For my parents," he says, "the typical career trajectory was like a steamship's—fire up the engines and full speed ahead. For my generation, the course was more like a sailboat's—through skillful tacking, we got pretty close to where we thought we would. But today's graduates need to be more like whitewater kayakers, quickly analyzing and responding to an ever-changing flow, knowing and trusting themselves so they won't panic."

The feeling of whitewater kayaking elegantly captures so many of the tensions we navigate at work today. We are alone in our kayaks, riding the currents of our immediate environment—but we also all sit downstream of significant global events that will impact millions at a time in some fashion. On the one hand, there are no limits to the opportunities available to those who can harness these rapids to their advantage; on the other, the constant uncertainty drives stress and panic that can thwart even the most industrious among us.

The whitewater metaphor also suggests that we are returning to some strengths of the forager's way of life. Like our hunter-gatherer ancestors, we must all be able to read the environment, scanning broadly for threat and opportunity. Once upon a time, the arrival of a herd of caribou would turn a whole tribe into hunters, butchers, and cooks. Discovery of a boon of wild berries might convert everyone back to foragers. We evolved to be generalists who could seize on local opportunity with great agility. That same recipe for success applies in the unknowns of today's market.

There is no precedent for either the *pace* or the *type* of change we face at work today. Successfully navigating this pace and type of uncertainty—not simply surviving, but also taking full advantage of the opportunity around us to thrive—requires a unique set of emotional, social, and cognitive skills. Understanding these two dimensions of challenge can help prepare us to respond.

The Pace of Change

During the Industrial Revolution, the world already seemed to be moving too fast for our forebears. How might we compare the pace of change around us today to what we experienced one hundred years ago?

One way to answer this is through the lens of job displacement—that is, the number of jobs replaced. In some cases that means those jobs disappear, perhaps taken over by machines. In others it means that the work transforms, so that some new type of employment—like "piecening"—replaces the old. In our very first labor upheaval, it took about ten thousand years for agriculture to fully displace foraging as a new way of working. Starting with industrialization, we have more precise data to rely on. According to a Bain analysis of data from the US Census Bureau, from 1900 to 1940, job displacement in the United States occurred at a pace of 40%. That is to say that, in the last forty years of the Industrial Revolution, 40% of American workers saw their work taken over or replaced by new technologies. It makes sense that the displacement would happen most quickly at the era's end, given the number and size of the factories up and running, and the abundance of urban areas ready with housing.

How does that compare to the pace of displacement today? By most estimates, the year 2020 still represents the first chapter of this new world of work. And yet according to the same 2018 analysis of US Census data, nearly 20–25% of the US labor force will be displaced by automation in the next ten to twenty years alone.

In other words, job displacement today, at the *beginning* of this transformation, is moving twice as fast as in 1900, at the height of industrialization. And that pace is only accelerating. As of 2018, an estimated 71% of total labor tasks were performed by humans, and 29% by machines. The World Economic Forum estimates that by 2025, this will shift to 50% of labor performed by humans and 50% by machines. According to the McKinsey Global Institute's models of new technology adoption, a full 80% of us will see job replacement or wage reduction due to automation by 2030.

Driving this blitz of change is the pace of technological innovation itself. Inventor Ray Kurzweil, winner of the National Medal of Technology and Innovation for his leadership in speech and text recognition, predicted today's exponential acceleration in automation, AI, nanotechnology, and more in 2001 with his law of accelerating returns. "It is not the case that we will experience a hundred years of progress in the twenty-first century," he wrote then. "Rather we will witness on the order of twenty thousand years of progress."

Twenty thousand years of progress in one century! And what of the individual experience of that change? How often will we need to "rebuild from zero" over the course of our individual careers? In other words, *Just how fast is the change that I will personally experience?*

A helpful proxy to set expectations for within-lifetime cycles of change is the pace of skill retirement. How quickly does something like a computer language, or best practices in marketing analytics, or a generation of customer management software, expire? Fifteen years ago, JSB pegged this at five years. Today he says it's closer to eighteen months. Groups like the World Economic Forum track the evolution of market demand for specific skills, grouped into larger categories, over a period of decades. Based on this tracking, the Forum estimates we'll be reinventing ourselves professionally more like every ten years. McKinsey Global Institute's tracking suggests that by 2030, not some but *all* workers will need new skills, as their work evolves beside sophisticated machines.

In the automotive world alone, massive breakthroughs in electric and self-driving vehicles have turned the field on its head in just a decade or two. By 2040, more than half of new cars on the market will be electric. For now, VanOrden and others can move from one factory to another. But automotive workers trained in gasoline engines will soon find their skills obsolete. Specialization expires fast.

On the one hand, this leads us back to generalism. Like our forager ancestors, we will find a broad base of generalist's skills to our advantage as we flex in and out of roles over time. Technological literacy, basic professionalism—these proficiencies will endure in value.

On the other hand, the true generalist in today's world of work specializes less in any technical skill—like hunting or fishing, once upon a time—than in enduring psychological capabilities. These used to be called "soft skills," as opposed to "hard skills," like coding. Soft skills have recently been rebranded "power skills" or "meta-skills" by those seeking to rehabilitate their image in a workplace that over-rotated on technical trainings. These psychological skills distinguish us from machines and transcend any specific job training. They speak instead to the deeply human capacities we need to thrive through change in a work environment so different from our forager roots. Defining and cultivating these meta-skills—the PRISM powers—is the project of this book.

Industrialization brought change generation by generation. The whitewater world of work brings change so rapidly we will feel it *within* each generation, several times over. We can expect to rebuild from zero not once, not twice, but many times throughout our careers. We can expect to learn new job skills, only to see them fall into disuse, or transfer to machines. We will be reinventing ourselves every day. And our children and our children's children can expect to do the same.

The Nature of Change

Alongside speed, inherent in the whitewater metaphor is the notion of constant unpredictability. Not only is the pace of change dramatically faster today, the change itself is of a different type than we have known in the past. Ours is "a world that is rapidly changing, increasingly interconnected," per JSB, "and where, because of this increasing interconnectivity, everything is more contingent on everything else happening around it—much more so than ever before."

This type of change, particularly the interaction of global and local events, first came to be of interest in military and policy circles in the late twentieth century. The acronym VUCA, for example— for volatility, uncertainty, complexity, and ambiguity—so often used today to describe our business environment, was originally coined by military leaders to describe the unpredictability of the changes triggered by the end of the Cold War. In the post–Cold War era, no longer were there two powers facing off—Us and Them; Democratic and Soviet; individualist vs. collectivist. Suddenly the geopolitical landscape looked less Rothko, more Jackson Pollock. Highly fragmented, nebulous, multilateral parties operated within and across national borders with dynamic motivations that couldn't be anticipated, let alone tracked. Soldiers had to be prepared for:

1. Volatility: Unexpected, unstable challenges of unknown duration
2. Uncertainty: Unpredictable events with potential for surprise
3. Complexity: An overwhelming number of interconnected variables influencing events
4. Ambiguity: Opacity of cause-and-effect driving events

The rise in usage of this acronym speaks to its increasing resonance with our current organizational reality. Many leadership training outlets offer VUCA-based tools leveraging military thinking to help leaders succeed in our world of work.

About a decade ahead of VUCA, planners and design theorists generated the related concept of "wicked problems" to describe complex social issues. By contrast to the simpler problems of mathematics or games like chess, wicked problems are difficult to solve because of incomplete or contradictory information or changing requirements. There may also be a large number of stakeholders and opinions involved, and the problems are often closely connected with other problems. Wicked problems by definition have multiple causes and lack a single "right" answer. Terrorism, poverty, and global warming are all examples of wicked problems.

Like VUCA, the concept has proven helpful in modern corporate strategy. University of Pittsburgh professor John Camillus, for example, specializes in "wicked strategy problems," which tend to "crop up when organizations have to face constant change or unprecedented problems."

Recall Mary Barra's decision to shutter Hamtramck. Barra had to contend with the wicked problem of global warming as a factor in shifting GM's focus to electric; with the local economic challenges in Michigan; with the pace of technological innovation giving competitors an edge while GM focused resources on traditional vehicles; and so on and so forth. Each of these challenges was daunting; Barra had to solve for the full, wicked nest of them.

In classic wicked problem form, upon "solving" for these challenges, when Barra closed Hamtramck and other plants, she created a whole new set of challenges for her industry. On September 16, 2019, 46,000 GM workers, all part of the United Auto Workers, went on strike, protesting recent shuttering of plants. Each week, the strike cost GM $450 million. Within a month, the two sides had reached an agreement: Hamtramck would reopen as an electric car factory, offering nine thousand jobs. By January 2020, that number had dropped to 2,200. At each strategic juncture, Barra's actions represented not a solution, but instead, a trigger for novel complexity from both within GM and without.

Displaced Hamtramck employees continue to wonder what any of this will mean for them. For his part, Robert VanOrden returned to work briefly for GM at another site, but wasted no time in applying elsewhere, not willing to hang his fate on one firm. Post-layoffs, with all the increasing volatility around the plant's status, its focus, its size, workers understand that they cannot rely on any single factory—or skill set—as a source of income.

The technology furnishing our daily dose of VUCA extends to all industries and forums. It sits in our homes, facilitating global communication and connection; and in our offices, enabling information sharing and faster work. In 2000, four hundred million people, primarily in North America, were online. Today it's five billion. That's five billion points of origin, five billion points of amplification and mutation, for any piece of information—for any ripples or rapids in the whitewater around us. The size of that ripple corresponds to the size of the impact that each piece of information, or each global event, will have. The ripples will interact—some will amplify each other, others may cancel each other out. Each of us sits amid these billions of ripples every day, deciding which to attend to, which to ignore, and which might signal a life-altering shift we must get ahead of.

What does it feel like to live with this change? The human experience was already fairly well described by the language of those late twentieth-century scholars studying VUCA and wicked problems. Volatility describes a "liability to change rapidly and unpredictably, *especially for the worse.*" And "wicked" could hardly be more vivid in encapsulating the negative valence these challenges provoke.

In the face of this sort of volatile, unpracticable change, we feel fear. Nauseated at best, terrified at worst. Humbled by the complexity we have created but can no longer control.

The Psychological Toll of Whitewater

Whitewater is not for the faint of heart.

We are, all of us, losing and regaining equilibrium with new tools, new markets, new intelligence quarterly. Today we know much more about the negative consequences of these conditions for our health than we knew in labor transformations past.

Employment instability, for example, and lack of job control—common by-products of VUCA—produce psychological disorders, poor health outcomes, and hundreds of thousands of premature deaths each year.

Actual unemployment, as we can now expect to periodically experience over the course of our careers, has worse consequences still. When we lose work, our physical and emotional health tank: Blood pressure, arthritis, and heart attacks increase significantly, as do rates of depression, anxiety, substance abuse, and suicide.

Another major risk to our well-being comes from the nature of the technological change around us, in that automation has profound implications for human loneliness. More and more of us can expect to spend our days with "co-bots" rather than people. Remote work, which became the norm in nonessential industries during the pandemic, causes social isolation. Rates of loneliness in the United States have in fact doubled since the 1980s. Physically and psychologically, it's bad for us to be alone. Loneliness is associated with higher rates of depression. It's more harmful than obesity to our health, and about as bad for us, in terms of mortality risk, as smoking a pack of cigarettes per day.

Loneliness is also bad for business.

In our lab's 2017 study of 1,600 American employees, we found that those who are loneliest feel most dissatisfied with their jobs, and they are more likely to want to quit within the next six months. We also learned that more educated workers are lonelier, even when you control for other socioeconomic factors. Some labor scholars predict that the increasing complexity of the next decade of work means we will all need to stay in school longer. This might mean that the prevalence and severity of loneliness worsens.

Right up until COVID-19, many companies still remained unconvinced that the new world of work was threatening our health. The pandemic shattered this illusion—irreparably, we hope. The dramatic increases in mental health needs among employees as a result of COVID-19 created a crisis for those in charge of organizational health. Employees found themselves reactively referred to unprepared, overwhelmed service centers. Some companies tried to offer support to those they had laid off; most were too preoccupied with trying to figure out how to help the workers still on payroll.

Our employers, just like all of us as individuals, are at a loss. We did not evolve to work in the VUCA of whitewater, and yet here we are. We know that if we do not take action, many will suffer. We can continue to do exactly what we did with our mental health response to COVID-19—that is, wait until the damage is done, and respond with basic palliation.

Alternatively, we can make use of our unique scientific knowledge— our historic edge—to position ourselves to not only survive, but also thrive, through the whitewater to come, as individuals, as leaders, and as a society.

CHAPTER THREE

Our Historical Advantage

The Science of Thriving

The science of psychology has been far more successful on the negative than on the positive side; it has revealed to us much about man's shortcomings, his illnesses, his sins, but little about his potentialities, his virtues, his achievable aspirations, or his full psychological height. It is as if psychology had voluntarily restricted itself to only half its rightful jurisdiction, and that the darker, meaner half. —Abraham Maslow, 1954

It was 2007, and the United States Department of Defense (DoD) had a four-letter problem. Post-traumatic stress disorder (PTSD) dooms as many as 15% of combat soldiers to a life of terrible anxiety, flashbacks, nightmares, and depression. Outside of the army, about 6% of the general population struggles with PTSD, triggered by accidents, abuse, assault, sudden loss, or acute and serious health issues. Many with PTSD suffer so severely that they cannot work, they cannot sleep, they cannot maintain long-term relationships.

In the beginning of this century, the DoD experienced a steep rise in PTSD rates, largely among veterans of the wars in Iraq and Afghanistan. In addition to the immense human toll, the disorder creates a financial burden that falls to the government in the form of lifelong medical and financial support for those afflicted. It also hampers America's preparedness: At any time, the pool of ready, active-duty veterans is about 15% smaller than it could be.

And so the Joint Chiefs of Staff appointed Colonel Jill Chambers special assistant to study and improve the problem. Chambers already had an illustrious track record of service, spanning assignments in Korea during Desert Storm and at the Pentagon in 2001. On September 11, Chambers was working four corridors down from where the plane hit. As military secretary it was her job to account for the whereabouts of three hundred people in the building that day. In the years that followed, Chambers slept poorly, suffering from nightmares. She had assumed it was normal in her line of work to sleep just two hours per night. Only in the process of building the military's PTSD program did she recognize that she, too, was afflicted with the disorder.

By 2008, Chambers had assembled a strong team and made the trek from DC up to Marty's home outside Philadelphia. Marty had by then established the study of learned helplessness, a broader phenomenon connected to trauma. How, Chambers asked Marty, could we better treat people struggling with PTSD?

For most of the last two centuries, psychologists and psychiatrists have been concerned primarily with helping people who are already ill—remediating existing disorders. Too often, however, treatment after the fact doesn't work very well. Despite many billions of dollars invested in the study and treatment of PTSD and related conditions over the last seventy to eighty years, it still has no cure. Once someone has developed the disorder, we use medication and therapy to provide partial relief from symptoms, but we cannot take away the condition. For most, symptomatic relief does not enable a return to normal life.

But there's another way to think about this problem, Marty advised Chambers and her team. Yes, it's true that 15% of soldiers return with PTSD. This means that 85%—the vast majority—*do not* develop the disorder. How? Why? What can we learn from the 85%?

What's more, amazingly, many of those 85% showed *post-traumatic growth.* Following a traumatic event, those with post-traumatic growth show measurably greater clarity on their priorities, a deeper sense of meaning and purpose, and an increased capacity to cope with setbacks.

Marty encouraged Chambers and the DoD to turn the very question on its head. Let's not wait until it's too late to fight off an incurable condition, he argued. Instead, let's give people the tools to withstand difficulty before it attaches to them.

This is an entirely different approach to mental health, one that comes from a relatively young branch of psychology, pioneered by Marty and others, called *positive psychology.* Along with neighboring disciplines like social psychology and behavioral economics, positive psychology upends the traditional medical model: Instead of putting all our resources into remediating illness, these disciplines focus on preventing illness from taking root in the first place. In the field of public health, intervening to prevent someone from developing a medical condition is called *primary prevention.* Let's prevent PTSD primarily before it develops, Marty advised. Let's shift the population curve toward post-traumatic growth.

Put another way: Imagine a scale of overall psychological well-being, on which zero is neutral, negative numbers indicate degrees of psychological illness, and positive numbers show just how much someone is thriving. For argument's sake, let's consider anyone from a negative two to a positive two "within normal limits"; anyone below negative two would be psychologically unwell; anyone above a positive two would be thriving. If traditional psychiatry and clinical psychology move people from a negative ten to a negative five, the positive behavioral sciences raise us from a negative two to a positive three and beyond. In so doing, they help people avoid falling to negative ten in the first place.

These fields allow us to train the sights of our vast, modern, scientific arsenal directly on the question of how to live better, not just less bad. They also open up an array of new possibilities for meeting the challenges that lie ahead in our whitewater world of work.

Origins

Two thousand five hundred years ago, when vast empires sprung up worldwide with a breathtaking consolidation of power in the hands of caesars, pharaohs, and kings, philosophers around the globe offered wisdom on the life well lived. Confucius, 500 BCE: "The more man meditates upon good thoughts, the better will be his world and the world at large." Simeon Ben Zoma, 200 CE: "Who is rich? He who is happy with what he has." The ancient greats presaged many of positive psychology's key tenets: The practice of better appreciating our lot, for example, is today called savoring, and is connected to gratitude, both of which have been shown in hundreds of scientific studies to improve well-being.

Given that psychological well-being has been a focus of philosophy and religion for millennia, how is it that it has become a topic of robust scientific inquiry only in the last few decades? To understand this, we'll take a brief dive back into the origins of modern behavioral science. For those eager to get to the practical applications of this new science, feel free to skip ahead to chapter 4.

Systematic empirical study of the natural world—aka "modern Science" with a capital *S*—emerged from the Scientific Revolution in roughly the sixteenth and seventeenth centuries. The works of Bacon, Copernicus, Galileo, Harvey, Newton, and eventually Darwin and others irrevocably changed our understanding of our planet, of matter, of nature, of the human body. The objective truth of our universe was, we realized, waiting to be discovered—but through observation, measurement, and experimentation rather than through scripture, reasoning, or intuition. Moreover, science could do more than just observe and describe. It could change nature itself.

The behavioral sciences came late to the party. Psychiatry grew out of the illness-centered medicine of the late eighteenth century. Early psychiatrists focused on the treatment of madness—those living at an abysmal negative ten while housed in asylums. In parallel, practitioners like Pierre Janet, Sigmund Freud, and Carl Jung began using case histories as a window into describing and treating the pathologies of individual consciousness.

The field of psychology coalesced at around the same time, but its orientation was different, drawing primarily on the philosophical and biological traditions to ask and test questions by experimental methods about not only pathology but also universal matters of human experience. Wilhelm Wundt (1831–1920), the first person to call himself a psychologist, was an experimentalist who tackled broad topics like sensation and perception. In the first half of the twentieth century, Edward L. Thorndike in America and Ivan Pavlov in Russia used animal models (Thorndike: cats; Pavlov: his famous dogs) to explore the learning process, giving rise to the school of study known as behaviorism. These and other discoveries provided the ideal template for what behavioral science should look like: inductive, falsifiable, and replicable.

In the early 1900s, psychiatry experienced its own first scientific successes in the development of medications to treat mental illness. General paresis, a deadly mental breakdown, was found to be caused by a tiny syphilis bacteria called a spirochete in the brain. By the 1940s, penicillin was being used to kill the spirochete and so treat neurosyphilis, and Australian psychiatrist John Cade had introduced the use of lithium for bipolar disorder. Psychiatric illness, it seemed, could be analyzed and treated just like any other wound.

By the middle of the twentieth century, then, both psychology and psychiatry had earned their medico-scientific stripes. Post–World War II America, replete with veterans struggling with the psychological consequences of battle, was ready to reap the benefits. In 1946, the Veterans Administration was founded, offering work to thousands of psychologists who would focus their clinical and research time not on general problems like learning, but instead on treating soldiers returning from the front. In 1947, the National Institute of Mental

Health was created. The hope was that all forms of mental illness would one day be curable.

The ensuing decades appeared to deliver on that promise. From 1940–1970, antipsychotics emerged that revolutionized treatment of those with schizophrenia; many who had previously required lifelong institutionalization were suddenly able to resume semi-normal lives at home. Sedatives, meanwhile, came to popularity among those with minor and serious ailments alike. By 1970, 20% of American women and 8% of American men were using sedatives regularly. In the 1980s, antidepressants like Prozac hit the market. Today we have Ritalin and Adderall for ADHD; Ambien and Lunesta to help us sleep.

One in six Americans use a psychiatric drug today.

Backlash

Amid these partial successes, some scientists began to argue that the focus on pathology had become too narrow and constraining. By only working on fixing the broken, we had neglected the many people who might benefit from what science had to say about human thriving. Starting in the 1950s and '60s, Abraham Maslow, Carl Rogers, and others called for their field to turn its sights to topics like love, creativity, meaning, and hope. Psychology, Maslow argued, had lost its way in the negative—"the darker, meaner half"—to the detriment of the field.

The movement they founded, humanistic psychology, dovetailed with the burgeoning counterculture of the 1960s. Self-actualization, quasi-spirituality, optimism, the quest for deep human truth—what more could a hippie ask for? Psychedelics? They studied those, too. Mass gatherings like Woodstock and the Human Be-In facilitated the rapid spread of the movement.

Ultimately, the popularity of humanistic psychology undermined its scientific potential. A vast literature of "self-help" spewed forth, driven by aphorisms and intuitions rather than research. The woo-woo vibes of the counterculture scared away the scientifically minded from studying humanistic ideas. In 1963, Harvard Psychology drew a line in the sand by firing Timothy Leary over the safety and ethics concerns around his LSD studies. The divide ran both ways, as hippies came to view the scientific establishment and the scientific method itself with suspicion. Abraham Maslow may have wanted science, but for many who took up his banner, science was a part of the problem that humanism needed to solve.

Carl Rogers gave voice to this tension in 1961:

> Let me see if I can sum up very briefly the picture of the impact of the behavioral sciences upon the individual and upon society; the increasing power for control which it gives will be held by some one or some group; such an individual or group will surely choose the purposes or goals to be achieved; and most of us will then be increasingly controlled by means so subtle we will not even be aware of them as controls . . . Man and his behavior would become a planned product of a scientific society.

Maslow's original call was for science to turn its attention to the promise of human potential. But his most receptive audience associated science with power. For a long time, the two sides seemed irrevocably at odds.

Crisis of Faith

In the beginning of the twenty-first century, the institutions of clinical psychiatry and psychology took a long, hard look in the rearview mirror.

The grand promise of psychopharmacy—Better Living Through Chemistry—was beginning to ring hollow. An extraordinary amount of money was being spent globally treating mental illness, with billions more poured into research and development. The National Institute of Mental Health today spends about $2 billion on research grants each year. Pharmaceutical companies' investments dwarf that.

Where, some were starting to ask, had all that investment in research and treatment gotten us?

The findings were damning. Although 17% of American adults filled a prescription for a psychiatric drug in 2013, prevalence rates of mental illness had hardly changed since the 1970s. There had been no demonstrable improvement in the morbidity or mortality associated with mental disorders, as evidenced by rates of hospital admission, suicide, and unemployment, during this era. Most tellingly, at the basic science level, little advance had been made toward understanding the fundamental causes of the disorders themselves. During this same period, not a single truly novel psychiatric medication had been developed. Nor did any of the drugs on the market cure psychiatric disease, they alleviated symptoms; and in many cases the treatment was no better than a placebo. The side effects, such as addiction and tic disorders, were sometimes worse than the psychopathology itself. Even the effectiveness of psychotherapy had budged little in fifty years.

The psychiatric establishment arrived at this alarming conclusion about a decade into the new millennium. The turning point came in 2012, when former NIMH director Steve Hyman dared to say out loud what so many were already thinking: The emperor had no clothes. The psychopharmaceutical model, within which miraculous drugs could effectively treat, if not cure, psychological disorder, was a "brilliant promise unfulfilled." The drugs had not improved in decades, nor had our scientific understanding of disease. "Overall," Hyman wrote, "industry has come to the justifiable view that with few exceptions, valid disease models do not exist for psychiatric disorders."

Consider the magnitude of that admission by one of the most important behavioral science leaders in the country. Despite one hundred years of research, despite billions if not trillions of dollars of investment, *valid disease models do not exist for psychiatric disorders.* We lack the most rudimentary understanding of how these disorders work—why and how they start, and what they do to our brains. What we do have are medications that help some people cope with some of their symptoms, some of the time. Even then, we don't really know why they help.

The next year, Tom Insel, who was head of the NIMH at the time, agreed. "Patients with mental disorders deserve better," he wrote, than the science that NIMH and the psychiatric establishment had been offering them. Core diagnostic and experimental methods were imprecise, unreliable, and invalid. Advances in neuroscience had not yet benefited psychiatric patients. The field needed a reboot.

Just two years later, Insel resigned his post.

Academic psychology had come to its own similar conclusions perhaps a decade earlier. In 1996, Marty was elected president of the American Psychological Association, the country's largest professional organization for psychologists. All presidents set their agenda in their annual address. For Marty, that particular APA convention in San Francisco was an ideal moment to herald change:

Since World War II, psychology has become a science largely about healing. It concentrates on repairing damage within a disease model of human functioning. Such almost exclusive attention to pathology neglects the flourishing individual and the thriving community . . . If it were indeed true that depression is caused by bad events, then Americans today, especially young Americans, should be a very happy group. But the reality is that a sea change has taken place in the mental health of young Americans over the last forty years. The most recent data show that there is more than ten times as much serious depression now as four decades ago. Worse, depression is now a disorder of the early teenage years rather than a disorder that starts in middle age, a situation that comprises the single largest change in the modern demographics of mental illness. And that, I believe, is the major paradox of the late twentieth century.

With Marty and flow psychologist Mihaly Csikszentmihalyi (pronounced Me-High Cheek-Sent-Me-High) at the helm, a group of leading psychologists began gathering to question their field's almost exclusive focus on psychopathology. None of the massive research investment in mental disorders had translated into more well-being. Longitudinal studies comparing psychological health scores across the decades showed no improvement, and the rate of psychological illness was getting worse, not better.

Homo sapiens today live longer than ever before, and, in the Western world, our standard of living has improved enormously in the last three hundred years. And yet, we are not happier, and we are not living *better*.

We suffer from more loneliness than any generation in recorded history. Anxiety, depression, and suicide among our youth are at or near all-time highs. COVID-19 has underscored for many just how fragile our well-being is, and how easily world events beyond our control can compromise it. Our focus on psychopathology has failed to translate into meaningful knowledge about how normal human beings can thrive.

Founding Positive Psychology

In response to this paradox, Marty, Mihaly, and colleagues founded a new field of scientific study: *positive psychology*.

Like humanistic psychology and all the humanistic traditions before it, positive psychology takes as its focus the life well lived. Meaning, happiness, love, connection, flow—all of these are front and center for positive psychology. Occupational thriving—accomplishment—is part of this vision as well.

Unlike its humanistic predecessors, positive psychology has positioned itself smack *within* the sciences. One can, today, get a PhD in positive psychology, but only after having demonstrated the same level of proficiency in the statistical and experimental methods expected of any other research psychologist. Fluidity with adjacent fields like social psychology, education, neuroscience, behavioral economics, and sociology has allowed for scientific cross-pollination. Positive psychology insists on careful empirical testing of key premises. Collectively we call these fields "positive behavioral science." Emerging today, for example, is the new field of positive psychiatry.

Science is not the enemy in this view. Rather, it is a venerable tool kit that can help us change reality. As Csikszentmihalyi wrote in 2000, "In this quest for what is best, positive psychology does not rely on wishful thinking, faith, self-deception, fads, or hand waving; it tries to adapt what is best in the scientific method to the unique problems that human behavior presents to those who wish to understand it in all its complexity."

Given the stalled progress of clinical psychiatry and clinical psychology, one might well wonder whether such a science can be relied upon. Perhaps, the argument goes, a scientific approach to the complexities of the mind is not yet within our reach. If fifty years of investment in studying mental disorders has yielded so little, why should the same investment in psychological well-being result in a different outcome?

The answer is twofold. First: clinical psychiatry and psychology have had plenty of wins between them. The fact that progress stalled toward the end of the twentieth century shouldn't diminish the true victories that came before. Scientific study of the brain's malfunctioning produced antipsychotics and sedatives that keep people out of the hospital; drugs that cured neurosyphilis; evidence-based techniques for psychotherapy that retrain the brain; and novel diagnostic technologies like brain MRIs. In some ways the field is penalized for its own successes: as soon as a psychiatric disorder is fully understood, like neurosyphilis, it becomes the purview of the adjacent field of neurology. Psychiatry is left, almost by definition, with the opaque. Within the realm of the opaque, there is so very much left to do that it can feel overwhelming. The marked plateau of these last decades should not lead us to lose sight of the much more abysmal sea level from which we began.

The second reason we should believe that the scientific method can uncover tools to help us flourish is that it has already done so. Applying the same methods of observation, measurement, and experimentation, the positive behavioral sciences have, in the last twenty-five years, taken the life well lived as their primary subject. Across positive psychology, social psychology, behavioral economics, and more, we have learned a great deal about both how to prevent poor psychological outcomes (avoid the negative ten) and how to attain greater degrees of thriving (hit positive ten). We have learned, for example, that our subjective well-being—happiness—centers on five components, PERMA: positive emotions (**P**); engagement in work, love, and play (**E**); positive relationships (**R**); meaning or mattering (**M**); and accomplishment, achievement, and mastery (**A**). More than eight thousand studies have defined these dimensions; have demonstrated how we can improve each; and have validated that improvements in PERMA align with improvements in our physical and psychological well-being.

We have learned, too, a great deal about how to withstand challenge. Forty thousand scholarly articles have been published on psychological resilience, the topic of our next chapter. We know how to measure it; we know what causes it to wane and to wax; we have a slew of validated interventions proven to build it up.

There are enough individual studies now that even meta-analyses—studies looking at the data from many individual studies—of positive psychology interventions (PPIs) abound. For example, a 2021 paper by Professor Alan Carr and colleagues at the University of Dublin analyzed 347 different studies of PPIs, covering 72,000 subjects. They found that the interventions had significantly improved well-being; built up strengths; and decreased stress, anxiety, and depression. These improvements were significant when tested both immediately after the intervention and also three months later.

None of which is to say that the work is done. But the most interesting questions to those who study PPIs today are not about whether they will work—that has now been established. They're focused instead on more deeply understanding why the interventions work, how to make them work even better, and how to make them last longer.

Thanks to these scientific investments, a robust literature now exists that can teach us how to live better than we ever have, despite the unique challenges of our era.

When Jill Chambers brought Marty to the Pentagon to share his perspective, he came ready to win hearts and minds. He'd been making the case for a preventive approach to well-being for a decade by then, and he knew what to do.

To his surprise, the audience was already on his side. By 2008, leading military thinkers knew all about positive psychology. For them, optimal human performance was a matter of national security. They had not missed the many findings documented by Marty, his dozens of colleagues, and their hundreds of students. They were ready to take action.

"The key to psychological fitness is resilience," General George W. Casey Jr., then chief of staff of the army, informed those in attendance, before Marty could begin. "And from here on, resilience will be taught and measured throughout the United States Army. Dr. Seligman is going to tell us how to do it."

Casey, Chambers, and team were not after ancient wisdom, nor religion, nor philosophical ideals. They wanted an evidence-based approach to human thriving. And that is exactly what Marty and his colleagues had been building. They had found that we can statistically predict who is most vulnerable to PTSD; lower the likelihood of mental disorders; and train for heroism and exemplary performance at work.

What the vast community of positive behavioral scientists have learned in the last thirty years is what offers us hope today of weathering the coming storm of change in the workplace. Without this science, we would be as vulnerable as previous generations to the psychological suffering of a labor transformation. With this science, we have the opportunity to not only avoid harm but also grow stronger through the challenges to come.

Embracing this science requires a dramatic change to the pathology-centered approach to psychology. If we view psychology as a way to fix people, we will wait until the damage is done, and then send them to a therapist.

There's an analogy here to short-term corporate thinking about maximizing quarterly gains, à la Milton Friedman's September 13, 1970, manifesto in the *New York Times*. It turns out that short-termism comes at a tremendously high societal and environmental cost. As a result, today's CEOs understand, at least in theory, that the corporation needs to preempt the challenges of tomorrow, rather than wait to respond reactively when the inevitable occurs.

We have yet to see this shift to long-termism translate to human capital management. Too many corporations still approach the struggles of their employees with a remedial, after-the-fact mindset. This mindset parallels that of society at large, which, for historical reasons, still views psychology itself as primarily a science for helping the sick.

If, by contrast, we can come to embrace the behavioral sciences as fields that can help us thrive and prevent illness from taking root, we will view their discoveries as the tools we all so desperately need today. These tools will allow us to proactively build a brighter future—for ourselves, for our corporations, and for society as a whole.

CHAPTER FOUR

The Building Blocks of Resilience

The Department of Defense had a second reason, alongside PTSD, to go all in on resilience training. Over the last few decades, VUCA-style warfare has only increased in its turbulence and unpredictability. This sea change in how wars are fought—from command-and-control to highly distributed, hyperlocal battles—has meant that time after time, US soldiers trained in traditional methods have found themselves unprepared for the new style of combat. As Major General Bob Scales (ret.), former commandant of the Army War College, tells it, we're fully entangled in a form of global conflict that "shifts from the traditional linear construct to a battlefield that is amoebic in shape; it is distributed, dispersed, nonlinear, and essentially formless in space and unbounded in time." Modern war is fought up close by soldiers who need to be ready at any moment to decide—*on their own*—to change tactics and try something new.

The shift from hierarchical, central governance to a distributed, dynamic, local, hyper-responsive one equally describes our post-Fordist workplace. The stakes for civilians are different, but the gameboard is the same. Like modern soldiers, in our daily work we need to flex on a dime as context shifts. Our organizations depend on each of us to make critical real-time decisions, and to ride the waves of challenge as they arrive without drowning.

Scales, like General Casey, has long looked to the behavioral sciences to better arm our soldiers for this VUCA environment. "Imagine how the psychological, behavioral, and emotional strength of soldiers in this moment might be amplified by better understanding of the human dynamics," he wrote in 2006. "We must begin now to harness the potential of the social sciences in a manner not dissimilar to the Manhattan Project or the Apollo Project."

For the DoD, the largest employer in the world, training resilience is about much more than preventing PTSD. Arming troops with the skills to thrive in the midst of uncertainty lets them perform at positive five, even in the most extreme environments. Resilience becomes the bedrock of psychological fitness for whitewater warfare.

So, too, at work. It all starts with resilience. Individuals and organizations with higher levels of resilience are happier, healthier, and more successful in this climate. Firms with higher levels of workforce resilience see 320% more year-over-year growth than those with lower levels. Hundreds of studies show psychological resilience can be taught. With the right tools, each of us can cultivate it, proactively building the psychological muscles that allow us to weather challenges and thrive. For all these reasons, resilience is our first, and most foundational, Tomorrowmind skill.

What We Talk About When We Talk About Resilience

At its most basic, resilience means "bouncing back" from difficult events. Something tough happens. Some people crumble. Others thrive.

The reality is a little more nuanced, in that resilience can refer to the way we respond to events as they happen in real time; it can describe the way we prepare for events that we *anticipate* happening; and it can describe the way we process events *after* they have happened. Resilience can also be used to describe the behaviors of an individual, a team, or an entire organization.

At the negative end of the resilience bell curve, people with low levels of resilience will struggle with challenge—even developing mental health disorders. At the opposite end of the curve are those people who grow stronger through challenge. Looking around in nature we find numerous instances of stress causing adaptation and improvement. The strengthening of muscle after exercise would be one example. Post-traumatic growth is another. Many types of learning follow the same curve: The struggle is what pushes us forward. The term for this process, coined by essayist Nassim Nicholas Taleb, is *antifragility*.

If the average person is like a dish sponge, able to absorb a certain amount of psychological stress before hitting capacity, antifragile people are more like those pellets that you drop in hot water and watch as they magically blossom into a brontosaurus. These individuals appear paradoxically to *thrive* on challenge. They soak it up, in the process becoming transformed for the better.

Since the 1970s, Marty and others have been researching the question: Is there some quality or skill that sets antifragile people apart, and if so, can we teach that skill to others?

The answers are yes and yes.

Marty's studies on learned helplessness at the University of Pennsylvania laid the groundwork for hundreds of resilience interventions to come. They demonstrated, for example, that our response to difficult situations hinges in part on our *beliefs* about whether we can do anything to escape those situations, and that healthier belief systems can be taught.

Because of how essential resilience is to workforce thriving, one of the most important projects of BetterUp Labs has been to understand its drivers. Resilience is a way of responding that spans our thoughts, feelings, and behaviors. It does not hinge on one single trait. As such, building resilience requires shoring up a complex set of psychological and behavioral skills. But how do we figure out exactly what they are?

Data scientists commonly use statistical regressions to break down the key drivers of an outcome. These sorts of analyses take large sums of before and after data and tell us what factors were most responsible for driving the outcome of interest. One of the ways we have studied the drivers of resilience is through one such relative weight analysis. Under the leadership of our psychometric assessment experts, we looked at the data from 1,800 full-time employees working to build resilience through coaching and practice on the BetterUp platform. We had administered our Whole Person Model (WPM) assessment, a 150-item scale, to each of them before, during, and after coaching. The WPM includes a full range of psychological mindsets and behaviors of interest to high-functioning adults, including dimensions of social, cognitive, and emotional thriving as well as essential workplace leadership behaviors. We then analyzed which of these 150 items most strongly contributed to the outcome of increased resilience. (For more on the WPM, see Appendix.)

Here's a look at our findings:

On the left-hand side, you can see all the psychological factors, of 150 total possible, that correlate significantly with how an individual scored on our resilience scale. The thickness of the "noodle" connecting the measure on the left to resilience on the right tells you how much that factor contributed to a resilient outcome for any given individual.

While all the factors on the left played a role in building resilience, you can see that five were especially important: *emotional regulation, optimism, cognitive agility, self-compasssion,* and *self-efficacy.* These align well to the existing literature on prime targets for building resilience. We will now examine how each of these drivers contributes to our capacity for resilience, and how they can be developed.

Emotional Regulation

Emotional regulation describes our ability to flexibly and productively manage our emotions—particularly negative emotions—as they boil up, in order to achieve our goals. Without emotional regulation, negative emotions can overwhelm our ability to think clearly. All those millions of years of highly evolved brainpower, hijacked by an emotional flood!

The seat of that hijacking is our limbic system, one of the oldest parts of our brains, responsible for our fight-or-flight response. Strong, sudden anger comes from the amygdala, a centimeter-wide, almond-shaped emotional center. In stress or fear, the amygdala triggers the release of cortisol and begins a cascade of intense physical responses that may be disproportionate to the original threat.

Many models of adult development hold emotional regulation as foundational to all higher-order functions. As we mature psychologically, even late into adulthood, we learn to manage our emotions with greater nuance and sophistication. Emotions have much to teach us, but they are blunt communicators. The most mature leaders and professionals know how to harness emotions to their advantage. They don't just react. For all the same reasons, great coaches will tell you that emotional regulation is essential to their work.

A word on what we mean by coach: Coaches come in many flavors—health coaches, sports coaches, life coaches. In this book, the coaches we talk about are what we used to call executive coaches, trained in helping professionals succeed at work and beyond. Today these professional development coaches work with all levels of employee, so the word "executive" is out of date. Like therapists, coaches work with clients on improving psychological health. Unlike therapists, they do not treat psychological disorders, focusing instead on helping their clients achieve their potential as people and as professionals. Many people seek coaching when they are foundering at work—struggling to perform, tiring of politics, burning out, or feeling unable to see their way forward through a tough chapter. Others partner with coaches to achieve specific personal or professional goals, like getting a promotion or improving communication in their family.

Emotional regulation is very often one of the first steps in taking control of our psychology so we can achieve those goals. Coaches are invaluable partners in helping us do this, because coaching sessions offer a structured and compassionate environment within which to examine and understand our feelings. Coaches teach targeted skills tailored to our unique trajectory of growth. Within just three months of coaching, people who struggle most with emotional regulation can improve by 92%.

Two of the most important emotional regulation skills are *slowing down* and *cognitive reappraisal*. We can see these skills in action in the following vignette:

Joy is a mid-career salesperson serving the Chicago metro area. She recently learned that her territory would be reassigned. Sales leadership had decided to shift focus to smaller cities, where new data had shown that its core product, a customer management software, was beginning to find market fit. Joy had spent three years developing relationships in Chicago. When she heard the news, she felt enormous resentment. Leadership, she thought, was disconnected and didn't care about its people. They were throwing away her blood, sweat, and tears without even asking for her input.

The afternoon she got the news of her reassignment, Joy drafted a resignation letter. She decided to call her coach before submitting it.

"I've got to get out of here," Joy told her coach, Carol. "They're making me start all over."

Carol's job, in this moment, is to help Joy slow down, creating space between her negative emotional reaction and her ensuing behaviors. She will first need to make Joy feel heard; then she will guide her through a series of questions to help Joy better understand what she is feeling.

"It sounds like you feel unappreciated," Carol says, after a few minutes of deep listening.

"To say the least."

"What else?"

"Angry. *Pissed.* Frustrated. Worn out."

Naming our emotions helps us gain insight, but also creates distance between stimulus and response. Joy can now stop the amygdala hijacking that was linking her feelings with her intended "flight"—quitting. In the pause between trigger and response, Joy can more carefully consider her options. She's putting the brakes on her amygdala so she doesn't run herself off the road.

"Quitting is certainly an option," Carol starts. "What information would you need to decide if that's the right thing to do?"

Carol is transitioning now into cognitive reappraisal. Cognitive reappraisal describes a group of techniques, first developed by Marty's mentor Aaron Beck (to whom he dedicates this book), that form the core of cognitive behavioral therapy (CBT). CBT is perhaps the most powerful evidence-based psychological therapy we have. In reappraisal, we step back from the urgency of our own thoughts, emotions, and behaviors to intellectually challenge our reactions. In so doing, we can reevaluate our situation, allowing for more nuanced interpretations than our emotions may have originally suggested.

Joy thinks. "I don't know yet if they will let me keep my active prospects."

"Is that a deal breaker?"

"I don't need to keep all of Chicago, but I would need to keep everyone who's at stage 3 and beyond." (Stage 3 is a stage in the sales cycle, which typically has seven stages from meeting a prospect to closing a sale.)

"That sounds reasonable," Carol says.

"And I need to know if this changes my commission structure. I can't land deals as big in these smaller cities."

Now Joy is fully into reappraisal, already planning for negotiations. Carol pulls her back to her emotions for a moment, however, to make sure she's not abandoning the lessons they have for her.

"What about feeling appreciated? That seemed important to you. Is there something there you need to know?"

"I need to know they want to keep me here," Joy says. "Like, do they even care if I leave? If they don't, I'm not sure I want to stay anyway."

They discuss how Joy can seek the recognition she is after and determine if she is appropriately valued by her employer. Joy may or may not end up staying in her role after the territory reallocation, but at least she will make a decision grounded in balanced information rather than knee-jerk reactions.

Coaches are phenomenal at helping us slow down and reevaluate. But you can improve your ability to regulate emotions without a coach, too. Try this two-step method next time you find yourself flooded with emotion and jumping to extreme action:

1. First, slow down. Create space between the emotions you are experiencing and any actions they might lead you to take. You

can do this by noticing your emotions; naming them; asking what triggered them. Notice your physical reactions—your heartbeat, any tension in your body. If you are too worked up to have clarity, focus on delaying action until your body has calmed down. Take a walk, meditate, call a friend, get the mail. You are buffering action from emotion so you can reevaluate.

2. Second, reappraise. Now, use that space you have created to think. What are your emotions trying to tell you? What parts of that message are helpful? What parts are less so? For Joy, for example, it was important for her to notice she was feeling unappreciated. She needed to know her leaders valued her if she was to stay and thrive in her new role. Next, consider your options. What choices do you have? What information do you need to decide among them?

You may need to repeat this two-step process many times for particularly charged situations, especially if you are new to these techniques. Over time we get better and better at regaining perspective and control quickly.

Optimism

Optimism describes the tendency to feel hopeful and confident about a positive outcome in the future. We have known for some time that optimism is a key predictor of resilience. During Marty's studies of learned helplessness starting in 1967, he found that even in the face of *inescapable* bad events, about one-third of subjects never became helpless. These resilient individuals tend to explain setbacks as temporary; as local and controllable: *It's going away quickly, it's just this onetime situation, and there's plenty I can do in the future to ward this kind of thing off.*

Notice that key word: *inescapable*. The stories these people told themselves in order to cope with discomfort did not conform to their experience. Nevertheless, they continued to tell the optimistic stories, and as a result, they kept trying and so fared better. The lesson is clear and powerful. How tolerable a situation feels grows out of our *belief* about whether we can do anything to escape it. That's optimism: the bias to expect a favorable outcome.

Why would we want to teach ourselves to think this way? Because—for the most part—it's good for us. Optimism predicts not only psychological but also physical resilience. Did you know that optimists live about eight years longer than pessimists? They are significantly less likely to die from a heart attack, when one occurs. They have more robust immune systems. Thinking optimistically is good for both mind and body.

There is powerful new evidence about how well optimists do at work. Researcher Paul Lester, along with the late Ed Diener and Marty, followed more than nine hundred thousand soldiers for five years, looking at exemplary work. Over those five years 12% of these soldiers received the army's much-sought-after award for "exemplary performance." The question was, could we predict, from their psychological testing when they first joined the army, who would win these awards? Yes, and strongly so. Soldiers who had high positive emotion, low negative emotion, and high optimism were four times more likely to win the performance awards, and the award for heroism as well. Since the sample population worked in more than 150 highly varied occupations, these findings are likely general to the American workplace.

One of the best studied interventions to help people think optimistically is called the "Best Possible Self." In this exercise, you pick a future time frame—perhaps fifteen years from now. Imagine yourself, in fifteen years, when everything has gone right: You're with a loving partner, if that's something you want; you have the career you've been working toward; you're living in the part of town you've always loved most. Then spend ten minutes writing about this future. How do you spend your time? What friends or family do you see most? What does it feel like? More than thirty studies have shown that this exercise improves not only optimism but also physical health. You can use different time frames to repeat the exercise. Each time you do this work you are strengthening your capacity for optimism.

Exercises focused on savoring success, on exercising gratitude, and on celebrating hard work all help us feel more optimistic about the future. Optimism can also be bolstered by monitoring our inputs, including on social media. During the pandemic, for example, many needed help tuning out unrealistic negatives—exaggerated reports of surging cases, for example—in order to more clearly hear the internal optimism they were working to nurture.

Cognitive Agility

Cognitive agility describes our ability to mentally move back and forth among many possible scenarios before focusing in and then acting on the most promising one. We saw earlier how essential cognitive agility, in the form of adaptability, was to our historical work as foragers. It went hand in hand with the generalist skill set we needed. Foraging relies on opportunistic identification of resources in brand-new topographies, followed by focused gathering or hunting. Without openness to evidence, foragers would miss valuable finds. But absent focus, and a generalist mindset, they would then be unable to harvest the food they identified.

We have come by these skills honestly, as a species, through millions of years of evolving for the forager life. But we have drifted from using them since the Agricultural Revolution. With farming, and then industrialization, our roles got narrower and our work activities more predetermined.

Today, once again, we need the cognitive agility and adaptability of a forager to flex in response to the rapids of the whitewater workplace. In this setting, we read currents, analyze context, and leave ourselves as many options as possible so we don't get stuck.

Recall Robert VanOrden's sudden job loss after the closure of GM's Hamtramck plant. His firing might have triggered a period of depression and extended unemployment. But this wasn't Robert's story. After a short period of grief, Robert pulled himself up and started figuring out a new way to live. With the agility of a forager, Robert scoped out his local environment for opportunity, and cobbled together a brand-new set of employment activities. First, he took advantage of the gig economy and began to drive for Lyft. Next, he employed his broader technical skills as a handyman, taking odd jobs around the neighborhood, and even installing a commercial kitchen for a Detroit church. Third, he turned his passion for restoring cars into a source of income, selling refurbished vehicles. Finally, playing into his love of music, Robert became a booking agent for local bands. Even when GM rehired Robert, he applied to roles elsewhere to keep his options open.

John Seely Brown has been writing about the importance of agility for decades, but he's been living these lessons even longer. Before kayaking, and before motorcycles, JSB traveled by hitchhiking. In the rural town of Hamilton, New York, where he grew up, hitching was the easiest way to explore. Trip by trip, car by car, JSB grew skilled in reading signals of threat vs. safety to determine which vehicle to get in and how to nonlinearly make his way from one point to another on the cheap. He learned to sleep anywhere, even on the side of the road.

In 1958, at eighteen, JSB hitched his way from New York to Cuba to visit his girlfriend. How, exactly, does one hitchhike to Cuba? In the middle of the Cuban Revolution, no less? Having made it all the way down to Key West, Florida, JSB lurked on the edges of the airport, observing, waiting for the right pilot with the right cargo, willing to "drop him off" on a runway near Havana. The return trip proved more eventful: Key West police arrested JSB on the way back, after his ride suspiciously left him on the runway, then took right off again. A recommendation letter in his pocket—saved there for just such a moment of crisis—enabled his release. Finding himself freed in the middle of the night, with nowhere else to sleep, JSB asked the police if he could crash in jail anyway. They obliged, leaving his cell unlocked.

It takes a certain kind of agility to get oneself out of jail; and a whole other kind to choose to stay there after release.

Cognitive agility gives us options. Where some people see a wall, those like JSB see hidden tunnels or room for a stowaway. Fortunately, cognitive agility is teachable, and those who struggle most at it also show the most dramatic improvements. People who start out in the lowest quartile of cognitive agility scores improve in this capability by 77% in just three months of coaching.

One of the bitter ironies of cognitive agility is that we need to be most agile in moments of crisis—when arrested in a shed on the side of a runway, say—precisely when our amygdala wants us to freak out. With our brain hijacked by fear, it's difficult to remain open to possibilities. Instead, we become overly conservative and narrow our field of vision. For this reason, we often need to couple work on emotional regulation with work on cognitive agility. Building optimism often comes into play here as well.

One of the most important predictors of poor resilience, for example, is **catastrophization**. People who catastrophize immediately jump to imagining the worst possible scenario in times of uncertainty. Among seventy thousand soldiers deployed to Iraq or Afghanistan, catastrophizers were much more likely to develop PTSD than non-catastrophizers, particularly when faced with severe combat. Catastrophizers are low on optimism, emotional regulation, and cognitive agility alike.

To assess your own tendency to catastrophize, imagine the following scenario: It's noon on a Friday. You're working away when a message pops up on your screen from your boss's assistant. Your boss wants to see you, one-on-one, at 4:30 p.m.

Where does your mind go?

Some people will have a specific automatic thought: "I'm getting fired." And, having that thought, they may freeze up, terrified, unable to focus on anything else for the rest of the day.

It's true that layoffs sometimes occur at the end of the week, and with little warning. In the absence of other cues as to poor performance, however, this is far from the most likely explanation. In a given year, your boss has a lot of 4:30 p.m. meetings on a Friday. Is someone getting fired at each? Probably not.

But for those of us inclined to catastrophize, that message reads like a death sentence. Catastrophizers allow their anxiety and fear to dominate their read on reality—a case of poor *emotional regulation* and low *optimism*. They also focus narrowly on a single outcome—a case of impaired *cognitive agility*, which would normally let someone remain open to multiple possibilities.

With training, catastrophization can be unlearned. The exercise "Putting It In Perspective" tackles this cognitive distortion by deliberately opening the aperture to the full range of possible outcomes. Here's how it works:

Putting It In Perspective:

For any scenario where you find your mind jumping to the worst possible conclusion, your aim is to more accurately predict different outcomes.

1. First, draw a line with the words "worst possible" on the far left and "best possible" on the far right. In the Friday-afternoon-call-from-the-boss example, "getting fired" would be plotted on this line to the far left.

2. Now that you have the worst possible outcome in mind, it's time to stretch all the way to the opposite end. What is the best possible outcome? What's the most positive scenario you can imagine? In the Friday afternoon example, this might be "getting a promotion." Plot this on the far right.

3. Finally, think of at least three "most likely" explanations and plot these in the middle of the line. "Boss needs urgent help on a project" might belong there. It's important to come up with several examples in this range because your mind is learning a more realistic distribution of likelihoods. There are so many more "most likely" outcomes than best or worst—that's what makes this part of the spectrum so crucial. A cognitively agile mind will be able to factor in these probabilities in imagining potential outcomes.

A version of this exercise was used to train forty thousand US non-commissioned officers to develop resilience for themselves and their troops. They learned to identify catastrophic thinking, challenge it, and develop new, more cognitively agile instincts so that they could respond with greater flexibility to future turmoil.

Self-Compassion

University of Texas at Austin professor Kristin Neff defines self-compassion, our fourth driver of resilience, as our ability to extend to ourselves compassion for our own suffering, failure, or perceived inadequacy. Self-compassion lets us take the playbook for comforting others who are experiencing difficulty—a playbook we know well, one our brains are very comfortable accessing—and simply apply it to ourselves.

A key aspect of this practice is understanding our own problems in the broader scope of the common challenges that face humanity.

Whatever adversity we face is usually not that different from what others have experienced throughout history. Self-compassion is also an effective tool for countering trauma-related symptoms in those struggling with PTSD.

A simple way to practice self-compassion is to imagine that whatever you are struggling with is happening to someone else. It's not you but your close friend Ollie, who botched his presentation to his executive team. What emotions would you feel toward Ollie? How would you support him and help him get back on his feet? It's not difficult to tap into these emotional and behavioral responses, and yet they are often dramatically different from those that we naturally apply to ourselves when we are the subjects of crisis. In accessing compassion, we counter our negative feelings of fear or shame with emotions of love and care.

Self-Efficacy

The final key driver of resilience is self-efficacy, the belief that we can succeed in a particular endeavor. First coined by psychologist Albert Bandura in the 1980s, self-efficacy is an incredibly powerful predictor of everything from workplace performance to success in dieting or exercise. Robert VanOrden's industriousness in finding a new, highly varied portfolio of work was a demonstration of enormous self-efficacy. He knew the work was out there, he believed he could find it, so he went and did it. Closely related to self-efficacy is agency, the belief that we can change future events. Agency protects us from learned helplessness.

Self-efficacy can be enhanced. According to Bandura, the best way to grow self-efficacy is through mastery experiences. Developing mastery in any area requires small, steady victories over time. Setting attainable, chunked goals helps us avoid the pitfalls of aiming too big and falling short. Small goals also help us build the confidence that will let us gradually take on greater challenges over time. When, after all this work, we arrive at a high level of skill—mastery—we then feel a higher degree of self-belief that will transfer to many other arenas.

Cognitive agility and self-efficacy work hand in hand, as we can see from the following story: Shaya is a product marketing manager for one of the world's largest technology companies based in the Bay Area. She grew up in Florida, daughter of Moroccan immigrants, attending public school and working in the stockroom in a local grocery to help support her family. Shaya became interested in marketing because of the advertising of the late 1980s. She recalls looking at the banal images on the Campbell's soup cans and wanting to help others imagine a better life through new products.

Fresh out of college, Shaya's early work for an office supply company focused on traditional marketing forums, including print ads and live events—conferences and customer gatherings not unlike those brand-building events of generations past. Her typical day then might include drafting copy, calling customers, and planning the agenda for a conference. She worked hard, harder than others on her team, eager for the financial stability her parents never attained. She saw that with focus and perseverance, she could learn wide-ranging skills across her field.

Three years after starting her first job, Shaya found out that her regional company would be filing for bankruptcy, unseated by more tech-savvy competitors. She had seen signals of the coming disruption but had not known how to raise the alarm for her leaders. Finding her next role was incredibly difficult, because hiring managers wanted digital marketing experience.

In the face of self-doubt, Shaya recalled how much she had learned in just the three years prior: *If I could do it once, I can do it again.* Her track record gave her the confidence to enroll in courses in online marketing. That's self-efficacy. Eventually Shaya's eagerness to learn and willingness to start at the entry level yielded her first digital marketing role.

In the last ten years, working for much larger enterprise technology companies, Shaya's work has shifted entirely to online marketing. Marketing today is heavily analytical and serviced by dozens of software programs at any one time: social media marketing tools, search engine optimization tools, lead generation and capture tools, email marketing tools, and much, much more. Monthly, weekly, even daily, new features and technologies emerge with the potential to make or break a business. Marketing technology—"MarTech"—is its own industry, alongside FinTech, Health Tech, and others. Shaya takes pride in keeping pace with the latest MarTech trends. She need not become expert in every new tool, but she needs to be open-minded enough to ascertain its relevance. This might mean watching demos, downloading free trials, or talking to early customers of new technologies to learn about their experiences. For those tools she deems worth incorporating into her team's workflow, she must then shift into the focused action mode to learn their ins and outs and influence others to use them.

At the same time, Shaya needs to keep pace with the more seismic shifts in the enterprise technology industry itself. From month to month, as leader of a large portion of her company's marketing portfolio, her focus may shift from promoting file-sharing products to North American customers to advertising imaging products to Asia-Pacific corporate buyers. Shaya's area of focus is determined both top-down—by superiors juggling resources across emerging products—and bottom-up, as Shaya and her colleagues advocate for greater attention to be paid to promising new opportunities.

Any single transition—from one very distinct product to another, from one geography to another, from one technological tool kit to another—challenges Shaya's self-efficacy, cognitive agility, and overall resilience. She must first and foremost be able to shoot the rapids of change without getting mired in helplessness. She must then balance openness to new opportunities with focused execution.

———————

Self-efficacy, self-compassion, cognitive agility, optimism, and emotional regulation are the building blocks for the psychological resilience we need to thrive in our whitewater workplace. Each of these can be taught. Personalized approaches like coaching or data-driven learning systems tailor the learning experience to each individual's needs. Some of us need to focus most on emotional regulation, for example, while others need to build the muscles of optimism.

With practice, all of us can build resilience and move ourselves further and further toward antifragility. And if you do it right, results come quick: we see a whopping 125% improvement in self-rated resilience scores in just three months for those who start out lowest in this skill. This increased resilience will help people avoid negative outcomes and thrive more stunningly in their personal and professional lives. That's shifting the curve.

So far, we've looked at how resilience benefits individuals and how we all can build up our personal reserves of resilience. Resilience also operates at the team and organizational levels, in ways that matter for workplace outcomes. Let's turn to the group.

The Resilient Organization

The COVID-19 pandemic offered an object lesson in workforce resilience. Overnight, tens of millions of workers found themselves working from home in tight quarters with roommates, partners, little children home from school. Service workers navigated business closures and constantly changing regulations. And these were the lucky ones. Millions of others lost their jobs altogether. We lost loved ones, day after day. Exhaustion, confusion, fear, and anger soared.

At work, organizations needed employees to pivot hard en masse. How quickly could they switch from making coats to sewing masks? From building cars to assembling ventilators? Leadership arranged furloughs for large portions of the workforce, while those remaining had twice as much to do.

And so the pandemic unmasked resilience as the true bedrock of any human capital strategy. Workers with low resilience scores slept less, ate worse, seldom exercised, and produced less; whereas workers with high resilience preserved not only their well-being but also their ability to perform for their employers. Their highs were higher, and their lows were blunted. Resilience prepared them to thrive even through this most challenging period of time.

In an effort to quantify this advantage, in the spring of 2020 we examined financial returns from the companies we work with and compared those with their population resilience scores. Companies whose workforce had the highest average resilience scores demonstrated 42% higher return on assets and 3.7x higher annual return on equity. In addition, they showed 3.2x higher year-over-year growth.

We also looked specifically at how the resilience of leaders drove those outcomes. We found that, from an organizational perspective, resilient leaders are the gift that keeps on giving. Employees who report to resilient leaders are themselves nearly three times as resilient as others. They're also 50% less burned out than employees whose leaders are not resilient. Teams with resilient leaders were 30% more productive. These teams were more innovative and more cognitively agile, too.

If any of that sounds hard to believe, call to mind your last few bosses. How resilient were they? Were they easily stressed?

Now consider your own degree of well-being while reporting to each of those individuals. Do you see the pattern?

As of May 2020, an estimated 22% of American companies had resilience included in their leadership competencies. Leadership competencies are the behaviors and skills that organizations expect to see in their leaders. Companies often design their leadership trainings to focus on these areas. Most of these trainings are not evidence-based, as we'll see in chapter 10. Nonetheless, 22% is a start.

The time to build resilience is and always will be *now*. The question most often asked of us is: How do we begin?

We know how. There are evidence-based programs available on the market today. They can target individual development needs in precise, data-driven ways, based on many decades of research and thousands of studies. These interventions move the needle on this most fundamental capability at the individual, team, and organizational level. And many do so on the order of not years but months.

Building resilience allows us to buffer the challenges of both today and tomorrow. The question is not how, but when. What are we waiting for?

CHAPTER FIVE

The Meaning Rush

Mattering in the Modern Economy

If you have your why for life, you can get by with almost any how.
—Nietzsche

In the 1970s, Pulitzer Prize winner Louis "Studs" Terkel did future generations the favor of preserving, on reel-to-reel tape, the voices of Americans talking about their work. Bookbinders, grocery clerks, steel workers, dentists, truck drivers, and gravediggers chitchatted with Terkel on his cross-country visits about how they passed the time on the job: the people they interacted with, the feelings their work provoked, the thoughts that flickered in their minds as they went about their day. The written version of these conversations was published in 1974 under the title *Working: People Talk About What They Do All Day and How They Feel About What They Do.*

Terkel did not realize then that his book would become an ideally timed "Before"—set as it was just before the onset of one of the most dramatic labor transformations in history. How did people feel about what they did just before the whitewater world of work?

In his introduction, Terkel summarizes the most potent wisdom he gleaned from his time with America's workers. Foremost among the themes that emerge across the diverse stories was the desire to find meaning at work:

> [This book] is about a search . . . for daily meaning as well as daily bread, for recognition as well as cash, for astonishment rather than torpor; in short for a sort of life rather than a Monday through Friday sort of dying. Perhaps immortality is part of the quest. To be remembered was the wish, spoken and unspoken, of the heroes and heroines of this book.

The observation was at once universal, and the unique, surprising product of its era. Terkel's contemporaries, humanistic psychologists Abraham Maslow and Victor Frankl, had come to similar conclusions about the essential role that meaning plays in our work. "If work is meaningless," Maslow said in 1962, "then life comes close to being meaningless." In 1969, educators Neil Postman and Charles Weingartner defined the project of "meaning making," today considered fundamental to education, work, and counseling. Something was in the air.

Silicon Valley itself was birthed in this ethos. We often think of the dawn of the Valley as the 1990s, but already by the 1970s, John Seely Brown's Xerox PARC team was developing the ethernet, the GUI, and laser printers. Engineers were lured to the area by the excellent Stanford Engineering department, great weather, and access to early computer processors. These engineers also dreamed of advancing space travel and pushing the limits of human progress.

This particular westward migration was not a gold rush so much as it was a meaning rush. These pioneering minds—the great innovators of their generation—were attracted to the work by money, sure, but also by purpose. In the words of early Apple employee and LinkedIn cofounder Reid Hoffman, in his forward to Fred Kofman's book on meaningful work:

What we see time and again in Silicon Valley is how the companies that grow fastest, execute most consistently, and become the dominant players in their industries . . . are the ones that define their corporate missions in big, noble, incredibly ambitious terms.

Today every corporation has a mission statement intended to both inspire workers and attract customers. Walt Disney employees create happiness through magical experiences. Sony inspires and fulfills your curiosity. Patagonia saves our planet. One hundred and thirty years ago, Coca-Cola was founded by a pharmacist who chose its name because the two Cs would look good in advertising. Now, Coca-Cola's purpose is to "Refresh the world. Make a difference."

Many such statements ring hollow. In a competitive labor market, employees can afford to hold out for the business whose purpose aligns most closely with their personal values. They can, similarly, afford to quit companies whose actions they find reprehensible. Musician Neil Young encouraged Spotify employees to do just that when Spotify refused to drop its biggest podcast star, Joe Rogan, over concerns that he was spreading misinformation about COVID-19 vaccines. "Get out of that place before it eats up your soul," Young advised.

Reciprocally, as part of their interview process, prospective hires should be prepared to explain their personal connection to a company's mission. Jobs are won and lost today on the basis of degrees of passion exhibited. Believers want to be surrounded by believers.

Why has mission, and meaning, become such an essential part of our work? This chapter examines the centrality of purpose-driven performance to our thriving, and examines the tools at our disposal to measure and nurture that sense of meaning.

Definitions: Meaning and Purpose

Psychologist Michael Steger analyzes meaning as having three components:

1. Comprehension: Making sense of one's experience
2. Purpose: Possessing highly valued goals or missions for one's life
3. Significance: Perceiving one's life to be worthwhile and to have value

These three components, while quite different, are each fairly implied by "meaning" as we use it colloquially.

Not all jobs are equally meaningful; nor do all of us seek to find meaning in our work in the same way. In a famous 1997 study of workplace attitudes, psychologists Amy Wrzesniewski, Clark McCauley, Paul Rozin, and Barry Schwartz showed that people view their work as either a job, a career, or a calling, as follows:

- A job: Focused on financial rewards and necessity. Jobs are means to the end of enjoying life outside of work. You quit when you find better pay.
- A career: Focused on professional advancement. Those of us with careers feel pride in our professional accomplishments and elevated social standing. You quit when the promotions stop.
- A calling: Focused on fulfilling work. You feel called to do socially or morally valuable work. You keep at it almost no matter what.

Three people in the same sales role might see their work as a job, a career, or a calling, depending on their orientation. These different types of motivations produce different types of work. Those of us who labor for money—extrinsic, or external, motivations—will do exactly what's required and no more. By contrast, those of us with a calling, a higher sense of purpose—an intrinsic motivation—see our work as deeply connected to who we are. Meaning fuels performance far beyond what is strictly required of the role.

How Widespread Is the Meaning Rush?

Billions of people the world over go to work every day. How many of them look to their work for meaning? You might assume that meaning is important to a small, privileged portion of workers, whereas most people are just fine having their job be a job.

We were skeptical too. In 2018, our lab set out to discover how many workers fell into each camp. We focused on America, where we have the greatest volume of data, and access to workers with the broadest range of economic backgrounds. We surveyed two thousand full-time US employees of all ages, industries, tenures, and incomes.

It turns out that the portion of workers who want meaningful work isn't small at all. In fact, in the US, it isn't even really a "portion." Virtually everyone we studied—across all generations and income levels, regardless of sector or position—craved more meaning at work. Everyone wanted work to be less of a job and more of a calling.

We also wondered how meaningful workers found their current roles. In the same study, using a ratings scale of 0 (no meaning) to 100 (maximal meaning), people gave their current jobs an average score of 49.

Which is to say: Our "meaning cups" are less than half-full.

We also asked these two thousand workers how much of their salary they would sacrifice for a job that was highly meaningful to them. The results were eye-opening. On average, people were willing to sacrifice a whopping 23% of their future earnings to have a job that would always be highly meaningful! This percentage held across income brackets from $40,000 per year up to $200,000 per year.

To put that in perspective, as of 2018, Americans spent about 17.5% of their income on their mortgage. We are willing to spend more on meaning than we do on the very homes we live in.

The Benefits of Meaningful Work

Why should meaning be so essential to our work lives that, as organizations, we recruit for connection to the mission; and as individuals, we crave meaning so much that we'd give up lots of money to have more of it?

It turns out to be more than just hype. We'll start with the organizational benefits. One of the holy grails of modern HR departments is "discretionary effort." Corporations seek to get the most work out of their employees. Psychologist Aubrey Daniels, who founded the field of performance management, defined discretionary effort as "the level of effort people could give if they wanted to, but above and beyond the minimum required." People in a *job* do not exercise discretionary effort. Those with a *calling* do. Discretionary effort is necessary for the creation of extraordinary work products— for levels of craftsmanship and innovation otherwise unattainable. This is the kind of work that comes from deep within, fueled by purpose.

How does that look on paper? Our study found that employees who find their roles meaningful work longer hours and miss fewer days. They like their jobs better, stay at their companies longer, and are more productive, creating about $9,000 more in value for their companies each year. For every one thousand employees who find their work highly meaningful, companies will save an average of $5.94M in annual turnover costs. These employees are also remarkable buffers for organizational challenge: In the face of poor management, or toxic environments, workers who find their work highly meaningful are able to push through the negativity with greater ease and are less likely to quit.

For us as individual workers, the rewards of meaningful work are even greater. On the professional side of things, those of us who see our work as highly meaningful get more raises and promotions than those who do not. So it turns out you don't need to take that 23% pay cut after all—quite the opposite: doing what you love, and loving what you do, accrues financial benefits.

On the personal side, meaningful work is good for our health. Pursuing work for intrinsic motivations—for reasons that come from deep within us, rather than for external reward—has been shown to have a positive impact on our overall well-being. In fact, the field of study known as self-determination theory (SDT), founded by psychologists Edward Deci and Richard Ryan, considers intrinsic motivation *the* essential ingredient for psychological well-being across all areas of our life. This deep well of intrinsic motivation is vital in the modern world of work. Navigating the whitewaters is no joke. We're out there daily, paddling furiously as the waves crash over us, facing challenge after challenge after challenge. Meaning and purpose motivate us to keep going.

Practically speaking, if resilience and cognitive agility are *how* we navigate change, meaning and purpose form the core of *why*. They are the fuel we need to power ourselves through the challenges ahead. Indeed, the data shows that our first two PRISM powers—meaningful work and resilience—go hand in hand. In the same 2018 study, we compared levels of psychological resilience of those who found their jobs most vs. least meaningful. The finding was unambiguous: Workers who found work to be most meaningful (with meaningful work scores in the top 25%) scored 23% higher on resilience items than workers who found work least meaningful (with scores in the bottom 25%).

By contrast: American anthropologist and anarchist David Graeber has described at length the negative psychological effects of pointless work. His 2018 book *Bullshit Jobs* argues that millions of people, from receptionists to marketing writers to bureaucrats, hold jobs that serve no purpose, and they know it. While Graeber's case is perhaps overstated, the negative psychological impact of this pointless work that his subjects describe bears mention. Anxiety, depression, and low self-esteem plague them. Psychosomatic illnesses mysteriously disappear as soon as they find more purposeful work.

We need meaningful work to help us perform and flourish through change. Our organizations need us to find our work meaningful to get the most out of the good times, and to buffer the bad.

Given all of that: Is meaning something that can be fostered? Or is it just . . . there?

What Makes Work Meaningful?

Another reason we undertook our 2018 study was to identify the most critical workplace factors needed for employees to find their work meaningful. Understanding these drivers gives individuals and organizations a point of entry for intervention.

The first key organizational factor that emerged is feeling like you're not in it alone. *Workplace social support* significantly influenced degrees of meaning. Workers who feel a greater sense of social support at work scored 47% higher on workplace meaning scales than those who did not. One of the most difficult challenges for organizations today, particularly post-COVID-19, is preserving community amid remote work, turnover, and job instability. But most of us don't realize that part of what's at stake is the very soul of work itself.

Another critical factor that emerged from the data was *values and purpose alignment with leaders*, particularly the company's most senior leaders. Employees who feel values-aligned with their colleagues were 33% more satisfied with their jobs—not bad! Employees who feel values-aligned with their leaders, though, were a whopping 46% more satisfied. Leadership's values matter, and not just to shareholders or board directors. They matter to the individual workers who need to follow that leader through the rapids. Shared mission statements are a decent place to start. To be most effective, however, senior leaders must live the values the company espouses.

We also uncovered some important differentiators in level of meaning based on type of work. Knowledge workers, for example, found their work more meaningful than others. Why should that be? Close analysis revealed that knowledge workers have a greater sense of *active professional growth*. All workers want, and deserve, to experience this sense of growth on the job. By seeking out these growth opportunities as individuals, and offering them more universally as organizations, we enable everyone to partake in that satisfaction.

Research by Harvard Business School professor Ethan Bernstein suggests that changes to the workplace can create an environment where all workers feel that their work is knowledge work. For example, employees perform better when given certain rights of privacy and the ability to experiment in judgment-free zones. Organizations that create these conditions can expect to drive a greater sense of meaning for their employees. Individuals benefit, both materially and psychologically, and organizations see outsized returns. Everybody wins.

Bolstering Meaning at Work: As Individuals

Call this the outside-in perspective on meaning—the organizational factors that influence how meaningful people will, on average, find their work. To arrive at those answers, we take people's scores on meaningful work scales and see how they correlate with organizational features.

The inside-out version of this same question asks, what parts of work do people *say* they find most meaningful?

Two professors at the University of Canterbury, in Graeme Payne's hometown of Christchurch, New Zealand, discovered that employees experience seven most common drivers of workplace meaning. Which of the seven best encapsulates what makes work feel meaningful to you?

1. Personal growth: You feel that work actively contributes to the development of your inner self.
2. Professional growth: You feel that work allows you to activate your full professional potential. (This was what we found knowledge workers experienced most.)
3. Shared purpose: You feel that you and your colleagues and your leaders are working toward a common purpose.
4. Service: You find meaning in acts of service for other people.
5. Balance: You find meaning in the work of balancing your personal and professional attitudes and priorities.
6. Inspiration: You feel inspired by your company's vision and leadership.
7. Honesty: You hold as a core value straightforward communication and the realistic assessment of work.

Much of the work of meaning-making must happen at the individual level. Helping people understand what creates that sense of purpose for them individually is a core function of a good coach.

Jinny is a mid-career R&D manager working on "next-gen" products who brought her coach, Patrick, an earful of frustration over a negative performance review from her boss. She knew she wasn't measuring up, but she also couldn't bring herself to do what was required. "He's asking me to do all this work on a project that may never even see the light of day," Jinny said. "And then I'm supposed to hire people to help me do this work that I don't even feel confident in."

Unwinding her frustration required retracing her motivations for staying in her role. In one of their first sessions together, Jinny had identified her core source of workplace meaning as *service*. She wants her labors to serve society. And as such, the idea that her products might now never get built felt threatening.

Patrick helped Jinny create two strategies to reconnect and reboot. First, Jinny needed to revisit and reaccept the level of risk built into working on cutting-edge products. On innovation teams, successes can produce substantial impact, while failures can be frustrating. Jinny needed to be able to tolerate the possibility of a dead end as part of the service she was performing. Second, Jinny was missing opportunities to perform smaller acts of service all around her. Hiring, for example, which made her anxious, was an opportunity to help someone early in their career learn key skills that only Jinny could impart. Even her boss could benefit from her help, she realized, as he had to tolerate that same frustration around the uncertain outcomes of their team's work.

We can also lean in to different sources of purpose in different roles and environments, affording ourselves greater agility. For some workers, for example, COVID-19 triggered a shift from a focus on professional growth to one on service. In times of transition and turmoil, service and honesty can be particularly powerful motivators.

The most common source of meaningful work across all worker populations in our 2018 study was *personal growth*. Over the course of our careers, we seek opportunities to develop our inner self, in the journey toward what Maslow called self-actualization. Increasing our sense of meaningful work can be as simple as gaining clarity on the ways we are striving to grow—in our thoughts, our relationships, our skills, our knowledge—and seeking opportunities to focus there.

One way to bolster your sense of personal growth is through regular review of your achievements. How often, at the end of the day, are you reflecting on a challenging task performed well? How about work that stretched you interpersonally—as a colleague, a friend, or a leader? Noticing and savoring your own growth will increase your sense of purpose and satisfaction.

On Mattering, as an Alternative to Meaning

A few years ago, pre-pandemic, Gabriella spoke to a gathering of Illinois senior human resources leaders about meaning and purpose at work in downtown Chicago. The event was hosted by a media company, at its sports TV headquarters. After appetizers and cocktails, everyone entered the speaking venue, which was the TV news studio itself. Under blue and orange fluorescent lights, behind the wide white news desk on the studio stage, it was hard to make out participants other than by raised hands.

"Here's the thing I'm not sure I buy," one man began. "As employers, is it really in our purview to make someone's job more meaningful?"

It's a fair question, an honest question, and an important question—if for no other reason than that some version of it inevitably arises in any talk on this subject. Gabriella's answer, in the moment, was to reiterate the organizational benefits of doing so.

But this gentleman wasn't asking why; he was asking *whether*. There are many reasons corporate leaders are hesitant to wade into the waters of workplace meaning. For some it feels uncomfortable. Meaning is so personal; is it really the boss's business? Meaning evokes spirituality. For many people, religion is still the greatest source of meaning in life. What place does the corporation have in that realm?

Part of the challenge is that the word "meaning" is so broad. It can legitimately mean so many different things. Even Steger's definition, provided on page 86, includes three diverse constructs: comprehension, purpose, and significance. This creates ambiguity—flabbiness, even—as well as confusion that makes meaning harder to talk about, harder to measure, and harder to improve than it needs to be, particularly for business leaders.

For all these reasons, over the years, in our work together, we—Gabriella and Marty—have gravitated toward the construct of "mattering" as a more concrete, measurable, and actionable alternative to meaning in the corporate realm. Mattering comes closer than meaning to the essence of what workers care about, and what companies can influence. Skeptics like the man in the news studio audience have no problem with mattering. Everyone understands, intuitively, that we all need to feel that our work matters; and that people other than us—our bosses, our leaders—are often better positioned than we are to help us see that impact.

We define mattering as one's sense of the difference one makes in the world. Of the three aspects of meaning in Steger's definition of meaning, "significance" comes closest to mattering, although mattering informs our sense of purpose as well. You can think of mattering as a highly concrete subset of meaning. Individuals who feel their efforts don't matter will be unmotivated to work at all, let alone to push through challenge. Organizations therefore have a vested interest in making sure their employees know why they and their work matter.

Philosopher and MacArthur "Genius" Rebecca Goldstein, originator of the Mattering Map in her brilliant and hilarious 1993 novel, *The Mind-Body Problem*, has argued extensively that one of our defining human features is our need to matter. Natural selection favors mattering. In Goldstein's words:

> If an organism—any organism—were to have the capacity to articulate its deepest motivation, the motivation that's a prerequisite for all its other motivations that drive it on in its ceaseless tasks and activities—its scurrying, hiding, roaming, raiding, mating—it would say that its own existence in this world, its persistence and its flourishing, *matters.*

This is what Goldstein terms the Mattering Instinct. Our need to matter is the primordial imperative of our very survival.

Why Does Mattering Matter?

Through the lens of Goldstein's Mattering Instinct, mattering is the story we tell ourselves to explain our own existence. It helps us make sense of why we feel we need to survive, even though our need to survive is in fact biologically derived.

Chicago resident Homer Martinez spent his career, much to his own surprise, as a gravedigger. In his interview with Studs Terkel, Martinez shared the narrative he used to explain why he should find his work important:

> I never had a dream to have this kind of job, but I believe that it is important, because not anybody can be a gravedigger. I mean, you can be a sewer digger, you can dig sewers, but sewers, you just can dig a hole anyway they come, you can throw dirt, you can make a mess of it, but when you dig a grave, it has to be neat and clean. All you see is a square hole and it's perfect.

The physical act of digging a hole is the same whether we dig it for a grave, a sewer, or no reason at all. Martinez's narrative tells how he makes sense of why he, Homer, is alive and digging holes day after day. Why the holes he is digging uniquely *matter*.

We know that our ability to explain our own actions through a narrative of mattering carries tremendous implications for our individual well-being. Without it, we falter. One of the hallmarks of depression is a low sense of self-worth. In depression, we believe that we do not, in fact, matter, and therefore there is no purpose to our activities. Why bother to try? We are drained of energy, and we have no desire to engage with the world. Meaning has always been one of the five pillars of well-being as defined by Marty and colleagues in PERMA. Today we replace meaning with its more actionable, specific constituent—mattering—as the *M* of PERMA.

Many of those looking ahead to the whitewater world of work fear for the loss of meaning we will experience as a result of repeated job loss and instability. As futurist and computer scientist Kai-Fu Lee writes in his celebrated book *AI Superpowers*, "tumult in job markets and turmoil across societies will occur against the backdrop of a far more personal and human crisis, psychological loss of one's purpose." Yuval Noah Harari shares this fear. "We need to protect the humans, not the jobs. The crisis here is a crisis of meaning, not employment."

We agree, with the amendment that, from an organizational perspective, this is, more specifically, a crisis of mattering.

Filling Our Mattering Cups

What it means to matter at work must look different for us today than in years past, particularly with job tenure decreasing to a few years or less. We need to feel that we matter sooner; and we need to be able to redefine that sense of mattering frequently as our roles change. Organizations and individuals need interventions to fill our mattering cups in this new context.

In the winter of 2018, we brought together Goldstein and a group of researchers to work with us on measuring and building mattering. While we all agreed that mattering offered a helpful alternative to the flabbier concept of meaning, much work had to be done to make mattering scientifically muscular.

Our first order of business was to create the Organizational Mattering Scale. Psychometric scales are necessary to measure whether any potential interventions are successful. We oriented our scale around the idea that mattering can be defined objectively or subjectively.

Goldstein explained that one can see mattering in classic terms as "arête" (ἀρετή), the achievement of excellence in one's actions; or as "kleos" (κλέος), the renown and glory earned through one's excellence in action. The former—arête—is an internal kind of mattering that an individual can achieve with effort, experience, and patience. The latter—kleos—is external and requires recognition by others. Both aspects of mattering are important for productivity.

This duality lends itself nicely to both measurement and intervention, as arête can focus on how individuals can help themselves arrive at a sense of mattering, while kleos focuses on how organizations support their employees in knowing the broader value of their contributions to others. Whereas the grand aspects of meaning may take months or years to cultivate, our sense that our work matters can be developed almost immediately through a combination of arête and kleos.

We use the scale to measure interventions to build one's sense of mattering. You can use it to evaluate your own sense of whether you feel your work matters. Higher scores on the scale—as measured by stronger agreement with each item—correlate with more promotions, more raises, and lower turnover.

Organizational Mattering Scale

Answer on a scale of 1 (strongly disagree) to 5 (strongly agree):

A. *Achievement* (Arête)
- My work contributes to my organization's success.
- The quality of my work makes a real impact on my organization.
- My work influences my organization's functioning.

B. *Recognition* (Kleos)
- My organization praises my work publicly.
- My coworkers praise my work.

- I am well-known for the quality of my work in my organization.
- My work has made me popular at my workplace.

Do you feel a sense of arête about your work? How about kleos? Scores above 13 for Achievement, or above 15 for Recognition, are exceptionally high.

With the scale in hand, we set out to build interventions to increase workers' sense of mattering. Taking our lead from *The Mind-Body Problem*, we created an Organizational Mattering Map that managers can use to help their direct reports more fully understand the importance of the work they are doing to others, targeting kleos. We designed the map to focus on the most essential areas of mattering. At the center of the map, the manager places the employee's name and photo. Around this are three concentric circles, each studded with three text boxes. In the innermost circle, managers identify three of the company values that the employee most embodies. These values sit closest to center to represent their connection to the employee's identity. Managers are asked to offer quotes and details explaining each value. Embodiment of values speaks to our deepest sense of significance.

The second circle lists the names of three business teams that the employee has helped. This allows the manager to help the employee understand how their work matters to others. Because of the pace of our work, and how quickly it shifts, we are not always individually aware of its broader organizational impact. This circle of teams allows the manager to highlight ripples of impact with quotes and testimonials.

Finally, the outermost circle focuses on the three organizational outcomes that one's work has produced. Here a manager might highlight that the processes an employee developed improved efficiency by $x\%$; that their customer service improved rating scores by $y\%$; that their sales activities drove bookings of $z. Some of these outcomes would be known to the employees. Others would not.

It's important that in each circle, the employee learn something new and concrete about how he has mattered to others. This expands his sense of mattering, and it helps him feel that these diverse dimensions of mattering are seen by his manager and others.

In the top corner, the company's senior leaders would include a quote, and a signature. This might be auto-generated but it offers a sense of official imprimatur that contributes to mattering, and to kleos in particular.

How will the whitewaters change our feelings of mattering at work? Will work become more or less meaningful in the future? As optimists, and as two individuals well educated about the new types of work ahead—work that is more human and less mechanical; work that is more varied and less rote—we see great promise for more, rather than less, meaningful work in the evolution of automation technologies. Greater volumes of data exhaust coming off our work also mean more potential to measure and recognize mattering.

Even amid these positive, humanizing tides, there will be many challenges, and we will need our mattering-driven motivation to help see us through. Fortunately, both good times and bad offer us an opportunity to reconnect with our purpose in life, so long as we are open to it. Indeed, the most horrendous conditions in world history yielded some of humankind's most profound meditations on meaning. In 1946, Victor Frankl encapsulated what he had learned from the torture of the concentration camps:

> Man *can* preserve a vestige of spiritual freedom, of independence of mind, even in such terrible conditions of psychic and physical stress. We who lived in concentration

camps can remember the men who walked through the huts comforting others, giving away their last piece of bread. They may have been few in numbers, but they offer sufficient proof that everything can be taken from a man but one thing: the last of the human freedoms—to choose one's attitude in any given set of circumstances, to choose one's own way. . . . It is this spiritual freedom—which cannot be taken away—that makes life meaningful and purposeful.

Mattering is the component of meaning that lets us explain to ourselves why it is important to wake up every day and do what we do. Mattering fuels our happiness, our productivity, our ability to withstand difficulty. Individuals, leaders, and organizations can nurture this, and will need to do so in order to successfully overcome the challenges ahead.

CHAPTER SIX

Rapid Rapport

Connection Under Pressure

> *Connect, George, Connect!*
> —Stephen Sondheim, *Sunday in the Park with George*

At 10:00 a.m. on December 14, 1970, a sunny day in Princeton, New Jersey, the first batch of volunteers arrived for a psychology experiment. The participants were seminary students at Princeton Theological, studying religion in preparation for a life of spiritual service.

Upon arrival at the study administrator's office, the participants were told that the experiment would examine career paths of seminarians. Each was asked to prepare a short talk on the topic and given some reading material for inspiration. Half the participants received a sheet of paper with questions and ideas about the best use of a seminary education. The other half received a copy of the famous New Testament parable of the Good Samaritan, who stops on the road to help someone in need.

All of this, unbeknownst to the volunteers, was mere prelude.

The administrator then informed each volunteer that, due to space constraints, they would have to walk over to a different building to share their talk. The participants were handed a map outlining a route that took them through an alley to the next building.

One by one, the participants set out.

Entering the alley, each participant encountered a startling sight: a pile of a man, slumped and motionless in a dark doorway, moaning in distress. Here was the experiment: Who would stop to help, like the Good Samaritan, and who would pass him by?

The groaning man, a disguised member of the research team, noted the reactions of each seminarian. Some hurried past without noticing him. Others looked or nodded but didn't stop. Some paused briefly to ask if the man was all right. And then there were a few "superhelpers" who guided the suffering man inside, refusing to leave until care had arrived.

Who stopped? Who rushed past? What determined whether a person took the time to help another human in need?

Study directors John Darley and C. Daniel Batson had hypothesized that priming the students to think about the Good Samaritan would make them more likely to help—a demonstration of the power of scripture to inspire moral behavior. However, analysis showed no statistically significant difference. Students who hadn't read the parable helped (or neglected to help) in similar numbers to those that had.

None of the other variables Darley and Batson tested—such as what type of religious beliefs the participants held—made a difference, either.

All except one.

Time.

Students who were told to *hurry* to their destination were significantly less likely to stop to help a man in pain. Students who were told they had a bit of spare time to make the walk stopped more frequently and offered more substantial forms of help.

We are hard-pressed to imagine people more likely to stay and help than seminary students. And yet, even among those who devote their lives to serving others, the perception of being short on time kept them from helping someone in obvious need.

Decades later, with life moving faster than ever, what hope is there for the rest of us?

———————————

Time is one of the most significant barriers to social connection today. We believe ourselves to be suffering from a "time famine": always with too much to do, and never enough time to get it done. The modern corporation enshrines this famine mindset. Human capital management systems monitor how and where employees spend their days. Employees keep "time pies" to track their allocation of this scarce resource against specific projects. The perennial struggle for work-life balance often comes down to one problem: I simply don't have enough hours in the day to do well at both work and home. Seventy percent of Americans eat lunch at their desks or don't eat lunch at all. Fifty-six percent of doctors think they don't have enough time to show their patients compassion. Lack of time—or our perception of lack of time—keeps us from connecting.

The pressure to be "on time" feeds all kinds of antisocial behaviors. Consider road rage—the volcanic tempers that flare when other drivers get between us and our destination. Or multitasking, the pervasive splitting of attention in the deluded hopes that doing multiple things at once won't produce mediocre or even deadly results. Every day nine people die and more than a thousand are injured in America by drivers distracted by texting or talking on the phone.

Alongside time, the unique social context of our whitewater world of work presents a number of additional barriers to connection. Seventy thousand years ago, we lived in small, stable, nonhierarchical groups, encountering perhaps a few hundred people over the course of our lives, all with similar skin color, accustomed to the same terrain, and working together collectively on the same narrow range of activities.

Compared with other species, of course, our social interactions have always been highly complex, to the extent that a huge amount of cortical real estate is devoted to puzzling out the great mystery of other people. As we sat around the fire with our tribe, how could we compose a sentence that would flatter Jenny, not be a put-down to Carly, not be boring to Mandy, and still get a laugh out of Darryl? English neuropsychologist Nick Humphrey was first to hypothesize a link between our rich social landscape and our unusually large brains. Numerous neuroscientific studies have borne this out, demonstrating, for example, that the larger the size of our social network—as reflected by artifacts like texts and emails—the larger the size of specific portions of our prefrontal cortex, our amygdala, and more. We are wired to grow through our relationships with others. We can recognize individuals and predict—and to some extent manipulate—what they will do. We have a "theory of mind" that allows us to intuit what others are thinking and act accordingly. We can negotiate, coax, flirt, sympathize, lie, command, and obey using this device. We can do this quickly and simultaneously with several conspecifics.

The complexity of our social context today is several orders of magnitude greater than it was in those moments around the fire, as attested to first and foremost by the number and variety of connections in our networks. Global professionals interact with thousands of people, all around the world, from different cultures—an unfathomably broad pool of colleagues, neighbors, servers, shopkeepers, caretakers, teachers, bridge partners, investors, mentors, gamers, and more each year.

As of 2019, before the coronavirus pandemic, 30% of Americans worked remotely. By October 2020, at least half of American employees worked from home some days per week. We stay with our employer for maybe three or four years before starting over somewhere else and gaining a whole new set of coworkers. We jump teams, we move locations, we switch roles. A manager based in Taiwan works while her team of contractors, based in Brazil and Canada, sleeps. They communicate via email and messenger apps, swapping code and documentation as the sun rises on each new continent.

But while the method, scale, and speed of social connection have changed dramatically, our *need* to connect is as strong as ever—if not more so.

In this chapter and the next, we'll examine the importance of social connection for our physical and emotional well-being as humans; for our performance in the modern global marketplace; and for the experience of our customers. Once we understand these benefits, we'll outline the barriers that make connection, as critical as it is, so difficult today. Finally, we'll explain how to overcome these barriers using the third of our PRISM powers—a set of strategies we call *rapid rapport*.

Connection and Well-Being

Well-being entails social connection. Risk for nearly every mental disorder, from depression to anxiety to schizophrenia to PTSD, increases with social isolation. When we are alone, deprived of the care of others, we are not well. Conversely, almost every positive activity done with another brings more joy.

Some of the most compelling evidence for the importance of social connection to human thriving comes from studies of physical, rather than psychological, illness. A vast literature draws a link between social support and better medical outcomes. Gerontology researchers at Brigham Young University compiled findings from 148 of these studies, encompassing thirty thousand subjects. Their conclusion? Having strong relationships in our lives affords us 50% greater "all cause survival." That is, *whatever* the cause of death we are facing, we are 50% more likely to survive if we have meaningful social support.

In a follow-up study, the same group turned the question on its head and asked how much more likely we are to die young if we are lonely. They found that people who are socially isolated carry a 26% higher risk of early death. Our very longevity depends on our connection.

What is the biological basis for this dependency? To understand the physiologic link between connection and longevity, we need to first define a few terms. Today one can "connect" with others on social media by clicking a lovely blue rectangle. That action will do very little for your brain or overall well-being. What does biologically significant connection look like?

Empathy describes our ability to experience the emotions of others, as if we were living them ourselves. When we empathize with another person, we actually feel, emotionally, some of what they are feeling. In this instant, a specific type of neuron, called a mirror neuron, fires in synchrony with our peer.

In the early days of online bridge, Marty got to witness the formation of surprisingly close bonds among people who had never met face-to-face. One evening, Marty was playing with Ming, a favorite partner, when their opponent made a small error. Scores of kibitzers noisily chatted away in the background.

Ming chimed in. "I've been under the weather lately."

"Something serious?" Marty ventured.

The chatter slowed a bit.

"Yes, Marty."

The chatter slowed some more.

"I have cancer. Pancreatic cancer."

Finally, kibitzer silence.

"I brought my computer to the hospital."

Dead silence.

"So I could die among my friends."

Long silence.

Moved, the kibitzers typed.

Deeply moved.

The devastation of playing cards online in a hospital room while dying hits us in the gut—we *feel* some small portion of Ming's pain as our mirror neurons fire. This stands in contrast to *sympathy*, which is the more cognitive exercise of recognizing someone else's feelings without experiencing them ourselves.

Wanting to put an even finer point on the biological nature of profound connection, psychologist Barb Frederickson of UNC Chapel Hill coined the term *positivity resonance* to describe the experience of shared positive feelings, mutual care and concern, and biological synchrony. When we feel deeply connected to others, we can feel it in our bodies. We are calmer, suffused with warmth, and time even slows down. Whereas empathy typically implies shared feelings of suffering, positivity resonance encompasses the full range of shared emotions, whose very sharing is an inherently positive experience. More poetically, positivity resonance can be thought of as the embodied feeling of love.

Compassion overlays all of this to describe a state of empathy that produces action. If *sympathy* means you understand what the other person is feeling without feeling it yourself, and *empathy* refers to actually experiencing what you imagine another person is feeling, then *compassion* means your feelings have prompted you to take action to relieve the suffering of another person. In the workplace, sympathy is less valuable than empathy, which is less valuable than compassion. We want our colleagues to take action to help us. We want our employees to take action to help our customers.

One final term: *rapport*. Empathy and compassion can be experienced and enacted as onetime events. Rapport, a close and trusting relationship between two people, results from the consistent practice of empathy and compassion over time.

With those definitions in hand, we return to the question of how connection influences our physiology. What is the biological basis for the "warm and fuzzies" of positivity resonance? The cluster of physiologic mechanisms that account for the many positive health benefits of connection are relatively well understood. When we experience emotional synchrony with others, by way of empathy or positivity resonance, our whole body shifts into a different way of being. Everything slows down. We relax, from the inside out.

Our nervous system has many subdivisions, each of which controls specific functions, such as moving our muscles or registering sensations like heat. Two important subdivisions are the sympathetic nervous system and the parasympathetic nervous system. (Note that *sympathetic* here is not related to the concept of sympathy mentioned above.)

The main job of the sympathetic nervous system is to trigger the fight-or-flight response, pumping us up, psychologically and physically, in the presence of a threat. We need this safeguard to survive true danger. But the fight-or-flight response is highly sensitive and can go off even when the threat isn't that serious. It's another mismatch: A car honking behind us doesn't present the same danger as a charging lion, although it might feel that way. Maximizing well-being, therefore, entails minimizing sympathetic nervous system activity—lower anxiety, lower stress, lower anger.

Remember, though, that our goal is to get to plus ten, not just avoid the negative. We don't just want less stress, we want more meaning, more connection, more joy.

That's where the parasympathetic nervous system—the "rest and recharge" system—becomes paramount. When we receive compassion from others, or feel compassion toward them, our parasympathetic nervous system sends signals that do all kinds of miraculous things, from lowering our blood pressure to slowing our breathing rate. These changes promote a greater sense of well-being and improve our physiology.

The star player on Team Parasympathetic is the vagus nerve. With good reason, the vagus has become the "it" nerve for well-being scientists. The vagus nerve inhibits sympathetic activity and lowers overarousal, paving the way for more well-being, not just less misery. Vagal tone is usually measured by heart rate variability (HRV), which measures how much a person's heart rate deviates in either direction from the baseline. You might assume that greater deviation would be worse—i.e., more irregularity produces more stress. It turns out the opposite is true. Higher variability indicates greater adaptability of our heart rate. Less variability means higher cardiovascular risk; more variability means greater well-being. People with high HRV have better memory, better control over their emotions, less depression, higher happiness, and more sustained attention.

A number of other mechanisms beyond the parasympathetic system contribute to the feel-good nature of connection. In a state of close rapport and positivity resonance, cortisol levels drop. Cortisol, aka the "stress hormone," mediates weight, cardiovascular status, memory, immune function, and much more. Although cortisol helps regulate the body during periods of peak stress, sustained high levels are bad for us and can produce a vicious cycle of physical ills that lead to the release of still more cortisol. Social connection disrupts this cycle and centers us.

A separate brain pathway triggered by connection releases the hormone oxytocin, aka the "love hormone." Oxytocin boosts our feeling of connectedness as well as overall happiness while lowering our blood pressure and increasing our pain threshold. It tells us when someone is part of our tribe, and makes us feel loved, loving, and safe.

Those who feel loved heal more quickly from all kinds of wounds, from burns to massive trauma. Feeling supported by others diminishes our sense of physical pain, making it easier to tolerate more severe discomfort. UC Riverside professor Sonja Lyubomirsky's lab has even demonstrated that performing acts of kindness produces improvements in the types of inflammatory genes we express. Connection confers not only immediate biological and psychological results, but also benefits that accrue over time.

What about more superficial connections? Neuroscientists have now demonstrated anatomic and physiologic differences between the experiences of helping others out of compassion versus out of obligation. As philosophers from Immanuel Kant to Martin Buber intuited, the nature of helping someone as a means to an end differs in kind from connecting with someone as an end unto itself.

Feeling authentically connected, befriended, and loved is an essential part of our humanity, without which, myriad forms of suffering ensue.

Connection and Workplace Performance

In 2008, thirty-four students at the University of Virginia were stopped while crossing campus and asked to estimate the steepness of a hill before them. Some of the participants happened to be walking by the hill alone. Others walked by with a friend. The team of psychologists took advantage of this condition to understand whether being with a friend influenced a person's perception of the steepness of the slope.

The results were positively metaphorical. When we estimate how steep a hill is, it turns out, we perceive the hill to be significantly less steep if we are standing with a friend than if we view it alone. The presence of a companion makes the task ahead less daunting to our mind's eye.

In jobs where required skills, embedded technologies, product portfolios, and market positioning change each quarter, every degree of lessened slope helps. We saw in the last chapter that workplace social support is an essential driver of the sense of meaning that we need to overcome challenges. Being able to establish that support quickly, in each new role, within each new team, matters.

Some of what's at stake professionally is clear from the loneliness literature. Our own research, published online in the *Harvard Business Review* in 2018, found that lonelier workers have lower job satisfaction, earn fewer promotions, and are more likely to quit. On the positive side, people who have a best friend at work are *seven times* as engaged as those who don't have a best friend. We're happier in our roles when we have a close buddy beside us.

Most discussions of workplace social support advocate for a broader umbrella of community than just one best friend. Psychologist Shawn Achor's *Big Potential* compellingly argues that we cannot reach our potential as professionals, or as creatives, without close partnerships with a variety of others. Studies of team collaboration, meanwhile, focus on how teams with more and richer social interactions do work that is more innovative and are generally more productive than teams with weaker relationships.

Histories of innovation bear this out as well. Jared Diamond has elucidated how Tasmanian Aborigines were at a cognitive disadvantage compared with Australian Aborigines. Tasmania is cut off by the almost impassable Tasman Strait, whereas social intercourse within Australia is not geographically inhibited. The sophistication of Australian tools increases across two thousand years, while the sophistication of Tasmanian tools deteriorates.

Indeed, crossroads thinking enriches understanding. Successful team collaboration in the whitewater yields tremendous benefits, but it's no small feat. In the Industrial Age, the same type of parts came down the assembly line, to be handled in the same sequence, by the same set of specialists. Today, new types of specialists emerge daily as technology evolves. Consider the proliferation of artificial intelligence roles: data scientist, data engineer, analyst, machine-learning engineer, data researcher. This dynamism means that collaborations become exponentially more complex to predict and navigate. Teams form and re-form quickly, bringing in workers with new skill sets, in never-before-seen combinations.

One of the secret ingredients to successful team collaboration across diverse backgrounds at work is a sense of belonging. Belonging describes the sense of being accepted and included by those around us. Without it, we won't contribute to our fullest. In other words, a company could assemble all the right experts in one room, and at great cost. If they don't feel they belong to the team, they won't give their all.

Many corporate leaders pay public lip service to the idea of belonging, but privately remain unconvinced. Because of this continued resistance to the idea that belonging is essential to successful work team functioning, in 2018 we ran a study looking at whether or not having a sense of belonging on a team actually *causes* individuals to perform differently. We recruited two thousand American workers from around the country to form ad-hoc virtual teams of three. In the first part of the study, teammates built group identities by playing a game together. In the second half, they worked on a task.

The trick was that only one member of each team was a human being. The other two were bots, although the human participant didn't know that. The team-forming activity was a virtual game of catch. In our inclusion condition, the bots passed the ball equally to each other and to the participant. In the exclusion condition, the participant almost never got the ball.

After the game, we gave the participants simple math problems, with monetary rewards at random intervals. Again there were two conditions. Some subjects were told they would keep the money—up to ten dollars, say—for themselves. Other subjects were told they would have to share the money with their teammates—up to thirty dollars, split three ways. We then let them work on the math problems until they decided to stop. Since the rewards were given out randomly, over time, the longer the participant kept at it, the more money they collected.

Note that in each condition, the participant could earn the same maximum amount. The only difference was whether the money went to them alone, or whether their teammates benefited too. (Note also that our analyses controlled for personality and other factors that could skew the results.)

Across three separate replications, we found, first, that feelings of inclusion or exclusion did not affect how hard people worked in the individual condition, when they got to keep everything for themselves. Being excluded by the group didn't dampen motivation to work solely on their own behalf.

Next we looked at the team condition, where participants had to split the reward. Subjects that had been included by their teams worked just as hard for their teams as for themselves. By stark contrast, participants who felt excluded worked significantly less—*even at their own monetary expense.* In a perfectly rational world, it wouldn't matter how many times a teammate passed you the ball, you'd work as hard as possible to get as much money as you could for yourself. But that's not what real people do. When we feel left out, we check out, with negative consequences for everyone involved.

So far, we've seen how social connection supports our well-being, enriches us as individual workers, and fosters successful teams. Now let's examine how it improves the experience of our customers.

Connection and Customer Experience

In 1994, Ken Schwartz was forty years old and in the prime of his life. A well-regarded health advocacy lawyer, he exercised regularly, ate well, and considered himself in generally good health—until a persistent cough sent him to the hospital, and tests revealed that he had advanced lung cancer.

Schwartz was in some respects lucky. He lived in Boston, home to several of the world's best hospitals. His brother, a physician who had trained at Massachusetts General, was able to guide him to the top experts. By virtue of his profession, he had extensive experience dealing with the healthcare system. He was, in short, an insider. But as his condition deteriorated, those advantages began to seem like cold comfort. Toward the end of his life, he looked back on his time as a patient and wrote movingly of what had truly helped:

> As skilled and as knowledgeable as my caregivers are, what matters most is that they have empathized with me in a way that gives me hope and makes me feel like a human being, not just an illness. Again and again, I have been touched by the smallest kind gestures—a squeeze of my hand, a gentle touch, a reassuring word. In some ways, these quiet acts of humanity have felt more healing than the high-dose radiation and chemotherapy that hold the hope of a cure . . . In such a cost-conscious world, with its inevitable reductions in staff and morale, can any hospital continue to nurture those precious moments of engagement between patient and caregiver that provide hope to the patient and vital support to the healing process?

Schwartz worried that the most asymmetric benefit he enjoyed as an insider receiving care was the time his physicians devoted to him—time they spent demonstrating compassion. He knew how rare that level of connection between patient and doctor had become because of the pressure on providers to see more patients each day. Shortly before his death, he founded the Schwartz Center for Compassionate Healthcare, the goal of which is to prioritize compassionate care in every facet of medicine: the provision of care, the structure of health systems, the measurement of outcomes, and the design of medical education.

Twenty-five years later, hundreds of studies have borne out the truth of Schwartz's words. We know today that compassionate doctors provide higher quality clinical care. They follow best practices more often, and their patients see better outcomes. Doctors with higher compassion scores also commit fewer major medical errors. Patients intuit all of this, as Schwartz did, without knowing the research. As the *Wall Street Journal* reported in 2004, in selecting a physician, people place a higher value on interpersonal skills than training—not because we don't care about outcomes, but because we understand at a gut level that a doctor who takes the time to establish a personal relationship will work harder and better for us.

Similar lessons apply to everyone whose work involves direct service to other human beings, from house cleaners to dentists to police officers to nurses to waitstaff. For many professions, social connection is the essence of the job.

Even in sectors like customer service, where automation is increasingly the norm, the trend serves to underscore the preciousness of human contact, as every interaction between employee and customer takes on greater significance. Consider the evolution of industry language. Thirty years ago, the goal was customer satisfaction. In the aughts, customer teams became units of "customer success." Today, we've gone beyond success to customer *delight*—"an extreme form of customer satisfaction." The shift isn't merely semantic. It reflects how global competition has intensified the demand for high-quality service. Customers are savvy. They expect more.

Companies spend aggressively to train their people to create customer delight. The Disney Institute trains non-Disney teams in the world-class service of Walt himself, offering workshops in "Exceptional

Customer Service" for $1,750 per person per day. These investments are not hard to justify. Measures of customer satisfaction often show a predictive relationship with a company's future earnings. Investors scrutinize metrics of customer turnover—a sign of *dis*satisfaction—as important proxies for firm sustainability.

The darker side of the customer delight imperative is the experience not of the customers but of the service representatives themselves. So many in the service industry, doctors included, suffer from high rates of burnout, depression, and even substance abuse. They find themselves drained rather than energized by the repeated requests from their clients. The depletion adds up over time. Corporations demand increasing levels of customer-centricity from their customer service employees without understanding the individual impact of the request.

Giving of oneself so fully to a customer requires what sociologist Arlie Russell Hochschild termed "emotional labor": the work of suppressing our authentic emotional responses in service of paid work. Hochschild's 1983 book *The Managed Heart* explored how flight attendants, for example, need to be "nicer than natural," and to suppress their own fear for the sake of their customers. During the pandemic, shop clerks took on the emotional labor of politely asking people to put on their masks, or show proof of vaccination, even in the face of vitriol. Hochschild said of essential workers at the time, "The internal task for the emotional laborer is to absorb—meaning to manage feelings about—immediate horrors while not feeling overwhelmed by them." Emotional labor significantly increases risk for burnout.

If we are lonely ourselves; if we lack a belief that our work matters; if we are failing to cope with the turbulent changes around us, this level of other-oriented service cannot be fairly expected. Given that the service industries account for 70% of the US GDP, this mounting problem of service industry burnout is a matter of national importance.

Barriers to Connection: Time, Space, and Us/Them

Connecting with others is essential for our personal well-being. It dramatically improves our professional outcomes. And it drives more delightful, successful customer interactions. All of that amounts to one half of the story for why social connection matters so much to each of us at work today.

The other half of the story for why this area needs special attention is that it's harder than ever to connect. Today's work context presents three major barriers that make rapport so much more difficult to achieve than it was in previous work environments. Achieving sustainably deep connections with our colleagues and customers hinges on our ability to overcome these significant barriers.

Time

Our brains, like those of the Princeton seminary students rushing to another building, treat time as a central factor in deciding whether to spend time helping others. Hunger, fatigue, and injury are some of the other determinants of how generous we are willing to be, but time is the resource most precious to workers today.

Ask doctors whether they have the time to interact with patients in the manner they'd most desire, and more than half—56%—will tell you they lack the time to treat them with compassion. Importantly, it's often not objective lack of time but rather our subjective experience of a "time famine" that drives this mindset. Connecting rapidly requires addressing and overcoming that perception.

Space

Never before has our workplace been as physically distributed as it is today. Pre-pandemic, 30% of Americans worked remotely; somewhere between 50–60% worked from home during the pandemic itself. In the world of software, it has long been the norm for team members to collaborate around the world, with just 40% of development teams collocated.

Needless to say, this is not the type of connection we evolved for. Touch, smell, and physical proximity trigger release of specific hormones in primate species, including humans, that contribute to the many health benefits of connection discussed earlier. No one has shown that hugging a computer can produce oxytocin.

In the meantime, the technologies that have evolved to bolster social connection across these divides may be doing more harm than good—and so yet another barrier to overcome are the very solutions we have put in place to help. Dozens of studies in countries from Estonia to Spain, from the United States to China, have demonstrated a link between social media use and both depression and anxiety. In 2016, for example, in one of the more important studies, Liu Lin and colleagues correlated social media use with depression symptoms for 1,787 representatively sampled American adults. They found that high social media use substantially increased one's odds of depression. Greater social media use also correlates with more social isolation— the more time we spend online, the less connected we feel. The mere presence of a cell phone, it seems, interferes with the depth of connection we can hope to achieve in conversation. Researchers have now demonstrated the causal nature of this relationship by showing that abstinence from social media improves subjective well-being.

Social media divides us even further than our geographic distance would suggest.

Us/Them

One of the less uplifting social realities of primates is our sensitivity to in-group and out-group dynamics. Evolutionarily, this was a matter of survival. We needed to be able to quickly determine whether someone was with us or against us, and process their actions accordingly.

Neurologically, connecting with "Us" looks different from connecting with "Them." When we see someone from within our group in pain, we feel for them empathically. Our emotional brain circuitry, most notably our amygdala, activates so we experience the emotions that our friend is feeling. When our kin expresses compassion toward us, their compassion actually lessens our pain.

By contrast, when someone we process as "other" experiences pain, we do not feel their pain in the same way. When we take the perspective of a stranger, we see activation of the brain areas responsible for theory of mind—a way of thinking about how other people perceive the world that is far less automatic and emotional than the way we process the perspective of a close loved one. In evolutionary terms, we are tribal creatures. We feel more compassion for people who look like us. The moral circle extends to "Us," not to "Them."

Crucial to global harmony of the future is lengthening the diameter of the moral circle. In the words of neuro-endocrinologist Robert Sapolsky, "Acting morally toward an Us is automatic, while doing so for a Them takes work." We've already seen that belonging is essential to team performance. It's more natural to help an "Us" feel that they belong than a "Them." As we switch teams, roles, geographies over the course of our career, we must learn to quickly and constantly overcome that sense of "Them," efficiently converting new colleagues to "Us."

Our social reality today is unlike anything our ancestors could have imagined. Our well-being and our performance alike depend on social connection. Yet we live far from one another; we are strangers; and we don't have enough hours in the day to build relationships. These challenges are daunting, but they are surmountable, as we will now see.

CHAPTER SEVEN

Rapid Rapport II

Connection through Time Affluence,
Synchronicity, and Individuation

Given how essential social connection is to our success in the whitewater, how do we overcome these three barriers—Time, Space, and Us/Them? How can we build rapport with our coworkers and our customers as rapidly, and meaningfully, as possible? This chapter picks up where we left off and offers solutions.

Time Affluence

Seminarians rushing from one building to the next didn't stop to help a crumpled man in an alley because they had been told to hurry. That instruction—"hurry"—triggers a mental script. Our focus narrows. We move quickly, ignoring stimuli that could deter us from our goal—including social distractions.

Hurrying is not inherently bad, but a never-ending time famine diminishes our quality of life and causes us to miss important opportunities. The trick is to disrupt this script to restore our sense of equilibrium. How?

Two distinct strategies can help us here. First, while we cannot add more hours to the day, we can make it *feel* like we did exactly that. A famous 2010 study by a trio of professors from Wharton, Yale, and Harvard examined four strategies for reducing our sense of time famine:

1. Giving people time back in their day that had previously been committed to a task
2. Asking people to spend that same amount of time on a task helping others
3. Asking people to waste the time
4. Asking people to spend that time on themselves

Only one of these interventions gave people the feeling of having time to spare—what the authors call "time affluence." Want to guess which one?

The title of the article sums up its conclusion: "Giving Time Gives You Time." When we help others, we experience that as time added to our day, rather than lost. Helping ourselves, by comparison, does nothing.

Internalizing this lesson takes practice. We need to push ourselves to give time to others in moments when we feel least capable of doing so. We also need to reflect on the experience after the fact by noticing our increased sense of time affluence. It's important not to overcommit—signing yourself up for a three-hour shift at a community event when you actually only have one hour available is not going to work. Start small and build—but start. Fight through the "hurry worry," because it's precisely when we feel least capable of helping others that doing so can do us the most good.

The second strategy addressing time famine does so by quantifying how long it actually takes to help. We have an unfortunate tendency to overestimate the amount of time needed, and therefore not to help at all. This is a particularly intractable problem in medicine: Healthcare clinics are so understaffed that workers there feel they can't adequately care for any one patient, let alone all of them.

A number of interventions have been tested to teach physicians how to efficiently, but effectively, show compassion. Researchers at Johns Hopkins, for example, tested a script that cancer doctors can use to bookend their patient encounters.

At the start of the appointment, the oncologists say, "I know this is a tough experience to go through and I want you to know that I am here with you. Some of the things that I say to you today may be difficult to understand, so I want you to feel comfortable stopping me if I say something that is confusing or doesn't make sense. We are here together, and we will go through this together."

Then, at the end of the appointment, the doctors said: "I know this is a tough time for you, and I want to emphasize again that we are in this together. I will be with you each step along the way."

Patients whose doctors share these words with them rated their doctors as warmer, more compassionate, and more caring. Perhaps more important, these patients have demonstrably lower levels of anxiety than patients whose doctors did not say these things.

The purpose of this study was not to demonstrate that compassion matters, however. It was to show just how *quickly* one can display compassion to a patient. All told, the script took an average of only forty seconds to deliver. Just ninety-nine words yielded significantly less anxiety for each patient.

Several other studies have reached similar conclusions. A Netherlands study on delivering bad news to patients, for example, found it takes only thirty-eight seconds to express compassion in a way that will lower the patient's anxiety. Several other studies have confirmed that it takes *less than one minute* to express the compassion needed to decrease patient worry. It's difficult to imagine a scenario more consequential than delivering bad medical news. If harried doctors reciting a prewritten script can move the needle in forty seconds, it follows that managers, call center agents, hosts, and airline stewards could expect similar results.

What's more, even smaller increments of time can matter. A 2017 study found that every compassionate statement a doctor made reduced patient anxiety by 4.2%, with a cumulative effect for each additional statement.

Try it for yourself at work. Ten seconds of compassion can connect you to a colleague, strengthen rapport, and improve well-being for both of you:

- *Great job today. I know it's been tough this past week. I see how hard you are working and I'm proud to be working alongside you.*
- *I really admire how you are rolling with the punches. I want you to know you're not in it alone. I'm here with you and we'll figure it out together.*

As time starved as we may feel, the sad truth is that we waste anywhere from thirty minutes to three hours at work each day surfing the web or in other ways. Who among us cannot actually spare a few seconds to connect with a peer or customer, with simple words of compassion?

Achieving time affluence requires challenging your own perception of time famine by first pushing yourself to give just a few minutes or even seconds to someone else, and then noticing—and enjoying!—the sense of expanded time that results.

Synchronicity

It's a relief to know that in a minute or less we can significantly strengthen relationships. But connection in today's world of work is limited not only by time but also space. Unlike the doctors delivering kind words in person, we need to catch our peer's ear across large distances. What is the recommended "recipe" for rapid rapport for a global, remote-first workforce?

Our lab recently investigated this question in partnership with Sonja Lyubomirsky's Positive Activities and Well-Being Laboratory at UC Riverside. Lyubomirsky is one of the world's foremost experts on social connection. For several months, we paid full-time employees across the United States to perform kind acts for others—strangers, colleagues, or family members. Some of the interactions took place in person. Others took place over video, phone, email, or various social media platforms. We defined successful social interactions as those that produce *positivity resonance*. As noted in the previous chapter, positivity resonance describes the experience of shared positive feelings, mutual care and concern, and biological or behavioral synchrony with another person.

Through this experiment, we uncovered an important "how" for modern connection. We learned that kindness performed synchronously—in person, by phone, or by video—works best, regardless of whether it's performed for a stranger, colleague, or family member. By contrast, kindness performed asynchronously—via email or text or social media—creates significantly less positivity resonance. Being together *in real time* is an essential ingredient for depth of connection. Shared time, shared experiences, matter.

This is also why email can be a disaster. Too much rich information is lost in the absence of immediate, corrective feedback. *Why did he use a period instead of a question mark at the end of that sentence? Did she misspell my name on purpose? Was that sarcasm or a typo? It's been three hours since I texted, why haven't I heard back?* The lack of context contributes equally to the toxicity of social media. At its worst, this type of interaction can produce the opposite of positivity resonance: negativity spirals.

Comparing outcomes from two versions of a popular positive psychology intervention yields a similar finding. For both the Gratitude Visit and the Gratitude Letter, you compose a short testimonial to a living person who helped you along your path, but whom you have never properly thanked. The testimonial has three parts: you describe first what she did or said, second how it affected you, and third where you are today as a result of her kindness. In the Visit, you phone her and tell her you'd like to visit without saying why. Then you show up on her doorstep and read the testimonial. This can also be done by phone or video. Typically, both people weep, and the giver feels a sizable increase in well-being and decrease in depression. In the Letter you merely send the testimonial. The Letter also produces a boost in well-being and lowering of depression, but smaller than that produced by the Visit.

In our study with Lyubomirsky, the fact that synchronicity allowed for deep connection regardless of physical location was surprising to us, and something we intend to investigate further. But the divide between shared time and asynchronous time was not. It's reassuring that in a virtual world, shared time can bridge geographic divide. By all means, employees should use email or messaging apps as methods of rapid information exchange. But to really connect, we need to get off social media and actually talk to each other, live.

"Them" Is "Us"

So far, we've seen that it doesn't take much time to connect, though we do need to alter our time-starved mindset to allow for it. We've also seen that the most effective form of connection is shared time, an important lesson for all managers and customer service centers that lean too heavily today on chat or email instead of live conversation.

What does it take to overcome the third barrier, our biological reflex to divide between Us and Them? How can we arrive more rapidly at feelings of unity across significant cultural, organizational, religious, ethnic, racial, and socioeconomic differences? How can we expand our Moral Circle?

This question deserves its own book, or several, and represents an area of rich and complex interdisciplinary research that sits beyond our qualifications. However, as behavioral scientists who help employees, teams, and organizations navigate difference every day, we have a few skills to share.

In chapter 6, we described our experimental game of catch in which teams either made the participant feel like an "Us" or a "Them." When participants were made to feel like a "Them," they withdrew as a kind of act of protest, leading the whole team to suffer.

The experiment didn't end there. Having proved that exclusion diminishes team productivity, we wanted to know if we could reverse those effects. We tested a number of specific interventions to see if they could restore the feeling of "Us," post-exclusion—and whether, in so doing, they could also undo the impact on team output.

Two of the interventions we tested bear mention. The first is **empowerment**. After someone had been excluded by the team, they were asked to share their ideas for how the game could be improved. Participants suggested more equitable turn-taking, monitoring of turns, and other behaviors to promote inclusivity. The result was remarkable. Simply having an outlet to express ideas for change fully reversed the effects on team performance. In fact, participants who were first excluded, then empowered to offer ideas for change, subsequently worked harder for their teams than participants who had been included by their teams to begin with.

How does empowerment reverse exclusion? Soliciting someone's opinion may foster in them a greater sense of control over their situation, which in turn reinforces participation. Asking for someone's input tells them their ideas can make a difference. A similar phenomenon has been observed in some of the studies of how and why physician compassion leads to better patient outcomes. It's not obvious why this should be the case: Why should having a kind doctor keep you healthier? In these experiments, patient self-efficacy—the belief that we have the ability to conquer the challenge in front of us—is a significant mediator of good patient outcomes. That is, when doctors act with compassion, this first inspires self-confidence in patients. Patients start to believe they can make the changes their doctor needs them to make—and then they make them. In a study of patients with HIV, for example, researchers found that those whose physicians expressed compassion experienced the greatest sense of confidence in their ability to adhere to their medication regimen, and then did so. Empowerment and compassion alike may foster self-efficacy, one of the more powerful predictors of positive psychological outcomes.

A second intervention we tested in the game-of-catch experiment was **perspective-taking**. When excluded participants read testimonials from other participants who had been similarly excluded, they felt less alone and more secure in their own experience. This, in turn, led them to work harder for their teams the next time around.

Perspective-taking exercises of many types can be used to build belonging and inclusion. A typical exercise might ask members of an in-group to work to imagine what the out-group's experience of the world might be like. It's much easier to imagine the experience of an "Us." With a "Them," we need to undertake the hard work of envisioning an unfamiliar world outside our own context in order to reach the same level of understanding.

At its most successful, perspective-taking allows us to not only cognitively access someone else's experience, but also, with enough imaginative effort, to emotionally feel what they are feeling. That empathic connection represents, at least momentarily, successful cognitive reprocessing of a "Them" as an "Us."

Empowerment and perspective-taking, then, are powerful tools for undoing exclusion. What are some ways to avoid exclusion to begin with? Kind, good-hearted colleagues want others to feel included, not excluded, right off the bat. Other than passing the ball fairly in a game of catch, how do we get there?

One important accelerator of shifting from "Us" to "Them" is **individuation**. Our brains designate someone as a "Them" based on group-level traits, rather than individual-level traits. Identifying someone wearing a yarmulke as a Jew indicates nothing of that person's individual identity, other than their membership in a particular religion. Intentional focus on individual characteristics—hopes, affinities, habits, personality traits—diffuses the generalities that lead to automatic classification as "other."

A related skill is **recategorization**. We all carry multiple identities. Two people can be miles apart in one dimension, but close kin in another. Shared identities abound: as caregivers, as experts in specific software languages, as fans of the same authors, as youngest children. The trick is to locate those points of commonality. Neuroendocrinologist Robert Sapolsky offers an illustrative anecdote from the Civil War:

> In the Battle of Gettysburg, Confederate general Lewis Armistead was mortally wounded while leading a charge. As he lay on the battlefield, he gave a secret Masonic sign, in hopes of being recognized by a fellow Mason. It was, by a Union officer, Hiram Bingham, who protected him, got him to a Union field hospital, and guarded his personal effects. In an instant the Us/Them of Union/Confederate became less important than that of Mason/non-Mason.

Psychologists Sam Gaertner and John Dovidio termed this a "common ingroup identity." Studies have applied this approach to helping employees from two corporations unify in a merger, for example.

Individuation and recategorization are two parts of the same process: getting to know someone for who they are both as an individual and as a member of society. The process comes naturally to many of us when meeting someone for the first time. At a party, for instance, when introduced to a friend of a friend, what most people do, automatically, is start probing for information that helps form a picture of who this person is in the world. This act of "small talk" is one of information gathering. The questions we ask, the way we ask them, the order they flow in—all of this will influence how we think of the other person, and how they think of us.

You can turn small talk into rapid rapport through thoughtful individuation and recategorization. Next time you find yourself meeting someone new at work, whether from your own team or another, take control of your reflexive drive for information by focusing questions less on roughing out general contours of identity and more on finding the fastest, most specific path to an "Us." Are we wearing shoes by the same brand? Did our preschoolers drive us both insane that morning? Do we listen to the same podcast on nutrition? Will we both be going camping this summer? When you find a thread of commonality, stay there. Mine that vein for deeper connection. Use it as a lens to learn more, leaning into your shared identity. This is much more than small talk: this is rewiring your brain and your conversant's, turning Them into Us.

Businesses informally employ these tools in a variety of different contexts for organizational gain. Psychologically-based negotiation strategies use recategorization to diffuse tension. Customer support staff learn to get to common ground quickly through their products. If they serve parents, they will establish their own identity as a mother or father. If they target the hospitality industry, they divulge that they once worked as a restaurant host.

Experienced sales professionals are remarkably adept at finding the shortest path to an Us. Watching them at work is a masterclass in the skill. Brad McCracken, senior vice president of worldwide sales at BetterUp, and a gem of a human being, thoughtfully navigates his way to commonality within minutes of meeting someone. He starts the work before the meeting happens—researching a prospect's background, geography, volunteer experience, and more. Prospective buyers today expect that new contacts will do this homework. Coming into the conversation, he'll introduce himself by offering an introduction relevant to that individual: "I grew up in Saint Louis . . ." (because he saw the prospect is from a nearby city) ". . . and I've got two kids, one is into sports . . ." (because the prospect volunteers as a soccer coach). "I used to work at SAP, but I love working for a startup . . ." (because the prospect just made a similar transition) ". . . and a fun fact about me is that my favorite part of leading teams is teaching them to do something better than I ever could" (because the prospect had a blog post on humility and leadership).

Everything he's saying is meaningful and true. Brad isn't making anything up, he's simply focusing on the parts of himself that naturally dovetail with parts of his new contact. The bonds Brad forms feel as authentic as they are. While salespeople and prospects are in some ways the ultimate professional Us and Them, Brad has made an art of highlighting aspects of his identity in ways that help him connect with each potential new customer.

Through individuation, recategorization, empowerment, and perspective-taking, we can more quickly arrive at connection with our peers and customers. But how do we deepen the rapport? Our final skill gets us the most relational impact for time invested: listening.

Deep Listening

Alongside sharing words of compassion, one of the simplest but most powerful actions we can offer another human being is deep listening. Present, generous listening. Not time-pressured listening. Good listeners create space for someone to fully express what's on their minds. Less-skilled listeners, by contrast, can be too emotionally reactive. They may jump into premature problem-solving or minimize the challenge in order to quiet their own anxiety. In so doing, they nullify the benefits of that conversation for either party: the speaker feels shut down, while the listener doesn't get to experience the expanded sense of time that comes from helping.

Communications experts distinguish five types of listening:

- Discriminative, in which we identify and isolate the type and source of the sound we hear
- Comprehensive, in which we focus on understanding content, as when listening to a news report
- Critical, in which we judge the value of information being shared
- Empathetic, in which we try to experience what the speaker is thinking or feeling
- Appreciative, in which we listen to gain pleasure, as when listening to music for enjoyment

Empathetic listening is the kind of listening that customer service centers hire for, and that great teachers do implicitly. We rarely train for this kind of listening, despite how essential it is to the work of these professions. But it can be taught. Here's an exercise you can use to practice this skill:

Next time you sit down with a colleague one-on-one, try listening in the same way you'd listen to a spouse or close friend. Allow your colleague to *dominate the conversation*. Don't interrupt, other than to nod or express alignment. She will gain clarity, and experience emotional relief, from being able to talk at length.

When she pauses, *ask open-ended questions*. Ask, "What happened next?" not "So did they ever get back to you?" Ask, "How are you feeling about it now?" not "Are you feeling better today?"

Make sure to *repeat back what you hear* to confirm your understanding. When we repeat back what we hear, we also allow our friend to hear their own words said differently. It offers them some helpful distance to reexamine their own ideas. Honor each statement as a gift of self-disclosure. At times, you may feel inclined to echo back a similar feeling or experience. Although you don't want to shift the focus, sharing vulnerably will meaningfully connect you in a more reciprocal fashion.

And finally, *allow for silence.* Silence for the speaker is likely full of thoughts. Give your friend time to process the conversation and whatever memories it's bringing up. She will feel that you are giving her the gift of time.

Importantly, empathetic listening is guided by the emotional needs of the *speaker*, with significant work being done by the listener to focus on the speaker's emotional state rather than one's own. Social psychologist and user experience researcher Anneke Buffone distinguishes neurotic empathy from mature empathy. In neurotic empathy, one asks oneself, "How would I have felt if I experienced that?" In mature empathy, one asks, "How would she have felt, experiencing that?" Mature empathy takes more time and thought and has better effects.

Empathetic listening sits at the heart of all good coaching or therapy. It cuts to the very essence of how we build rapport. And, in a climate in which more and more corporations are asking their managers to serve as coaches to their reports, it is an essential skill for modern managers. In a hierarchical work context, managers give orders. In today's highly agile, dynamic, and increasingly flat corporate structure, managers coach their reports to self-direct toward progress against their goals. Done right, empathetic listening can be transformational for speaker and listener alike.

For all these reasons, listening carries risks as well. Recall Hochschild's emotional labor: the work of suppressing our authentic emotional responses in service of paid work. Repeated deep listening at work while suppressing one's own emotions can indeed be considered emotional labor. How do we balance taking other-oriented actions with the risk of emotional burnout? How do we set the right boundaries so we don't harm ourselves in the act of giving?

Appropriate boundaries in relationships are one of the hallmarks of adult psychological health and maturity. Boundaries at work vary depending on the relationship in question—be it with your boss, your customer, your colleague, or your close confidant. A simple way to think about boundaries is through the lens of our old friend Time. Because there is a reasonable, and an unreasonable, amount of time to spend emotionally supporting each person. This amount will be greater for a close friend, lesser for a distant colleague. It will be more in cases where the listening and self-disclosure is reciprocal, less when it only happens one way. The right amount of time to listen to a customer varies by business and industry. Some companies will have standards at the ready. At other companies, if you don't know what's reasonable, you will need to ask your boss or senior colleagues to tell you.

Once you have clarity on this essential parameter of time, you can feel safe knowing that your deep listening is finite; that you will not drown in hours of it; and that the time you do spend receiving the other person's words will deliver outsized returns in terms of the strength of the connection you are building. Limit the amount of time appropriately to each person, and then focus it on the synchronous acts of compassion and listening that will most effectively bolster your relationship.

We need each other. We need to matter to each other. We need each other to feel well, to be well, to live well. We need each other to succeed personally and professionally. And our organizations rely on our social behaviors to drive productivity, innovation, and customer success. The barriers to connection presented by the modern way of work are significant and will become even more so in the decades to come. We will continue to feel that we have no time for each other. We will continue to feel physically distant, because we are. And we will continue to struggle to feel like we belong, because of the real differences that divide us.

In the face of this, we are being asked to connect with more people, more quickly, across a wider gulf of backgrounds, on tasks that are increasingly complex.

The solutions are not simple, but they are effective. We will need to fight our own perception of being starved for time, so that we can pursue the social behaviors that will, in fact, help us feel that we have time to spare. We can then devote the time we do have—even just a few seconds—to shared synchronous experiences, small words of kindness, and generous listening. And we can employ the many evidence-based strategies at our disposal—individuation, recategorization, empowerment, and perspective-taking—to find a rapid path to a feeling of Us.

The work is hard, but it is its own reward.

CHAPTER EIGHT

Prospection

Our 21st-Century Superpower

The Great Data Bonanza began on April 21, 2010, at Facebook's marquee F8 Developer Conference. Mark Zuckerberg, onstage in signature hoodie and baggy jeans, unveiled a product that, in Zuck's words, would be "the most transformative thing we've ever done for the web."

The product, Open Graph, increased the connectivity between Facebook users. They would now be able to see, for example, what articles their friends were reading or what restaurants they had reviewed. Each individual in a network thus became a portal to every other member of that network, making it simple to amass large amounts of data on people's online habits—the content they engaged with, the places they went, how they spent their money. The product also included an API (a connection between computer programs) that allowed developers to transfer this information in and out of Facebook. Developers could preserve access to the information indefinitely.

At the time, these features were presented as obvious goods—selling points. The goal of Open Graph was to "create a web that's smarter, more social, more personalized, and more semantically aware."

For Aleksandr Kogan, it was a gift from the gods of Menlo Park.

Kogan, a psychologist and data scientist, was the founder of the University of Cambridge's Prosociality and Well-Being Laboratory. He had a reputation as an astute thinker, interested in applying novel methods to investigate age-old questions of human connectedness.

Open Graph enabled him to ask them on an unprecedented scale. A 2015 study published in *Personality and Individual Differences* demonstrates how the process worked. Kogan and colleagues examined the relationship between wealth and global networks: Does having more money mean you have more, or fewer, international friends? His lab offered subjects one dollar each to complete a consent form providing researchers access to their Facebook profiles. Eight hundred fifty-seven people signed up.

That would be a decent number of subjects for any psych study. But because of Open Graph, each of Kogan's recruits brought along information for several hundred friends, causing the pool of data to explode.

Legally, and for the bargain price of $857, Kogan and team bought Facebook data for just under three hundred thousand people.

And that was just one study. Suddenly, and with startling ease, Kogan could construct detailed profiles of *millions* of people, from every corner of the planet, across every demographic category.

It's important to note that—to begin with, at least—his intentions appear to have been noble. No individuals were targeted or identified, and his team was mining the data for insights about well-being, in service of the broader social good.

Had Kogan continued to use the data exclusively in this way, the world might never had heard his story. His life might look more like that of fellow Cambridge professors John Rust, David Stillwell, and Michal Kosinski. Rust, Stillwell, and Kosinski had been the first to bring Facebook research to Cambridge. They developed an app called myPersonality to understand the relationships between personality types and online social activities. That group opted to keep their research exclusively academic, even once its commercial potential became clear.

Alex Kogan chose another path. In 2013, he built his own app, called Thisisyourdigitallife, which it seems he initially intended for academic work. By 2014, however, he had started a commercial firm, Global Science Research, using the app to administer personality tests. People who signed up to take one granted access to their—and their friends'—Facebook profiles, often unwittingly.

All told, Kogan paid an estimated 270,000 people to complete tests, thereby obtaining data for eighty-seven million Facebook users.

That data set was eventually sold to the parent company of election consultancy, Cambridge Analytica (CA). In a 2016 interview with Sky News, Cambridge Analytica CEO Alex Nix boasted that CA possessed "somewhere close to four or five thousand data points on every individual" in the United States.

The rest is history. Cambridge Analytica used the data to target and manipulate voters during the 2016 US elections. They used it to influence Brexit voters in the UK. CA's electoral involvement has now been alleged in Mexico, Australia, India, and Argentina, among others. The US Federal Trade Commission eventually fined Facebook $5 billion for violating consumer privacy, a settlement that included restrictions on how the firm would handle data privacy moving forward.

In retrospect, it seems obvious that the data could and would be misused. Human beings will always be prone to greed and corruption. But Alex Kogan did not build Open Graph; he merely seized on its potential. By all accounts, the developers who actually designed the product did not have the faintest idea they were opening a Pandora's box. Facebook not only condoned Kogan's work but participated in it openly, proud to be able to advance scientific understanding of well-being through its platform. Among the coauthors on the "wealth and friends" study were academics from Harvard and UC Berkeley, venerable institutions with proud histories of behavioral science research. Plus two authors from Facebook itself.

Why didn't they see it coming?

Before we allow ourselves to get too smug, we should remember that our species is notorious for solving one problem, only to discover that the solution has opened up a new and unforeseen set of problems. We tend to focus on present needs and conditions. Early man tamed fire to keep warm and cook food. He could not have known that it would lead to burning at the stake and the atomic bomb.

What distinguishes our era from its predecessors is its incredible complexity and the dizzying speed with which new things arise. Ours are wicked problems in a VUCA world. A million and a half years elapsed between the discovery of fire and Hiroshima. Getting from Open Graph to Thisisyourdigitallife took three years. And the pace of change continues to increase, so that nowadays we seem to face upheaval—technological, cultural, economic—every few months. Too often we're playing catch up, struggling to solve problems several versions out-of-date.

In that sense, Facebook's mistake was a characteristically twenty-first-century one. It was, above all, a failure of human imagination. They could not see the *could*, let alone the *would*.

As we each confront a volatile and uncertain future, the ability to anticipate change and plan for it becomes particularly urgent. The question of "why we didn't see it coming" yields to another, more pressing and actionable: *How can we do better?*

Prospection: A Defining Psychological Capability for Our Era

Our ability to imagine and plan for the future is an extraordinarily powerful human capability. Prospection *metabolizes* the past and present to project the future. Like digestive metabolism, the prospecting mind extracts the nutrients from the past and present, then excretes the toxins and ballast in order to prepare for tomorrow. Prospection encompasses everything from our thoughts about what to eat for lunch, to our ability to sign a "Do Not Resuscitate" form, to our collective efforts to curtail global warming. Drawing on the work of Dan Gilbert, Tim Wilson, Peter Railton, Chandra Sripada, Roy Baumeister, and others, we define prospection as "the mental process of projecting and evaluating future possibilities and then using these projections to guide thought and action." In 2013, Marty, philosopher Railton, psychologist Baumeister, and neuroscientist Sripada published *Homo Prospectus*, arguing that the defining feature of our species is our ability to envision and plan for the future.

As foragers, we needed to prospect about proximal, concrete natural events. The Agricultural Revolution heralded a new kind of labor rooted in prospection—planting seeds in spring to harvest in fall, growing a balanced set of crops, breeding docile livestock, and storing food as a hedge on famine. As we saw in chapter 1, the farmer's prospection also carried the shadow of anxiety.

With the Industrial Revolution, laborers shifted their focus away from prospection to consistent execution of discrete, here-and-now tasks. The machines dictated pace, order, and outcome. Human hands carried out repetitive, in-the-moment tasks. Thinking about the future would still have benefited us outside of work. But inside the factory, prospection mattered very little as a core labor skill.

Now the tide has turned again. With today's labor transformation, prospection has shot back up to the very top of the list of essential workforce skills. Workers today need prospection more than ever before, and in new ways, because our whitewater world is one of constant, rapid change. The capacity to get ahead of that change through effective prospection offers enormous advantages for individuals and organizations alike.

For individuals, prospection allows us to emotionally and logistically prepare for change before it arrives. In 2021, we examined how the prospective abilities of 1,500 workers relate to their personal and professional thriving. We found that the more skilled prospectors, as assessed through a battery of prospection scales, had greater optimism, self-efficacy, and resilience and significantly less anxiety and depression. Prospective ability also correlates with both productivity and life satisfaction—better prospectors are 21% more productive at work and experience 25% greater life satisfaction overall. Prospection allows us to anticipate the downstream impact of our decisions, which, in our highly connected environment, also ripples out across our teams, our companies, and our markets.

At the organizational level, prospection is essential because strategy no longer looks like a twenty-year plan. Markets and technology evolve too quickly. Firm-level prospection relies on real-time, bottom-up inputs that can feed a dynamic set of approaches to possible futures.

One version of this story: Let's feed all the data to machines and they will tell us what to do. According to this story, it's not humans but machines that need to be good at prospection. The catch is that all those machines still rely on human inputs in critical ways. During the 2016 election cycle, the Democratic Party used a cutting-edge digital polling arm to predict victory on Tuesday, November 8. But it was human beings who chose what data to collect and how to interpret it. Many pollsters decided to use the same models from the 2012 election, rather than evolving new models to account for how voters had changed in the interim. Others used data from press coverage of rallies to inform their predictions, without accounting for the political bias of the press to under- or overestimate attendance. It's also humans who are telling the machines what to predict. Machine-learning algorithms typically still rely on human hypotheses that they may prove or disprove. *We* decide what might be true; machines tell us if the data are compatible with our hypotheses. For the moment, anyway, we remain subject to a more sophisticated form of "garbage in, garbage out."

Organizational prospection, then, requires that we as human employees be more skilled in foresight. In that same 2021 study, we also looked at how prospection relates to group-level business outcomes. We saw that teams whose leaders score higher in prospection perform better in a number of critical dimensions: team engagement is 19% higher; team innovation scores are 18% higher; and team agility, as measured with a cognitive agility scale, is 25% higher. One of the most important differences between team leaders who are stronger vs. weaker in prospection was the sheer amount of time they spend planning. Leaders with high prospection scores spend 159% more time planning at work than their less-prospective peers. These leaders are also more committed to their employers—they're 33% less likely to quit.

The concrete individual and organizational benefits are clear. There is also a more philosophical side to our need for prospection today. In an era of constant change, our ability to anticipate what's coming offers us hope for preserving our sense of agency. Like Graeme Payne, we need to keep our ears to the ground, reading cues as to what's next. Where capacities like resilience and agility help us cope with the onslaught of change—resurfacing from the crashing waves quickly and consistently—prospection offers us the potential to spot the biggest breakers before they arrive. For all these reasons, prospection is the fourth of our PRISM powers, a defining meta-skill for thriving at work today.

Prospection for Software Teams

Software teams—usually small working groups of engineers, product managers, and designers—offer some of the most compelling examples of the pivotal role of prospection in the modern workplace.

Consider today's operating systems for public safety, privacy, healthcare, financial, and political institutions. Software squads, adept at building digital tools, will be hired or contracted to develop these platforms. These teams are not, however, equally expert in civil realms—understandably so. Ideally, engineers and subject matter experts like demographers or public health officials or law enforcement administrators or voting officers would sit side by side, navigating each decision as it arises. Occasionally that is the case. More often, due to limited resources and rushed timelines, the builders of these systems are asked to figure it out on their own, making game-time decisions with wide-reaching implications for how society will function. And sometimes, they fail to anticipate the ways it can all go wrong.

On April 9, 2014, at 11:54 p.m. Pacific time, eighty-one 911 emergency call centers across California, Washington, Florida, Minnesota, Pennsylvania, South Carolina, and North Carolina went down. For six hours, no one could get through. Eleven million people lacked emergency support. Imagine yourself, in your most urgent time of need, calling 911 . . . with no answer. Heart attacks, suicides, burglaries, car accidents, house fires—no one picked up. An estimated 6,600 emergency calls went nowhere.

Forces mobilized rapidly to diagnose the problem. Had cellular service been lost? What had malfunctioned?

The Federal Communications Commission ultimately deemed this event the result of a "software coding error." But it would be more accurate to call it an error of human prospection. "Software coding error" implies that someone missed a semicolon. The engineers in question didn't err in their code; they—and the teams they were on—erred in two specific *decisions* that informed their code: First, in building the call system, the team created a total capacity limit, beyond which incoming calls aren't taken. In setting the limit, the team estimated too low. Second, for every potential system dysfunction, the team built an alarm system to trigger concern for those watching over operations. But because they didn't imagine the system would ever exceed its limits, the alarm they designed for this issue was both too slow and too low level to be effective. To those monitoring the system, both the source of the error and its severity were invisible.

Should this software team have been able to foresee this issue? Yes, clearly. We can confidently call their work an error, because there was better information available to guide their decisions. Any given developer or product manager could not have instinctively guessed that the system would quickly surpass a limit of forty million calls. However, by accessing subject matter expertise and accurate demographic inputs they could have avoided this outage altogether. At the heart of the issue is not coding skill but poor modeling of the future. Eleven million people lost access to emergency help because of an error of prospection, not of coding.

Whether we are trying to make the best use of our predictive tools, considering the potential effects of a new product, or navigating turbulence in our professional lives, prospection starts with the individual. It all goes back to a specialized part of that three-pound football of flesh.

Let's see how prospection looks in the brain.

Prospection and the Default Mode Network

One of the most important neuroscientific discoveries of our lifetime was that of the default mode network (DMN), a set of brain regions involved in our mental downtime. Like many of the most significant scientific discoveries, it was made by accident.

Functional imaging researchers were mapping out the brain's "task positive" networks, those regions that light up when we engage in focused tasks like anagrams or arithmetic. In most of these experiments, there was also a control condition, consisting of rest periods ("just lie there and don't do anything"). We might expect the brain to go dark and quiet while resting. Instead, a reliable network of midline and medial temporal lobe brain structures would consistently light up, suggesting not stasis but vibrant activity. This same network activates whenever we let our mind wander, as when we daydream.

Consider the significance of that. When nothing else is going on, the brain doesn't just "power down." Instead, it switches into a new mode of thinking, one so vital that it is our *default*—the activity our brain jumps to in every free moment. What is so important about this activity? It specializes in two processes: imagining and planning.

Chandra Sripada describes what it feels like to experience the default mode as follows:

> The content is quasi-perceptual and imagistic: autobiograph-ical memories of remote events, replays of more recent events, prospections into the near and distant future. The transitions between individual thoughts are discursive. There are often thematic associations between adjacent thought items but also substantial discontinuities. This kind of meandering thought stream is ideal for identifying interesting patterns and rela-tionships. Thoughts are juxtaposed next to others in unpre-dictable and partially random ways, thus enabling implicit learning systems to "observe" these novel thought streams (in the same way they would observe actual unfolding events in the world) and extract new patterns, generalizations, interpre-tations, and insights.

We are all familiar with the spontaneous oscillating of our atten-tion. It's happening to you as you read this book, in fact. Every minute or two, your attention will drift off into a daydream. You'll stay there for maybe a minute, then catch yourself and go back to attending to the reading. During mind-wandering, the default network is on and at-tention veers away from the specific task toward daydreaming. In this realm, our mind breaks the bonds of space and time, blending mem-ory and fantasy. When we then return to our task at hand, the task positive network turns back on and attention shifts away from day-dreaming. These oscillations—on the order of seconds or minutes—recur all day long.

Sripada understands this oscillation as an eternal cycle between exploitation and exploration. Task positive thinking is efficient; it respects space and time, gathering existing information about the world and *exploiting* these knowns. The default network *explores* new possibilities by imagining scenes that can differ radically from the actual past and the actual present. Such vivid, fantastic imagery allows us to discover and learn deeply about what does not yet exist.

Using the task positive network, we attend to the history book and we encode the fact that Franklin Roosevelt succeeded Herbert Hoover as president. But when, in the next moment, we picture Herbert Hoover as a giant vacuum . . . which leads us to the vacuum of space . . . which leads to wondering about what it would feel like to live on Mars . . . we're doing something critically important for our brains. In our next chapter, we'll see how essential this interplay is to creative work.

Mind-wandering, in this view, is a feature of the mind, not a bug. As we feel increasingly starved for time, we might be tempted to rein in our attention tighter and tighter, to grind ceaselessly and cut down on mental "downtime." Even if that were possible, it would be undesirable. The default mode is often where our best ideas come from. It's the default for a reason, and we ignore it at our own hazard.

How does that mental meandering shape our understanding of the future? And how can we leverage it to plan even better?

That's what our colleague Roy Baumeister wanted to know.

The Two-Phase Model of Prospection

Baumeister, professor of psychology at the University of Queensland, is one of the most highly published of all psychologists. Tall, laconic, with a working knowledge of behavioral science research to rival PubMed, Baumeister has published seven hundred articles and more than forty books. Over the years, he's examined prospection from a number of angles. In one labor-intensive study, he had five hundred participants track their thoughts at random, prompted moments throughout the day, over three days, in order to better understand how we think about past, present, and future. These thoughts spanned both task-positive and mind-wandering modes. Baumeister defined the present as within five minutes of the current moment. Everything else was past or future.

The resulting data tell us a tremendous amount about the "when" of our daily thoughts. Do we live most in the past, present, or future?

Baumeister discovered that people spend most of their time thinking about the present . . . but much more time thinking about the future than about the past. Prospection, in fact, occupies at least one-quarter of our waking thoughts.

He also hit on an interesting paradox. Thoughts about the future feel more meaningful and exciting, compared to thoughts about the present or the past. But thoughts about the future also carry more negative emotions than those about the present. Additional experiments served to deepen the contradiction. Although people often experience optimism when thinking about their future, the actions they actually choose to take while in this future-mindset reflect aversion to risk, and pessimism.

How can we make sense of this? When it comes to imagining the future, it seems we are at once both our most optimistic and pessimistic selves.

To address this conundrum, Baumeister, together with Minnesota marketing professor Kathleen Vohs and NYU psychology professor Gabriele Oettingen, proposed that prospection occurs in two distinct phases:

- **Phase one** is fast, sweeping, and optimistic. In this initial phase, our thoughts tend to focus on the questions "What do I want the future to be?" or "What hopeful outcome might lie ahead?" Phase one typically lasts on the order of seconds to minutes. It is also more exploratory, reflecting participation of the default mode network.

- **Phase two** sets in quickly after phase one and entails a much slower, more specific, more deliberative, and more realistic— even pessimistic—assessment of the pictures that phase one has painted. The question now becomes "How will I get there?" In phase two, we engage in detail-oriented planning—which can quickly start to feel overwhelming.

The two-phase model helps reconcile the contradictory experimental findings on the experience of prospection—the fact that we derive meaning from thoughts about the future but also fear and anxiety; the fact that we can project optimism about what's to come, then make risk-averse decisions. It's immensely meaningful and exciting to imagine where we'll go next. And it's frightening when we begin to think about what it will take to get there. That fear can propel us toward the safe route.

This two-phase model also suggests how best to go about improving prospection. People have different natural strengths as prospectors. For this reason, the interventions that we use address each phase separately.

Building the Prospection Muscle: Phase One

For the optimistic daydreamers among us, phase one prospection is *the best*. We think expansively, we project our ideal selves into exhilaratingly bright futures. Our DMN hums with possibility.

For others, however, phase one prospection is downright uncomfortable. Such individuals don't like ambiguity; they'd rather get down to brass tacks as quickly as possible. As we'll see in the next chapter, some of this tendency likely has to do with low levels of a personality trait called *openness to experience*. A person who struggles with phase one will jump right into planning without fully considering all the options available. In doing so she commits a kind of mental "error": she may foreclose brighter opportunities for herself, her family, or her organization without realizing it. She also deprives herself of the immense fun—the joy!—of fantasy.

Another similar type of phase one "error" appears in people prone to post-traumatic stress disorder. As we saw in chapter 4, among the automatic thought patterns in those with PTSD is catastrophization. Catastrophizers immediately identify the worst possible outcome and declare it inevitable, shutting down the exploration of alternatives.

A helpful intervention in this case is the "Putting It In Perspective" exercise from chapter 4. This exercise allows people to hone their prospective skill in a structured way, opening the aperture to a wider range of possible outcomes. Moreover, by spending more time in phase one, the exercise lets people feel some of the positive emotions it offers. Exploring highly divergent, exciting possibilities in an open-minded way feels good. Everyone should get to experience that.

In severe cases of PTSD, it can be difficult for people to access *any* positive thoughts whatsoever about the future. A few years ago, Marty's then students David Yaden and Anne Marie Roepke experimented with different types of interventions to address this difficulty. In their study, they asked individuals who had recently been exposed to adversity to perform different tasks. One task worked best, when done once per week for a month. Here are the instructions:

After difficult experiences, many people feel a sense of loss:
It feels that certain opportunities or "doors" have closed in

their life. Sometimes, people also find that new doors open and new opportunities present themselves. These new opportunities could be almost anything (new activities, goals, role models, friends, job-related changes, ideas, or ways to help people). The existence of new opportunities does not mean that losses are unimportant or less painful; important losses can exist alongside some potentially important new opportunities. We would like to know if you have noticed any new doors opening in your own life in the past six months. For the next fifteen minutes, please write down whatever comes to mind about the new opportunities or "new doors" that have opened, or might open.

The task explicitly acknowledges the negative thinking trap and honors the reality of painful experiences. *Your losses are real. We see them too.* This simple message of solidarity has a powerful effect, establishing a shared mental "holding space" for negative thoughts. Participants now feel permission to step back from those thoughts, which makes it easier to resist their pull and clears space for positive thoughts about the past, present, and future.

Roepke, Yaden, and colleagues found that this expressive writing task, introduced with these specific words, improves the ability to grow from adverse events, and decreases negative outcomes in the face of challenge. It strengthens phase one muscles, allowing us to uncover possibilities previously buried in negativity.

Another tool for improving phase one prospection is called *scenario planning.* First developed in the 1950s by futurist Herman Kahn for the think tank RAND, scenario planning guides groups of leaders to envision widely divergent futures (phase one), and then asks them to work backwards toward plans for preparation (phase two). The first portion of the exercise regularly produces visions that would never have otherwise surfaced, and which prove surprisingly useful in near-term planning. In one famously successful application of scenario planning, Royal Dutch Shell Corporation used the method to prepare for the 1973 oil embargo, and resulting price shocks, before they occurred.

The elaboration of stories about vastly different futures leverages our extraordinary default mode network for exploration. Imagining the future more vividly allows us to better prepare for what is to come.

Building the Prospection Muscle: Phase Two

For others, it's phase two prospection that's hardest.

Phase two involves the careful, deliberative *evaluation* of potential futures in order to inform action. And we have some core brain functionality working against us in this effort.

The planning fallacy, first described by Daniel Kahneman and Amos Tversky in 1979, is our tendency to woefully underestimate the time and cost required by a future task. If you've ever done a home renovation project, you probably know what this is.

Importantly, the fallacy only occurs when we're planning for our *own* future tasks. When we observe others' plans, we are more accurate. The next time you're budgeting for that major reno, ask a friend who's finished a similar project to predict the cost and duration of yours. They will likely be more accurate than you will.

Helping people get better at phase two prospection entails training a more realistic assessment of what it will take to arrive at any given outcome. One intervention supported by robust evidence is NYU professor Gabriele Oettingen's "WOOP" framework. The framework sounds simple, but it has produced an impressive array of results, from successful weight loss for patients with diabetes, to increased student effort and attendance in schools.

WOOP is a four-step process:

1. Identify the Wish
2. Consider the Outcome
3. Focus on Obstacles
4. Determine your Plan

Many coaches employ a similar method called GROW. GROW uses four basic steps to help individuals identify goals and plan for obstacles. The coach then holds the individual accountable for executing their plan. GROW can be adapted for individual use as well.

Exercise: The GROW Model of Coaching

G—Goals: Step one is identifying your goal. Goals should be SMART—specific, measurable, attainable, relevant, and time-bound. In this stage, you answer the questions:

- What do you want to achieve?
- How will you know when you've reached your goal?
- Within what time frame is it realistic to achieve this goal?

R—Reality: Step two is understanding the reality that is holding you back from achieving your goal. The coach will help the coachee identify key obstacles and use careful examination of each to drive self-awareness. Questions to answer in this step include:

- What has made it hard to achieve this goal?
- Under what circumstances are these barriers most/least prominent?
- What strategies have you tried?
- Does this remind you of anything you've experienced in the past?

O—Options: In step three, we imagine options for overcoming these obstacles. This is the most generative part of the GROW model—a bit of exploratory phase one prospection in service of phase two deliberation. Some helpful prompts include:

- What could you try differently this time?
- What are the pros and cons of these options?
- Imagine you are telling the story of how you reached your goal. What was the secret to your success?

W—Will: In step four, you choose an option and convert it into an action plan.

- Which option will you take to reach your goal?
- What are the steps you will need to follow?
- How will you overcome obstacles *a*, *b*, and *c*?
- Where will you go for help if you get stuck?
- Who will you tell about your plan so they can help hold you accountable?

The **GROW** method helps people make substantial progress toward their goals. Whether with GROW, WOOP, or other similar methods, developing a muscle around anticipating obstacles and planning to overcome them helps improve our phase two prospection.

Correcting the Innovator's Bias

The planning fallacy is just one of many cognitive biases discovered by Kahneman, Tversky, and others. A cognitive bias, defined simply, is a systematic error in thinking. These errors are hard-coded into our minds and affect us all.

Why would we come with built-in errors? Biases aren't all bad. Under the right circumstances, they act as mental shortcuts to save us time or resources. The problem is that they are always operating, regardless of circumstances, which can lead us to some strange places.

In 2021, BetterUp Labs researcher Andrew Reece and his team proposed a new type of bias, one that specifically hampers our ability to accurately prospect about a novel product's potential for harm.

The idea came from observing a pattern in the real world: Highly innovative people who excel at phase one prospection can get stuck there, unable to remove their rose-colored glasses. Think back to Mark Zuckerberg's promise for Open Graph: It would be "the most transformative thing we've ever done for the web." Open Graph was transformative. Just not in the way Zuck hoped for.

Andrew and team called this *innovator's bias*: our inaccuracy in assessing the potential for harm for any product we ourselves create. This differs from confirmation bias—the tendency to seek out information that supports existing beliefs and to disregard information to the contrary—in that it relates not to how we integrate existing information but how we imagine the future.

The team tested this theory with a series of experiments. First, they had subjects rate a list of hypothetical inventions for their potential to cause good vs. harm. The goal was to identify neutral inventions, products that large groups of people with no vested interest felt were equally likely to produce good or harm. Examples of inventions rated neutral included a booster shot that could improve IQ and a lost loved one hologram. Step two involved a brand-new group of six hundred participants. All of them were primed with an exercise: They were given a description of a neutral invention, like the hologram, then asked: How would you market and promote the hologram for purchase? Participants had to think deeply about its value proposition, come up with names and slogans, and decide how to position it for potential consumers. This exercise was intended to put them in an "ownership" mindset over that specific invention.

In step three, they split the same group of six hundred participants into two groups, a control group and a group of "owners." Owners were told to rate the hologram's potential for harm vs. benefit. Those in the control group were given a new neutral invention (the IQ-boosting drug, for example) and asked to rate its potential for good vs. harm. Note that the control group had not spent any time working on this second invention.

Andrew's team hypothesized three possible outcomes:

1. **Viral enthusiasm.** Both controls and owners would have been primed by the marketing exercise to feel optimistic about inventions in general. Both would overestimate the potential for good of any product they evaluated.
2. **Competitive juices.** Owners would rate the hologram as having a higher potential for good than for harm. Controls, by contrast, would be in a competitive frame of mind from having worked hard on the hologram. They would therefore overrate the potential harm of the booster drug.
3. **Innovator's bias.** Owners would see a higher potential for good in the hologram. Controls would rate the booster as neutral, as had unbiased raters in step one.

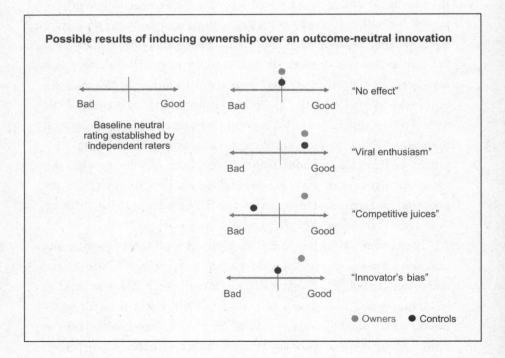

Possible results of inducing ownership over an outcome-neutral innovation

Possibility three was the winner. The priming exercise biased owners in favor of the hologram, while controls remained neutral on the booster. Andrew's team then replicated the findings with a second group of five hundred participants, across multiple inventions.

One possible conclusion is that organizations should seek outside parties to assess a product's potential for harm, or else create siloed internal teams. But what if we can reverse the innovator's bias?

The final phase of the team's research focused on this question. They quickly discovered that there are also risks involved in trying to bring people around to a more realistic point of view. One is that you can dampen their enthusiasm for potentially important work. Positive, activating sentiment is critical for innovation. We don't want to snuff out that passion.

They tried several interventions to help owners course correct without losing momentum. The winner was what they called "worst-case scenario": Owners and controls were instructed to *intentionally* catastrophize by imagining the most disastrous outcomes for the invention in question. Given how much ink we've devoted to the negative side of catastrophization, it might be surprising to learn that this had a desirable effect. Priming controls to think about the most severe consequences of an invention did not sway their neutral rating of impact-neutral inventions. For owners, however, priming them to think about the severest outcomes for the inventions they "owned" brought them back down to earth a bit, leading them to correct their overly optimistic ratings to neutral. Best of all—this correction happened without dampening the innovator's enthusiasm.

Based on these findings, we now have in our tool kit the beginnings of a new, specific intervention that may be able to help innovators and organizations more accurately prospect about future outcomes for their work.

Measurably Improving Prospection

Because prospection is so essential to thriving in the whitewater, measurably improving it for clients has become an increasingly important part of BetterUp's work. In 2018, BetterUp's psychometrics team validated a three-item pragmatic prospection scale that assesses the frequency and effectiveness of people's thoughts about the future. This assessment yields a baseline for all clients. After coaching, the assessment is repeated.

Hundreds of thousands of people have now taken this assessment before and after coaching. Because of this, we now know that prospection can be taught. Those who are bad at prospection are not doomed to remain so; those who are good at it can continue to improve. In fact, across all the Whole Person Model dimensions we track, prospection grows most significantly. On average, within three to four months of coaching, coachees see 24% improvement in prospection skills. Those who start out with the lowest scores as prospectors see an astonishing 115% improvement in the same time frame.

The results are encouraging. Regardless of your initial skill level, you can build prospection to position yourself—and your organization—for success. Prospection underlies corporate strategy, product development, commercial partnerships, investment portfolios. It's a capability we have yet, as a species, to express to our full capacity, because never before has our work demanded it to such an extreme extent. Simply surviving at work today requires prospection. But *excellence* in prospection is what will separate those of us who thrive from those who merely get through the day.

A few years ago, Facebook launched a new function for "responsible innovation," reporting to Vice President of Design Margaret Stewart. The function was charged with bolstering efforts "throughout the product development life cycle to anticipate and minimize potential harm and ensure we are building responsibly."

Gone was the Open Graph–era hubris about transforming the web. In its place, an admission of a failure to prospect.

Facebook is not alone. Other companies have also begun to build training for product and engineering leaders in advanced prospection. Over time, we can expect that all R&D organizations will have a function like this one; that credentials in engineering and product management will include courses in prospection; and, ultimately, that legal expectations for good prospection will be put in place to ensure that any harms that can be avoided will be.

As an analogy, consider the role of the chief information security officer. A few decades ago, the field of "information security" did not exist. Now, having learned from twenty years of data leaks and hacking, including those Graeme Payne lived through at Equifax, every major company has an InfoSec team monitoring data privacy and storage. These teams coordinate closely with both legal and engineering leaders. Corporations are held responsible by law for failure to uphold best practices.

Lessons in failed foresight may yet yield a chief prospection officer. In the interim, this emergent corporate capability will be needed most urgently by those building, launching, and servicing new technology products. Leaders in this field need expertise in prospection, in decision-making, in stakeholder management, in data analytics, in public policy, and in the behavioral sciences.

There is much work to do between here and there to entrain these prospective abilities, at scale, for our workforce. But we *can* get there. Doing so will reinvest us—as individuals, and as organizations—with the agency so easily dissolved by the whitewater.

CHAPTER NINE

When We Are All Creatives

The arrival of AI will at least remove what cannot be our reason for existence on this earth . . . One very valid reason for existing is that we are here to create . . . We invent things. We celebrate creation. We're very creative about the scientific process, about curing diseases, about writing books, writing movies, creative about telling stories, doing a brilliant job in marketing. This is our creativity that we should celebrate, and that's perhaps what makes us human. —Kai-Fu Lee

In November 2006, at the age of forty-two, Martha "Marty" Cobb found herself on the top bunk in a basement dormitory, staring at a ceiling so low she couldn't sit up in bed.

Newly divorced and bankrupt, Marty had few options. Her friends in Lubbock, Texas, where she was raising her three kids, had recommended working for Southwest Airlines. It would mean grueling hours and living away from home. But the lack of good local jobs had made the difficult decision clear.

The "David Koresh compound" is what Marty calls the three-story house in Baltimore where Southwest packs in its flight attendants like sardines. Each floor has bunkbeds and a refrigerator. The most junior attendants get the worst spots. Twenty-six women shared the home, which was owned by a male pilot (hence "Koresh"). That

Thanksgiving, as Marty ate cold turkey out of a Styrofoam container, she thought, "What have I *done?*"

It wasn't her first time starting over. As a college student, Marty had set her sights on becoming an event planner for luxury resorts. She'd cultivated this dream in Hawaii, where she'd attended summer school ("I got an A in hula and a C in economics") and then in Santa Barbara, working at the Biltmore. It was a property unlike any she'd seen, and she'd pictured the black-tie galas she might one day orchestrate.

Not long after returning to Texas to graduate, though, Marty had gotten married. Then came three babies. And Lubbock had no hotels like the Biltmore, not even close. So for ten years, Marty had focused on raising kids. "I had no gifts," she says. "I could do nothing except the splits."

In fact, Marty is as gifted as she is humble. Creatively bringing joy to others is her superpower, fueled by a wickedly sharp sense of humor, with a knack for improvisation. She credits her father for instilling her passion for service. On Thanksgiving, he would deliver turkeys to ten of their closest friends. On Christmas, the whole Cobb family rose early to bake cinnamon buns for the same group. Her father taught his daughters to show up for people, especially during hard times. "Doing something is better than doing nothing," he'd say. "You're not doing it for you, you're doing it for them."

In her decade as a homemaker, Marty tried her hand at various part-time occupations, gravitating toward service roles where she could add her own flair. She taught aerobics, for example, and made her classes laugh so hard they forgot they were working out.

Change came knocking once more: Her first marriage ended. Marty found her way to a marketing role for an orthodontist, one who let her throw big parties. The orthodontist was from Louisiana, so they planned a New Orleans–style party for their clients with étouffée, crawfish, a band. Concocting elaborate new ways to entertain customers was right up Marty's alley.

And so, after a second divorce left her in financial distress, Marty knew how to pick herself back up. "I always taught my kids, 'Keep moving forward and upward, and if you make a mistake, you dust yourself off and get back out there.'"

Starting out at Southwest wasn't easy. The training was extremely intense. The first six months were a probationary period, with Marty always "on reserve." The company could call her in at any point, and she would have to show up two hours later, ready to fly. As a new employee, she worked weekends and holidays. Plus, her colleagues were instructed to keep a close eye on her in-flight performance and report any issues. A bad report could lead to immediate dismissal.

As anxious as she felt, however, nothing compared to the stress radiating from her passengers. People fly for all kinds of reasons. For every honeymooner, there was someone going to a funeral. She accompanied fallen soldiers. Plenty of passengers were terrified of flying altogether.

With the onset of the pandemic, the screws turned tighter still. Suddenly *no one* wanted to be flying; the only passengers left had to be there for some unpleasant reason. Every sniffle or cough set the whole plane on edge. Airline employees, equally terrified of the virus, bore the weight of their industry crashing around them. In April 2020, passenger traffic was 96% below what it had been in April 2019.

Crisis, everywhere.

Marty felt the air thick with unhappiness. She wanted to help. So she did what came naturally: She cracked jokes.

Position your seat belt tight and low across your hips, just like my grandmother wears her support bra.

To activate the flow of oxygen, simply insert seventy-five cents for the first minute.

And if you're traveling with small children, we're sorry. If you're traveling with more than one child, pick out the one you think might have the most earning potential down the road and put their oxygen mask on first.

The surprised laughter came in clusters first, then spread uproariously throughout the plane. "Giving to other people, making other people laugh and smile, and forgetting about what was on the ground that I couldn't change or fix, it made me smile," she recalls. "You start to realize you are kind of making a difference. The more you give, the more you get back." With just a few words, she could lift the mood of an entire planeload of customers.

Encouraged by the responses she got, Marty started to push the envelope. One of her more experimental bits went like this:

Y'all, it's been a really long day for us flight attendants, and we know it has been for you, too, so we're going to go ahead and take our union break. But before we do, we're going to pass out refreshments for you. At Southwest, we believe in working smarter, not harder, so this is what we call Southwest Express coming to you . . .

At which point Marty would start launching bags of pretzels and peanuts around the plane. Passengers would leap out of their seats into the aisles, grabbing for the snacks, climbing over one another. When enough people were down on all fours, Marty would get back on the speaker:

All right y'all, now look up here.

They'd look up.

Cuz here come your drinks.

One day after her opening "set," Marty went to perform her walk-through, inspecting the cabin before takeoff. She found a young woman of twenty-five or thirty bawling her eyes out.

"Are you okay?" Marty said. She laid a hand on the woman's shoulder. "Can I help you?"

"I've been afraid of flying my whole life," the young woman sobbed. "And I think you just cured it."

Laughter heals.

Over time, improvisational humor became Marty's go-to tool for solving all kinds of problems. For example, a perpetual challenge for Southwest is the tight turnaround between long-haul flights, the result of a business decision that keeps costs low. Southwest's flight attendants are their own cleaning crew. They must collect garbage and tidy up during an unusually short window in order to board the next group of passengers.

Marty's solution: Enlist the passengers for help. But how? Toward the end of long flights, she requests everyone's attention.

There's a rumor that Southwest has hidden a four-hundred-dollar free-flight voucher somewhere on this plane, y'all. I want you to look deep down in your seatback pockets, look behind your tray table, look under your seats—it's a voucher for four hundred dollars. And while you're down there, pick up any trash you see and just hand it on over to us in the aisle.

It almost always works. Once, a passenger took Marty seriously, mistaking an old, buried note with the Southwest logo on it for the voucher. When he learned it was just a tall tale, he complained about Marty's tactics to her gate attendants.

Here was a critical moment for Southwest: Would its leaders reprimand Marty for her improvisation, out of fear? The airline had invested dozens of hours training Marty in exactly what to say in her announcements. Many other major airlines prefer to keep their flight attendants on script.

But Southwest has always been different. Founder Herb Kelleher believed that if you treat your employees well, they will treat your customers well, too, by bringing their best selves to work. The strict training-up-front provides staff with guardrails and weeds out those at risk of pushing too far. Once attendants nail their training, the airline knows it can trust them to give their work their own twist, and even recommends that they do so. Yes, everything is done on the cheap, including Marty's claustrophobic Baltimore quarters. That's part of how they maintain industry leadership. But frequent outings, parties, and pranks—all, once upon a time, instigated by Herb himself—are the truer representation of what it feels like to work at Southwest, once you're in. There's a reason its stock exchange symbol is LUV.

Early in her tenure, having graduated from her probationary on-boarding, Marty had taken her cues from other Southwest workers imagining their way to fun, creative service solutions. At the corporate level, one of Southwest's most radical innovations has been relying on flight attendants to provide in-flight entertainment. Case study after case study has demonstrated that Southwest's approach to "human resources"—aka staff—is a huge differentiator in a highly commoditized industry. Southwest has one of the highest operating margins of any airline, thanks in no small part to this innovative approach to customer service.

"Herb had such a high view of humanity and people that he didn't want automatons," says Kevin Freiberg, a management consultant who wrote a book on Southwest's success. "It was like, 'Come be yourself and express your creativity.'"

Marty was never reprimanded for her voucher bit. Instead, she and her supervisors shared a sympathetic chuckle at the passenger's reaction. Today, Marty helps perpetuate Southwest's culture of creativity expression by modeling for others. And she's become a celebrity: A 2014 video of Marty's announcements has nearly three hundred million views on YouTube. Her material even earned her kudos from comedian Ellen DeGeneres, plus an appearance on Ellen's show. Inspired, Marty's peers use her material to make their own flights easier, safer, and more enjoyable for each and every passenger. All of this was possible because Marty Cobb was allowed—encouraged—to get creative.

Creativity: Our Uniquely Human Gift

Human creativity, in all its recombinant, unexpected splendor, is a gift uniquely ours. AI thought leader and former president of Google

China Kai-Fu Lee has gone so far as to suggest that creativity may be the very *purpose* of human existence. In some views, the only work that will be left to us once everything else has been automated will be, by definition, creative.

According to creativity researchers, to qualify as creative an idea must be:

1. Original
2. Surprising
3. Useful and desirable for an audience

The third qualifier distinguishes creative ideas from purely imaginative ones. Children are highly imaginative, but they are not necessarily creative, as they often lack a sense of audience. Marty Seligman's five-year-old's idea of paving his driveway with salami was original and surprising—delicious, even—but it was not creative.

One common challenge to this definition is the "artist ahead of her time," ignored by her public and appreciated only posthumously. In art it's possible, though uncommon, for creative ideas to emerge ahead of audience readiness.

In the business realm, however, the third criterion of this definition holds nicely. Our original ideas are only helpful, professionally, if they create value for ourselves or our organizations.

For many decades, corporations have ascribed creativity to discrete segments of the organization—units literally designated "Creative." Designers, prototypers, marketers, and a few others get to—*have* to!—be creative. Everyone else just does their job. This model is a holdover from the Industrial Revolution, where creativity was even more limited to the small number of inventors of machines and products that would roll down the line. For the vast masses of factory workers in that era, creativity was a liability, not a strength.

When a large multinational technology company recently unveiled a new leadership framework that included a pillar on creativity, many of the employees were befuddled. Wasn't creativity the purview of their creative division? What could it mean for every leader to be creative? Were their jobs changing? Would they all be replaced by so-called Creatives?

The days of thinking of creativity as a specialized skill are numbered. Such models are not only outdated, they are also insidious and highly maladaptive for leaders looking to equip their people with the skills they will need to succeed in the modern workplace. In the whitewater, this essential forager's skill has been restored to prominence after its assembly line decline.

Creativity is an essential work capability today for two reasons. First: Given the growing automation of work, the work that remains for humans to do will be inherently more creative. McKinsey Global Institute identifies creativity as the one skill that will be least impacted by automation between now and 2030, estimating an overall 13% increase in workforce hours devoted to creativity, with an additional 16% increase in hours spent on other types of innovative thinking. The World Economic Forum likewise projects that innovation will be a critical work skill in the 2020s because of automation.

Think about the role of the journalist. News outposts today use bots to create short articles like coverage of sports events. The *Washington Post* used bots to generate much of its coverage of the Rio Olympics. On the corporate side, dozens of firms use AI-generated blogs, many powered by the impressive language model GPT-3, to replace human content. If simple narrative assembly can be replaced, what's left for human reporters to do? Investigative journalism—making subtle observations; hypothesizing connections between wildly disparate events based on nuanced social cues—is an example of the subset of reporting that may be protected from automation in the years to come.

The second reason creativity is essential in today's world of work is the pace of change itself. Today, entire industries are rapidly disrupted by faster-moving entrepreneurs. Look at what Uber did to taxis; what Netflix did to Blockbuster and then movie theaters; what Amazon did to . . . everyone. Whether an organization is seeking to disrupt, à la Stripe, or seeking to avoid disruption, à la financial industry legacy players like Visa, it can only compete if it's leveraging the full innovative capacities of its people.

This begins, first and foremost, with those on the front lines— people like Marty Cobb, who can pick up signals of emerging need and experiment with new solutions. Cultures that don't position every employee as an innovator will rapidly fall behind.

We are all creatives now. In our own ways, from our own functional seats. Creativity need not be like rain, something we pray for and hope to receive. It's inside each one of us—native to our species and bound up with our very humanity. While creativity research is not as far along as many other areas of psychology, with much still to be learned, decades of studies offer important insights into how we can nurture this power and harness it for our benefit. In this chapter we'll start by understanding some basics on how our brain powers creativity. Then we'll look at what we know about why some people are more creative than others. Some of this has to do with differences in the types of creative thinking— we'll look at those types next. Next we'll shift to understanding how creativity works in groups. Finally, we end with a new set of behavioral tools to help build creativity for individuals, teams, and organizations.

The Creative Brain

Growing our creative "muscle" means, first, understanding it. Creativity is not like your biceps—a localized mass of cells devoted to one function. Instead, it's the symphonic product of many different cognitive abilities, orchestrated by three distinct large-scale brain networks. You can think of a brain network as a highway system sending messages from one group of brain centers to another.

In the last chapter, on prospection, we met the default mode network (DMN). Recall that the DMN is associated with spontaneous, self-generated thought, most often planning for or fantasizing about the future. The DMN breaks the bounds of time and place. Creativity can be understood as a subtype of prospection—a glimpse into what might be. And so it's not surprising that the DMN is one of the three networks central to innovation.

Two other brain networks show up consistently alongside the DMN in studies of creative tasks: the salience network and the executive control network. The salience network monitors our internal and external environments for signals that require conscious attention. When it finds those priority signals, it directs the flashlight of our attention—a precious neural resource—toward them, and shifts other networks on and off accordingly. When you are driving and hear a distant siren of an ambulance, your salience network shifts your attention there so you know to pull over. The executive control network, by contrast, oversees specific, externally directed tasks. For example: Name your two closest friends from elementary school. You've just activated your executive control network.

How do these three networks come together to support creativity? The theory is that our innovative ideas, often novel recombinations, emerge first from the DMN, where spontaneous, preconscious ideas can connect and attach. Many of these will be gibberish—think salami driveway—but a few will offer enough value to pique the interest of the salience network. The salience network then recruits the executive control network to refine and develop this idea. The executive control network also loops back to the DMN with relevant information about the creative problem to be solved.

This exchange between controlled and spontaneous thought processes may remind you of Baumeister's two-phase model of prospection. The executive control network is crucial for phase two deliberation, while the DMN drives phase one daydreaming. This model may even help us better understand the two systems of thinking described by Daniel Kahneman in his book *Thinking, Fast and Slow*. Kahneman's system 1 involves fast, emotional, automatic, nonconscious thought: intuitions. System 2, by comparison, is slower, more effortful, more deliberative. We can think of creative images as arising from what Danny Kahneman calls system 1 (intuition), and then, once taken seriously by the salience network, being placed into system 2 (deliberation) for refinement into a creative idea by the executive control network.

The dance between intuitive, spontaneous thought and highly controlled, focused effort cuts to the heart of a long debate among creativity scholars: Is creativity conscious? Sigmund Freud, philosopher Daniel Dennett, and others have argued that it is not, and their view resonates with many artists, for whom creation can feel mysterious or romantic. The science tells another story, however, given the important role of our salience and executive control networks. You can see it on imaging tests, and you can demonstrate it in a lab.

Roy Baumeister has done just that. In one experiment, he invited jazz musicians to improvise a solo over a piece of music they'd never heard before. One-third of these musicians had to count backwards by 6 from 913 while playing—a cognitively demanding task that absorbs most if not all of our conscious attention. Another third of the participants counted up by 1s from 15 while playing—a near-automatic task that requires less attention. The final third were left to improvise without any additional tasks burdening them. Expert musicians then blindly judged the quality of the improvisation.

Solos improvised when the musician was counting backwards by 6 were significantly less creative than those performed by either of the other groups. Counting itself was not problematic for creative output, so long as it could be done by 1s. This finding suggests that conscious attention is essential to creative output. As Baumeister and colleagues write, "The unconscious generates the pieces. Consciousness puts them together into a creative product." Interfere too much with consciousness, and creativity suffers.

Excellence in creativity requires, then, on the one hand, the generation of novel and surprising ideas by the DMN; the identification of marketability by the salience network; and finally the exploitation of the surfaced idea by the executive control network. The executive control network also loops back to the DMN, which is important for focusing the nonconscious ruminations in a direction that is most likely to yield useful results.

The Creative Person

So far, we've spoken in universals: All of us can be creative. And all of us use three key brain networks in our creative acts. But we are not all equally creative. Some people's brains seem better suited to creative output. Why is that, and how can the rest of us get there?

Studies of highly creative people seek to uncover the secret recipe for creative genius. What is it that Van Gogh and Juliana of Norwich had in common? Psychologists typically sort individual differences into two buckets: *traits* and *states*. Traits describe aspects of a person that are relatively stable over time, like personality. States describe more fleeting features. These are not hard and fast categories. Some states last longer than others, while traits are more malleable than we once thought. Today, many understand even personality as one end of a spectrum of malleability of individual patterns—meaning that one's personality can change, but to a lesser degree than, for example, one's mood.

In the realm of traits, research has revealed five classic dimensions of personality—the Big Five—which correspond to the acronym OCEAN:

1. Openness to experience: Curiosity and appreciation for new ideas and opportunities

2. Conscientiousness: Self-discipline and adherence to external constraints
3. Extraversion: Extraverts enjoy social interactions and typically are highly energetic. The converse is introversion.
4. Agreeableness: The general disposition toward getting along with others. Disagreeable people value self-interest over social harmony.
5. Neuroticism: Emotional instability, typically with negative moods like anxiety, anger, or depression

The personality trait most significantly, and consistently, associated with creativity is openness to experience. It has even been called "the core of the creative personality." Many definitions of this trait of openness to experience include creativity in them. But how does openness lead to creativity in the brain?

A fascinating 2016 study by a group of American and Austrian psychologists used fMRI data to examine the role of openness to experience in the functioning of the DMN. They found that people with high degrees of openness are able to more efficiently process information in the DMN so it can be shared with other networks. This would help foster creative output. Moreover, one of the ways networks communicate with one another is through chemical messenger molecules called neurotransmitters. Dopamine is one of the neurotransmitters that couples the DMN and the executive control network in particular. Dopamine, known as the "reward molecule," responsible for both normal and drug-induced states of pleasure, is also the neurotransmitter that shows up most in studies of the genetics of both creativity and openness. Both highly creative people and people with high degrees of openness show significant genetic variation in numbers of dopamine receptors, dopamine pathways, and levels of dopamine in the prefrontal cortex. One theory is that highly creative, open people pursue novelty because they experience so much pleasure, by way of dopamine, in new ideas.

These findings outline an important story about openness to experience, creativity, and the brain changes that go along with them. But do they mean that only those born with this trait can be highly creative?

Not so fast. Of all the Big Five personality traits, openness to experience is the one most heavily influenced by genetics. And yet even it only shows 21% heritability. Meaning, *most of what determines how open we are to experience has nothing to do with genetics.* Aspects of openness can indeed be trained.

For example, one facet of openness to experience that is essential to creativity is cognitive agility, the ability to flexibly balance open exploration with focused attention. Creativity tests commonly gauge cognitive flexibility as a core skill: Can we shift frames of reference to generate new approaches to a problem? Revise ideas based on new information? Tolerate conflicting pieces of information at once? Being mentally flexible allows us to let information in and out of consciousness as needed to allow for varied inputs, but then to focus where we need to. Chapter 4 explored some of the ways we can build cognitive agility in pursuit of resilience; in doing so we reap the very powerful secondary benefit of expanding our openness to experience and our creative capacity.

As it turns out, many of the drivers of resilience we analyzed share this dual role in driving creativity. Take optimism and emotional regulation. Activating, optimistic, positive moods stimulate creativity. At the same time, even certain types of negative moods can work in service of creativity if one is skilled at emotional regulation. Emotional regulation allows us to lean in to a sense of urgency without getting overwhelmed by the potential negative outcomes ahead, channeling the negative energy into creative fuel.

Self-efficacy was another driver of resilience. Alongside openness to experience, *creative* self-efficacy—our confidence in the value of our creative effort—is one of the most significant individual predictors of successful creative output. Highly creative people must be able to hear criticisms, to fail . . . and nevertheless push forward. They must be able to dwell in ambiguity and uncertainty without discomfort, even though many aspects of the creative process can be daunting. As such, a number of educational approaches focus on guiding teachers to increase creative self-efficacy for students. Like cognitive agility, optimism, and emotional regulation, creative self-efficacy can be developed.

This high degree of overlap in drivers of creativity and resilience was not entirely surprising to us. Sustained creative success involves failure after failure, the so-called overnight success that's really twenty years in the making. It makes sense that the ability to bounce back and try again would increase our odds of creative triumph.

In the spring and summer of 2020, as the pandemic tested our resilience as never before, BetterUp Labs decided to test this relationship empirically. We already knew from our own research and from the research of others that more resilient workers would maintain higher levels of productivity and well-being. But how would they fare creatively?

The results were astonishing. Across a wide range of creativity measures, more resilient employees showed substantially higher scores. In the arena of novelty—how new are the ideas you can think of?—highly resilient individuals outperform those with low resilience by 20%. Resilient individuals' ideas were also 11% more useful. Plus, their influence extended beyond themselves: The teams they sat on were 18% more creative. The connection between resilience and innovation was so strong, in fact, that we developed a Resilience and Innovation Index, an assessment that allows individuals and organizations to measure common underlying drivers across resilience and innovation.

So far, we've seen that cognitive agility, optimism, emotional regulation, and creative self-efficacy are all malleable sources of individual differences in creativity. There's one more important individual-level variable worth mentioning: motivation. Highly creative people often describe themselves as driven to create. Where does that come from?

Harvard Business School professor emerita Teresa Amabile has been studying this question since the 1970s. Recall from chapter 5 the difference between two different kinds of motivation: intrinsic and extrinsic motivation. In creative work, intrinsic motivation is our internal drive to innovate: because of the challenge, the satisfaction and meaning we draw from the work, the passion we feel for it. Extrinsic motivation comes from others, often in the form of monetary compensation. What Amabile has found is that, when it comes to fostering creativity, intrinsic motivators are far more powerful than extrinsic ones. In fact, in her famous 1998 *Harvard Business Review* piece, "How to Kill Creativity," Amabile advised that the wrong type of external reward structures can diminish, rather than increase, creative output.

Amabile's findings dovetail with those of Richard Ryan and Edward Deci, the founders of self-determination theory. Their definition of intrinsic motivation could double as a definition for creativity itself: the spontaneous tendency "to seek out novelty and challenge, to extend and exercise one's capacity, to explore, and to learn." They have demonstrated that this tendency is one of the strongest predictors of well-being and performance.

We saw earlier that meaning, mattering, and purpose are some of the key drivers of intrinsic motivation at work. Just as with resilience, interventions or conditions that increase our sense of mattering will have the virtuous secondary effect of enhancing our incentive to create. Marty Cobb never got paid more because of her jokes. (Well, not by Southwest. Eventually Ellen DeGeneres gave her a check . . . but that's another story.) She's fueled to improvise by her desire to brighten her passengers' day and to ease her colleagues' workload. She thinks, from time to time, of the young woman bawling in the aisle, and how much her humor *mattered* to that passenger. And she feels, from her organization, supported and celebrated for her initiative. That sense of mattering translates to a happier, more innovative employee who will pay it forward to everyone around her.

The Creative Idea

Just as creativity varies across individuals, creative ideas come in different shapes and sizes. Maximizing creativity requires recognition that there are different ways to be original. We have identified four distinct types of original thinking. Understanding these types positions us to better understand our own creative talents.

Type I: Integration

Integration is the idea that things that look different are really the same and that there is an underlying process that explains them all. Integration can be local, stitching together a few concepts, or it can be sweeping—a grand unifying theory.

Isaac Newton (1643–1727) was a genius of integration. He co-invented calculus, itself enormously integrative. The story of Newton and the apple is likely true, but not the way we learned it in school, with an apple falling on Newton's head. Back at the family farm during his self-imposed isolation from Cambridge in the plague years of 1665–66, Newton, twenty-two years old, noticed that a two-inch apple situated twenty feet from his head occupied the same visual space as the rising moon viewed through his window.

"Could it be," Newton thought, "that whatever draws the apple to the ground is the same thing that holds the moon in orbit?"

This astounding integrative idea gave rise to the elegant inverse square law: that the gravitational attraction between two bodies is inversely proportional to the square of the distance separating them.

True of all bodies, moons, and apples, the inverse square law is a paradigmatic example of sweeping integration. Sweeping integration brings order to chaos—one of the loftiest goals of science.

Integration is a central form of innovation in industry today. The iPhone is an example of a series of more local integrations that culminated in a single, profoundly powerful tool. The first phase of integration was popularized in the early 2000s, as cell phones combined the telephone, the internet, the music player, and the camera in one centralized device. The integrative victory of the first iPhone is both technological and conceptual. The process of digitizing tools like cameras and phones required recognizing that they all capture and transmit data; and that inventions like semiconductors and liquid crystal displays that were invented for one specific type of data capture and transmission could be repurposed for what had previously been thought of as an entirely different machine. That technological victory was shared among the many hundreds of inventors who brought about the digitization of each device. The conceptual half of the iPhone's initial integrative victory entailed recognizing that consumer interactions with each of those tools represent analogous acts of capturing, storing, and retrieving data; and that as such they may as well happen on a single device. Forty years ago, your phone, hanging on your wall, had nothing to do with your boom box, sitting on your console, or your camera, whose film you'd just dropped off at the drugstore. Today, thanks to our phones, we understand intuitively that all these tools traffic in data, and we are grateful to have it all in one place.

The second phase of iPhone integration came by way of the App Store, introduced by Apple in 2008. Here Steve Jobs needed help from others in seeing the integrative whole: Initially Jobs wanted to limit the App Store to apps built by Apple, and not third-party developers. The fully realized vision of the App Store recognized that an infinite number of web applications—from travel sites to media players to content houses to coding platforms—all required similar services to work smoothly with one's cell phone; and that they also entailed similar consumer interactions, such that it made sense to group them in one place. Jobs had commercial reasons for wanting to limit this new space to Apple products only, but other stakeholders prevailed upon him to allow the App Store to achieve its full potential.

Type II: Splitting

The opposite kind of creative thinking, splitting, is also common in both science and industry. Splitting describes recognizing that things that look the same are really different; or that an item typically treated as a whole can be more usefully split into component parts.

The history of medicine is full of examples of splitting. Smallpox was one. This contagious, disfiguring disease presents at first with back pain, sudden high fever, headache, then a rash on the skin and lesions in the mouth. Smallpox is deadly, usually within a week or two. The germ theory of smallpox had pointed to a single virus, *variola major*, as the cause. But it was discovered that some people who had the symptoms did not die. Why? Closer examination revealed that these individuals were infected with a different, more benign form of the virus, *variola minor*. Thus a single disease became two, one fatal and one not. The practical significance of this distinction was that if you survived smallpox, you would be much less likely to get the disease again. Meaning: *variola minor* infection, inconsequential though it was, would be protective against *variola major*. The similarities between the viruses would build up immunity, while the differences would lead to distinctive courses of the disease.

One of the greatest industrial innovations of all time stemmed from splitting: the assembly line. Prior to the Industrial Revolution, one craftsperson might oversee the entire production process from start to finish. Division of labor allowed for faster, more consistent, and more scalable production. Splitting up labor in this way hinged on the revolutionary manufacturing concept of *interchangeability*, first introduced by Swedish inventor Christopher Polhem for the production of clock gears. Interchangeability meant that the parts had integrity separate from the whole. Many didn't believe, at first, that components could be swapped among different tools. Guns, for example, were seen as holistic productions of individual craftsmen skilled in woodworking, metalworking, and more. When, in 1785, Frenchman Honore Blanc first demonstrated that he could assemble a working gun by selecting from a large pile of interchangeable parts, audience members were shocked. The French government placed orders. Thomas Jefferson shared the news with Eli Whitney, in hopes he could generate the same results for the United States. It was harder than it looked, and Whitney failed for many years before finally succeeding. Warfare would never be the same.

Quantum mechanics splits matter down to its smallest components and delineates the multiple states of being of a single particle. Applying quantum theory to industry has yielded advances in electronics, cryptography, and quantum computing. The latter promises to outperform classical computing for certain problems. Whereas in classical computing a bit can only occupy a single position at once, quantum computing's qubit can occupy multiple positions simultaneously, exponentially increasing computing power. Google demonstrated "quantum supremacy" in 2019 with its quantum processor Sycamore, which took two hundred seconds to finish a task that would take a classical computer ten thousand years to complete.

Type III: Figure-Ground Reversal

The term "figure-ground reversal" comes from the study of vision and refers to our ability to shift our attention from the foreground to the background, producing a different overall picture. Images like the one below demonstrate how our minds can toggle back and forth between the two:

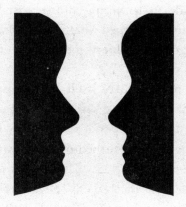

Figure-ground reversal is the type of creative genius that made Sherlock Holmes famous. In the story "The Adventure of Silver Blaze," Holmes is discussing the case of a nighttime intruder with a detective from Scotland Yard.

> The detective asks, "Is there any point to which you would wish to draw my attention?"
>
> Holmes replies, "To the curious incident of the dog in the night-time."
>
> "The dog did nothing in the night-time," the detective objects.
>
> "That was the curious incident."

Sometimes what's missing is most important—a source of immense value, hiding in plain sight.

Figure-ground reversal is Marty Cobb's signature form of creativity. She takes the task no one wants to do—listening to the announcements, moving to the back of the plane, cleaning up trash—and thrusts it into the foreground as a source of not misery but delight. In the case of the hidden voucher, she used playful subterfuge to entice passengers to not only see but also remove the trash everyone would prefer simply didn't exist. In the case of her witty announcements, she turned what product managers call a "pain point"—the drudgery of a safety message—into a side-splitting source of customer value.

The discovery of the DMN itself came from a figure-ground reversal in neuroimaging. As we saw in the last chapter, researchers were studying the neural networks activated by focused tasks. But the more interesting finding turned out to be what the brain does when "at rest."

Another example we've touched on: The field of positive psychology came about as a figure-ground reversal of clinical psychology and psychiatry. For decades, these disciplines emphasized remediating illness. That focus on the negative side of the human experience did little to improve our well-being. The insight of positive psychology was that happiness and sanity are real achievements and not merely the *absence* of pathology. It's not sufficient to eliminate illness. The skills of building positive emotion, engagement, good relations, meaning, and accomplishment are often different from the skills of fighting depression, anxiety, and anger. Positive psychology puts building those in the foreground.

We see figure-ground reversal all the time in industry. Amazon Web Services was developed by a team working on Amazon's internal need to efficiently scale up its own infrastructure. Software developers

Chris Pinkham and Benjamin Black, who led the work, envisioned a solution that they quickly realized others would want: that it could be a highly compelling product in and of itself. Today, technology created in response to a background infrastructure need has become a foreground business of its own, doing $45 billion in revenue in 2020. Similarly, Slack, the ubiquitous messaging platform, started as an internal product to help Stewart Butterfield's company Tiny Speck develop a video game. The video game fizzled out, but Slack went public in 2019 with its messenger app. In 2021, Salesforce purchased Slack for $28 billion.

Type IV: Distal

Finally, distality is the skill of imagining things very different from the here and now. Many a creative genius has been described as someone who can envision something radically different from what the rest of us see today. The great Nikola Tesla once described his process of invention as follows:

> When I get an idea, I start at once building it up in my imagination. I change the construction, make improvements, and operate the device in my mind. It is absolutely immaterial to me whether I run my turbine in thought or test it in my shop . . . When I have gone so far to embody in the invention every possible improvement I can think of and see no fault anywhere, I put into concrete form this final product of my brain.

Among Tesla's distal brain children were the radio, the neon lamp, AC power, and hydroelectric power.

In some cases, an innovator's imagination runs so far ahead that the market isn't quite ready for it. In other words, it's still imaginative, but not yet creative, as it has not yet found its audience. Computer scientist and cryptographer David Chaum invented anonymous digital cash in a 1983 paper, just as personal computers were coming into vogue, and well before the entrenchment of the internet as we know it today. In 1994 the first such electronic payment was sent, by Chaum's company DigiCash. But the economic and technological ecosystem needed to support widespread adoption of digital currency did not yet exist, and the company folded in 1998. Like many "first movers" in new technologies, Chaum paved the way for successors like Bitcoin, but only benefited from a small fraction of its commercial success.

The trick for distal inventors ahead of their time is to bridge the gap. They can do so in one of two ways. The first is by accelerating market maturity, through promotions, partnerships, and focused launches. One example of this is PayPal. Today we use PayPal and other digital wallets to pay for almost anything. But when PayPal was launched, in 1999, adoption of its full slate of intended uses was low. Rather than continue to hopefully advance an ambitious vision prematurely, the company focused its strategy on eBay, a platform where digital payments were becoming the norm, to develop its user base. The symbiosis was so perfect that eBay would eventually acquire PayPal in 2002. By 2014, the two companies once again split. Their interests were no longer aligned, as broader PayPal usage now outstripped its initial use case. Today PayPal is used in two hundred countries. The company's annual revenue in 2021 was $25 billion.

A second strategy for distal innovators ahead of the market is what we call backwards innovation—developing intermediary technologies that are immediately marketable and which will move stakeholders along the maturity curve toward readiness for the original invention. (This is different from reverse innovation, which refers to the practice of building products for developing economies before adapting them for Western consumers.) Here, self-driving cars offer a helpful example. There are many reasons autonomous vehicles are not yet prevalent, including technological, infrastructure, and regulatory barriers. One major obstacle to widespread adoption of the technology that does exist is consumer distrust: The buyer is not yet ready to hand over the wheel. Backwards innovation involves stepping-stone products that sit between driver and no driver—products like autopilot and self-park. These incremental offerings people *will* use. Tesla offers drivers both traditional autopilot and a version they call "Full Self-Driving Capability," the latter of which gives the car even more control. Truly driverless operation, which Tesla terms "full autonomy," is not yet available, but the company positions both autopilot and Full Self-Driving Capability as its precursors. Consumers can start where they are comfortable, then progress. Musk and Co. are training us to eventually embrace the full vision.

Integration, splitting, figure-ground reversal, and distal thinking: Which of these creative styles do you recognize in yourself? Maybe it's more than one. Each offers a unique advantage—as well as potential blind spots. To maximize the former and minimize the latter, we need to find others whose skills complement ours. In practice, that must happen at work, on a team. Let's turn now to the dynamics of successful innovation in a group.

The Creative Team

The classical view locates creativity in the mind of a single genius: Leonardo da Vinci, Georgia O'Keeffe. Another view, popularized by Joshua Wolf Shenk in his book *Powers of Two*, emphasizes the creative pair, or dyad: Marie and Pierre Curie, George Balanchine and Susan Farrell, Warren Buffet and Charles Munger. Dyadic creativity emerges from the back and forth of suggestion, exploration, critique, and refinement.

The third creative unit is the team. While this route is less romantic than the lone genius, it's how almost all business innovation happens today. The personal computer, artificial intelligence, and smartphones all emerged through collective elaboration. Team-level innovation is far more complex to model and understand than individual innovation because multiple brains are involved. Over many years of research, however, we've identified a set of characteristics common to successful creative teams.

The first is that good creative teams are heterogenous. As we just saw, there are multiple ways to be creative, and we get the most out of our teams when skill and knowledge sets complement each other. Moreover, a team with a broad set of experiences widens the range of accessible ideas, expanding what biologist Stuart Kauffman describes as the "adjacent possible." Kauffman notes that complexity in nature evolves incrementally, via frequent recombination that draws on the resources that happen to be readily at hand. At the individual level, we have seen how brain networks function to surface the adjacent possible from the DMN. At work, the creative team is the human collective instantiation of the adjacent possible. An environment rich with opportunity for recombination—a diverse team with a wider array of references and experiences—is more likely to give rise to innovation.

All the ideas in the world are of no use if team members can't or won't share them. For this reason, it's not surprising that excellent communication and information sharing is the second characteristic consistently exhibited by successful creative teams. Communication is particularly important in the middle stages of creativity: taking initial ideas and fleshing them out into usable products. It also leads to more effective evaluation of creative ideas.

One of the biggest barriers to open communication is low psychological safety. Conversely, high psychological safety is a third key feature of highly innovative teams. Psychological safety is the belief that you won't be humiliated or punished for making a mistake or taking a chance. Innovation is replete with risk. Feeling like you might be humiliated or punished for a bad idea would naturally result in team members volunteering fewer concepts. Psychologist Amy Edmonson and others have shown experimentally that higher psychological safety produces better team learning, innovation, and overall performance.

Some of what it takes to create psychological safety we explored already in our discussion of belonging in chapters 6 and 7. In the setting of creative collaboration, much of the responsibility for setting a safe tone will fall to the team leader, whose reactions to new ideas will be watched closely by everyone on the team. Leaders may need training in how to give constructive feedback that will sharpen those ideas without compromising the team's sense of safety.

Imagine, for instance, a product manager—the leader of a team developing a new software product—whose lead designer presents a proposal for a more inspiring, outside-the-box visual direction . . . but one that will be impossible to execute in the time frame allotted. This exact scenario plays out every day in companies around the world. Often the product manager reacts in frustration: *"What are we supposed to do with this? We only have three weeks to ship this thing . . ."*

While the product manager's reaction might be understandable, it can have the unfortunate consequence of triggering defensiveness, fear, and creative shut-down. The designer will think twice about offering a bold idea the next time. Her unease will spread to others on the team—who wants to speak up only to get slapped down?— leading to a negative feedback loop of creative stagnation.

A better approach is for the product manager to ask questions, seek to understand the essence of the proposed approach, and then ask the designer to zero in on its best features so those can be prioritized in the time available. Leaders who offer this type of feedback—curious, positive, constructive—sharpen a team's creative output without compromising its psychological safety. And this style can be taught. It starts with the rapid rapport strategies we explored in chapter 7.

A final characteristic of successful creative teams, alongside hetero-geneity, excellent communication, and psychological safety, is adequate planning. Precisely because teams are so complex, with so much poten-tial for missed opportunity, it's crucial to establish clear roles, respon-sibilities, and milestones that everyone can understand. Here, again, the team leader plays a pivotal role. Leaders need to decide who owns which part of the problem; which team members will work together and with what resources; which creative processes are paramount for each challenge—integration, splitting, figure-ground reversal or distality—and what the criteria for success are. Phases of the project should be clearly mapped out, starting more divergently and then converging, with each team member playing the appropriate role at each phase.

Under the leadership of psychologist Michael Mumford of the University of Oklahoma, the Mumford Research Group has broken down the creative planning process into four stages:

1. Identification of the necessary skills and resources needed for the project
2. Identification of possible obstacles, along with mitigation plans
3. Creation of a framework for backup plans, to guide team adaptation
4. Definitions of success

Planning of this kind is, in essence, phase two prospection. You can think of it as a team innovation version of GROW. In creative work we often focus on phase one prospection—the generative, divergent intuitions that produce an array of novel possibilities. But as Mumford and colleagues have demonstrated in their research, in a group setting, with so many minds in play, the slower, more deliberative work of phase two prospection is just as important—if not more so.

You may have noticed that so far, in reviewing characteristics of highly innovative individuals and teams, we have touched on each of the four other components of PRISM:

- Resilience (**R**): Cognitive agility, creative self-efficacy, optimism, and emotional regulation, all drivers of resilience, are likewise drivers of creativity.
- Mattering and meaning (**M**): These fuel our intrinsic motivation to innovate.
- Rapid rapport for social support (**S**): The skills we use to establish trust and communication among diverse individuals, allowing our teams to innovate at their best.
- Prospection (**P**): Creativity is a subset of prospection, leveraging both the divergent, DMN-rich imagination of phase one and the more deliberative planning of phase two.

It is not by accident that we have here uncovered fundamental relationships between creativity and all the capacities covered in preceding chapters of this book. **When we work on these skills, we're doing double duty, increasing our ability to thrive in the whitewater as well as indirectly boosting our creative capacity—which gives us yet another competitive edge.**

There are also techniques that more directly improve innovation—at the individual, team, and organizational level. To these we now turn.

Building the Creative Muscle: Introducing Creativity "Hygiene"

Honing our creativity requires venturing to the edges of the conscious mind and peering over the border. One hundred years ago, Moldovan-born physiologist Nathaniel Kleitman made a similar journey for a different purpose. As a young immigrant to New York City, Kleitman followed his curiosity about everyday consciousness to its opposite: sleep. Surely, if he could better understand the mind in sleep, he might gain deeper insight into our waking hours.

Kleitman's work resulted in the birth of the brand-new field of sleep studies. He helped discover REM sleep and demonstrated that the sleeping mind moves through cycles of rest and activity. One of his most influential ideas was that of "sleep hygiene"—the collection of habits and practices that enable quality sleep. For example, we now know that having a fixed waking time, even on weekends, helps our brains keep a steady sleep rhythm. We know that naps interfere with nightly patterns. For many, avoiding screens before bed—the blue light from cell phones interferes with the release of melatonin, which helps us feel tired—can be life-changing.

Sleep hygiene provides a model for how we can use conscious behavior to affect our nonconscious minds. One cannot simply command oneself to fall asleep or stay that way. Instead, sleep hygiene focuses on factors within our control.

The parallels to creativity are striking. Like sleep, creativity is highly complex and requires brain function that is not fully conscious. (By not conscious, we simply mean mental processes that we are unaware of and cannot voluntarily control, but which influence behavior nevertheless.) The creative brain balances intense focus with daydreaming, guided problem-solving with divergent brainstorming. We cannot just order ourselves to be creative any more than we can order ourselves to sleep. We can, however, identify behaviors and conditions that facilitate creativity and others that inhibit it. We can, in short, improve our "hygiene" around creativity—as individuals, teams, and organizations.

Individual Creative "Hygiene"

For people who want to directly amp up their creativity, we offer three strategies:

Seek novelty

As David Epstein has demonstrated so compellingly in *Range*, our most talented innovators are not specialists. Instead, they draw from a wide breadth of experiences that helps them see unusual connections. Creativity and intelligence researcher Robert Sternberg has written, too, of the tunnel vision that can result from too narrow a lens of expertise, impairing creative divergence. Recall that a primary function of the DMN is to juxtapose concepts differing across time and space in surprising ways; and that people who are most open to experience seek novelty naturally. It's therefore essential to stockpile as much divergent raw material as we can. In Stuart Kauffman's language, we want to enrich the adjacent possible for our DMN.

Finding novelty doesn't have to entail large-scale life changes. You don't need to go skydiving or climb Everest or sign up for SpaceX. The aim, rather, is to break old patterns and pave the way for new ones. Novel stimuli may come in the form of reading books at the edge of one's discipline; or of making new friends with knowledge and experiences relevant to your pursuit. Even something as basic as taking an alternate route home from work can wake us up from ingrained habits.

Here are some simple ways to embrace novelty in your daily life:

- Branch out socially. At a party, seat yourself next to someone you don't know. Introduce yourself to another parent at the playground. Talk to people in elevators. Reconnect with old contacts who now inhabit different corners of the world. At a dinner party a few years back, Gabriella sat herself next to the person she knew least. This remarkable individual turned out to be an illustrator and puppet maker, and . . . her own undiscovered third cousin!

- Take a different route. Drive home a new way. Carpool rather than commute alone. Wherever you are walking, turn down a new street. Look for ways to make the same old routine new.

- Browse broadly. Go to an actual, real-life bookstore—they do still exist—or a library and browse sections you have never explored. Challenge yourself to find a book in any section that relates to the problem you are solving. A similar approach has been shown to work in education: students tasked with making connections between data in diverse fields produce more creative work. Browse Wikipedia. Used right, the web can be a friend, not a foe, to the type of serendipitous discovery required for innovation. Follow links down rabbit holes. Be patient. Use unusual language in your web searches, language that will shift, or broaden, Google's lens.

- Go deep strategically. Read a work of fiction with a character inhabiting a problem space close to your own but set in a different era or culture or geography. If you are working on a dating app, spend some time with the works of the Brontë sisters. If you are building a product for college students, try *Norwegian Wood* by Haruki Murakami. (If you are just starting out and building your fund of knowledge, of course, fiction or nonfiction set closer to your topic matter would be the place to start. We do need to know enough about our specific area of innovation to be dangerous.)

Dial in incubation periods

The conscious and nonconscious work of creativity exist in fine balance. Focused research or brainstorming, for example, needs to be offset by less focused incubation, time for more spontaneous, generative mind-wandering. Research suggests that the more complex the creative job to be done, the more it will benefit from these incubatory periods. A wide body of studies has also found that mind-wandering is most productive when the focused work comes first: start with the deliberate problem-solving, then follow it with downtime. In our focused time, our executive control network is consciously planting ideas for our DMN to harvest. Recall that the executive control network loops back to the DMN; this is why that loop is so crucial.

It's also important to note that incubation is not the same as rest. Creative "ahas" don't typically arrive when we're lying in bed doing nothing. Instead, it seems that they happen most often when we are engaged in undemanding tasks. UC Santa Barbara professor Jonathan Schooler's lab has spent more than a decade studying mind-wandering. In an important 2012 study, they tested different types of incubation to see which worked best. After giving participants a few minutes to try a creative problem-solving activity, they then paused and assigned them to four groups: take on a new demanding task; engage in an undemanding task; rest; or no break. Everyone then went back to the same creative problem-solving. Of all four conditions, those in the undemanding task condition performed best, post-incubation. The key takeaway is that incubation is not about doing nothing. It's about doing *just little enough*.

Most common workplace activities—writing emails, attending meetings—are too demanding to facilitate incubation. Our executive control network is fully focused, so by definition the DMN is off. By contrast, activities like walking, reading, bathing, exercising, and free writing are all undemanding enough to create space for the DMN to activate and hit its stride.

One activity that, somewhat surprisingly, *won't* work: mindfulness. Mindfulness is in some ways the opposite of mind-wandering. Mindfulness directs the full spotlight of our conscious attention to sensations and feelings in the moment, whereas mind-wandering is the more intuitive, free-flowing, future-focused, unexamined spontaneous generation of ideas. Mindfulness is an excellent tool for achieving emotional regulation and can be transformative for coping with anxiety. Increasing evidence from Schooler's lab suggests, however, that it will undermine creative mind-wandering by absorbing too much conscious attention. Mindfulness fails our "just little enough" test.

Embrace ambiguity

Many people find ambiguity, a defining feature of the early phases of a creative project, uncomfortable. We saw in chapter 8 that this type of person typically needs the most help with phase one of prospection— divergent, expansive, intuitive—lest they prematurely foreclose on important options. Highly creative people tolerate, and even enjoy, this ambiguity. Robert Sternberg has targeted ambiguity tolerance with creativity interventions in schools.

One simple way to increase ambiguity tolerance is to structurally extend the period of exploration before selecting a solution. Merely by prolonging the time in which we sit in ambiguity, we expand our capacity for it and give ourselves a better chance of coming up with that big idea. We're extending time spent in phase one prospection.

Rian is a product manager for a social media company based in Northern California. He thrives in highly structured environments and gravitates toward the role of product manager because it is the product manager's job to turn messy problems into clear specifications. Some PMs love the early discovery phases of product development, in which teams collaboratively brainstorm problems to be solved. Rian instead prefers implementation, the phase in which the team's approach has been distilled into very clear product requirements, and building is underway.

Unfortunately, Rian has hit a ceiling in his advancement at his company, having been passed up for a promotion in the last cycle. Rian's manager explains that, while Rian is excellent at leading small squads in the rapid, reliable development of defined product enhancements, he has struggled with anything more complex. She recommends that Rian work with a coach to support his growth.

After an introductory session, in which Rian describes his goals and background, Rian's coach, Hana, gives Rian an assignment. Hana asks Rian to reflect on his experience leading a team through one of the more complex assignments he had had, namely, figuring out how to get users of his social media app to refer more friends. What went well? What went wrong? And, importantly, what emotions did Rian experience in each phase of the project, from discovery to completion?

"What did you learn from doing the assignment?" Hana asks Rian in their next session.

"That I really hated this project." Rian laughs. "It was kind of a nightmare from start to finish."

"That's a good thing to know!" Hana says. "It sounds like, if you wanted to, you could stick with less complex products and stay in your current role. Do you want that?"

"It certainly would be easier. But no. I want to become a leader of a larger organization. I've just got to get better at this."

"Good. That's clear," Hana says. She's now established the intrinsic motivation Rian will need to press forward. "Then tell me, in your assignment, what specific emotions were coming up for you in which phases?"

Throughout the project, Rian's dominant emotion was anxiety. He feared they wouldn't be able to solve the problem. He panicked when he couldn't see clearly to the solution. Once the team arrived at implementation, he worried that what they were building wouldn't achieve its intended aim.

"And it didn't," Rian says. "It didn't increase referrals at all. We should have spent more time figuring out the right solution."

"Okay." Hana nods. "Why didn't you do that?"

"We needed to move on. To start building. We'd wasted too much time trying to come up with ideas."

"So on the one hand, you said you should have spent more time figuring out the right solution," Hana reflects. "On the other hand, you're saying you wasted too much time coming up with ideas. What's the right amount of time for discovery?"

"Well, normally it's quick, a week or two. And I typically know what we need to do beforehand. I'm more or less bringing the team along with me."

"How about when you don't know what needs to be done?"

"Yeah . . ." Rian thinks. "I guess I don't know how long it should take when we start from truly not knowing what needs to be built. I definitely did *not* know what to do in this case. I still don't."

"Should you have known?"

Rian thinks. "No. No one knows."

"Okay then. So how does the team get there?"

Step-by-step, Rian comes to understand that discovery is where he struggles most because uncertainty makes him anxious. His strong impulse is to rush his team through the messiness to start building. With this new self-awareness in hand, Rian can begin to work on tasks that will help increase his tolerance for ambiguity. Hana will have Rian begin with less complex products, by extending the length of their discovery phases. Even if Rian can see his way to a solution alone, he must learn to sit in phase one prospection—generative, divergent, unpredictable—and take seriously unconventional ideas proposed by his team even if they don't align with his preconceived conclusions. He must also challenge himself to come up with alternatives of his own, increasing his internal openness to ideas. Once he has mastered discovery on more straightforward products, he can begin working on products with greater complexity.

Initially, the goal is to make ambiguity less unpleasant. Over time, with greater mastery, Rian might even be able to enjoy it.

Team and Organizational Creative "Hygiene"

Because Rian is a manager, his work to increase ambiguity tolerance will not only help him as an individual, it will also aid his team as a collective. Managers are the single most critical point of leverage for improving the creativity of teams. So far, we've seen four characteristics of highly creative teams, including:

1. Heterogeneity of skill sets, creative thinking types, and backgrounds
2. Effective communication
3. High psychological safety
4. Careful planning by team leaders

To this list, we add two strategies managers can use to more directly enhance team creativity:

Build creative self-efficacy of team members

"The principal limitation on what creative people can accomplish," management professors Paula Tierney and Steven Farmer have found, "is what they think they are capable of accomplishing." We've seen how creative self-efficacy influences our creative output. The more we believe in ourselves, the more dazzling our innovation.

Managers, teachers, parents all sit in privileged positions of power from which they can exert outsized influence on a person's creative self-efficacy. Managers can improve creative self-efficacy of their team members most directly through recognition, either public or private, of the team member's creative accomplishments. Notice the little things like small iterations. Make sure your people know that you appreciate these improvements.

Conversely, when things go wrong, tread carefully with your feedback so you don't inadvertently undermine an employee's creative self-efficacy. Missteps are learning opportunities. Honor the thinking that led to the negative result while pointing out how to do it differently next time. Managers must not dampen their team's enthusiasm for innovation. When team members are secure in their creative identity, they will be better able to take the creative risks required for important discoveries.

Broaden the realm of the possible

Group norms for all kinds of behavior form quickly, far more quickly than we are aware. When a group of people gets used to working together, it can stagnate, failing to generate divergent enough thoughts in the early stages of innovating. One of the biggest challenges for cohesive creative teams is breaking old patterns.

Michael Arena, vice president of Talent and Development at Amazon Web Services, and a PhD in organizational dynamics, is a preeminent scholar of how new ideas emerge in companies. One of four key factors is what he calls discovery connections: individuals who bridge multiple networks within a company and can therefore give their teams access to a broader set of ideas. They're extending the team's adjacent possible. And in so doing, they're inspiring greater divergence in others. Managers should therefore proactively introduce discovery connections onto creative teams.

Jeizzon "JZ" Viana Mendes is a design lead at BetterUp who regularly plays this role on the various product development squads he joins. He sits on both the Design team and the multimedia Studios team, and also regularly collaborates with the scientific BetterUp Labs crew. When staffed to a creative squad, JZ bridges ideas with clarity, confidence, and warmth, which makes others listen rather than dismiss them as too far afield.

In addition to bridging multiple teams, JZ is a distal thinker. He diverges widely and freely, introducing the metaverse, wormholes, and ancient artifacts to more conventional product brainstorms. Team members like JZ—and they need not be the team lead—will enlarge the circumference of adjacent possibles that the team feels they can inhabit. Teams that circumscribe their efforts too tightly, by contrast, are doomed before they begin.

Broadening the realm of the possible for creative groups means finding or hiring these discovery connections and distal thinkers, and strategically staffing them on worthy teams.

So much of creativity at work lives and dies at the team level. But the surrounding organization can create a climate that generally fosters or inhibits that work. Firm-level creative "hygiene" is transmitted most powerfully by culture—the set of shared assumptions that guide behaviors. Southwest's culture, for example, included the assumption that employees should bring their humor and creativity to bear to solve problems. Here are two organization-level strategies to help increase firm-wide innovation:

Celebrate risk-taking

Great creative strides are always risky. Ensuring psychological safety at the team level is one way to empower employees to take chances. Celebrating risk-taking at the company level is another.

One way some companies model risk-taking is with failure awards. At Castlight Health, a digital health company where Gabriella worked, there was once an award for spectacular failures—initiatives that were risky and well-conceived yet failed. Large segments of the company would gather to hear this award announced. The winner's courage and brilliance would be celebrated by a senior leader, before he or she was welcomed to the front of the room to share a few words. Usually the winner would include shout-outs to contributors, and funny-in-hindsight anecdotes about what went wrong. The assembled crowd would cheer, pat the winner on the back, and return to their teams to continue the hard work of innovation.

At BetterUp, quarterly Insightful Idea awards serve a similar purpose. Any employee can submit these business improvement ideas to the founders for consideration. Ideas range from ways to improve the product to new methods for recruiting top talent. Employees can offer them for any department in the company. Winners are announced by the founders at All Hands meetings, and given a spot bonus, regardless of whether the idea will be enacted. The purpose is to celebrate people for going out on a limb.

Treat everyone as creative

In corporations where one area is labeled "creative," it should not surprise anyone to find that other teams are less creative on the basis of that characterization. In the meantime, the Southwests of the world embolden all employees, at every level, to contribute creatively to their organization's success. These companies will have the edge in volatile, increasingly global competition. Their employees will offer their spare time to shepherd innovations in from the edges of the business with confidence. They will seek greater and greater challenges, as each success is rewarded with even more stimulating problems to solve.

———————————

Every worker has the hardware we need to be creative. And we will need to do so. The work ahead promises tremendous complexity. The joy to be had in cracking a particularly hard puzzle; shipping a particularly groundbreaking product; or unwinding a particularly gnarly nest of customer complaints is there for every employee with enough confidence, optimism, and resilience to accept the challenge.

On the one hand, creative work is personal and introspective. We need to benefit from our own nonconscious processes, as personal as fingerprints. Our creative ideas derive from our individual experiences, our unique imagination, juxtaposed and interpreted through the lens of our values, and powered by our sense of purpose.

And yet, at work, innovation does not typically happen alone. We need access to the adjacent possibles of our colleagues, with their complementary styles of integration, splitting, figure-ground reversal, and distal thinking. We need the encouragement of our managers, and the support of the organizational climate around us. This complex ecosystem, spanning individual, team, and organizational levels, ultimately determines the success of creative work.

Some of this change has begun at leading corporations—places like Southwest, or Adobe, where creativity is a core leadership skill.

There is, in addition, a different type of organizational change that most corporations are not yet aware needs to occur. Corporations that want to access the full potential of their employees need to reflect that aspiration in their organizational design and processes. To this topic we devote our final chapter.

CHAPTER TEN

Future-Proofing the Workforce
The Proactive Organization

In 1880, Agnes McClure Dunn, pickler at the H. J. Heinz Company factory, got a promotion.

Just thirty years old, Aggie already had several lifetimes in her rearview. The first she'd spent in Ireland, where she was born. After immigrating to America, she entered the workforce as a teenager, toiling on the line at a Civil War munitions factory. But the factory shut down when the war ended. Scrambling, Aggie found her way to the more traditional role of seamstress, a job she kept for ten years, until the opening at Heinz arose, along with the promise of greater growth and stability.

Plans changed, then changed again: Soon after joining Heinz, Aggie left to marry and run her household. Or so she thought. Her husband died suddenly, leaving her the sole provider for her ailing father and infant son. Aggie Dunn returned to pickling.

Her story is at once remarkable and ordinary. Beside her, in chairs lining the Carrara glass tables at Heinz, sat hundreds of other women, scooping up pickles with wooden spoons, nimbly filling spotless jars. They were immigrants, war widows, country girls making a go of the new industrial life. Each was surfing the tides of social, political, and personal upheaval. Each had walked a path littered with innumerable obstacles.

Henry Heinz was not naive to these challenges. Like most nineteenth-century industrialists, he found his business plagued by high turnover rates caused by the human toll of factory work. Unlike most, however, Heinz believed he could help.

And so, in 1880, Henry Heinz promoted Aggie Dunn to general forewoman of the "Home Plant girls." In doing so, he created the factory's first full-time role devoted to improving the welfare of workers. "Mother" Dunn, as she came to be called, presided from a rocking chair near the dressing room. Despite her elevated status, she wore the same factory apron and cap as her wards. She did the recruiting, the interviewing, the hiring, and the counseling for all the Heinz women. When there were medical bills, Aggie routed them to the right executive. She made house calls. One month, she attended no fewer than twenty workers' weddings.

"These girls Mr. Heinz wanted me to look after were just so many Aggie Dunns over again!" Aggie said once. "They were just traveling that same old bumpy road over which I had just come. I understood these folks, plain like myself, and they understood me."

Aggie Dunn died of pneumonia in 1924, having worked for Heinz for fifty-one years. On the afternoon of her funeral, each of Heinz's sixty plants across the United States, Canada, and England shut down in her honor.

The legacy of Mother Dunn lives on today in the Human Resources function of every major corporation. Hundreds or even thousands now fill the many varied roles Aggie once occupied all alone. Modern corporations universally believe that they can enable greater success for their staff through key investments in workers' health and well-being. Henry Heinz's disposition is today the rule, not the exception.

We need the help now more than ever. Half of US workers are burned out. Hundreds of thousands die unnecessarily each year due to workplace stress. That stress is also destroying our relationships, so essential for our well-being. We are languishing, not flourishing, in the whitewater. Human Resources is the part of the corporation most explicitly tasked with supporting employees. As we have now seen at length, in order to succeed at work today, we need to be armed with the PRISM powers of a Tomorrowmind. HR will be our greatest corporate ally in this endeavor.

Universally, however, as the stress and burnout statistics reveal, corporations are falling short. There are many reasons for this failure. One of those reasons is so deeply embedded in the fabric of HR departments that few notice it. It's a structural problem, rooted in Aggie Dunn's era, when the two HR functions most closely connected to employee thriving—Benefits on the one hand, and Learning and Development on the other—evolved from two distinct historical traditions, each of which remains somewhat siloed today.

In this chapter we'll begin by outlining the contours of the problem, as it is unfamiliar to most. We'll show why we believe that this two-pronged structure makes it challenging for corporations to tackle thriving holistically, and why each approach is insufficient on its own. We then examine additional organizational barriers to flourishing, before offering solutions.

Helping the Suffering: The Social Welfare Tradition

In chapter 1 we learned how the harsh conditions of industrial factory work created a steep rise in alcoholism in the late nineteenth and early twentieth centuries. We also met Chicago businessman Robert Law, who in 1863 brought an alcoholic employee into his home to get sober. Like Aggie Dunn, Law viewed employees as wards under his care, and he hoped to protect them from physical and psychological harm. The HR function that grew out of this paternalistic tradition today goes by the name of Benefits. A vice president of Benefits (or Benefits and

Total Compensation, if they also oversee pay scales) usually reports to the company's chief human resources officer (CHRO), who in turn reports to the CEO.

Historically there have been two types of services administered by the Benefits team that are most relevant to employee emotional well-being: the Employee Assistance Program (EAP) and the health plan. You'll recall from chapter 1 that as Alcoholics Anonymous and corporate sober living programs like Law's became more widespread, organizations embraced them under the euphemistic umbrella of the EAP. Over time, this program came to encompass organizational support for an ever-widening circle of psychological ills beyond substance abuse. Modern EAPs offer counseling for depression, anxiety, parenting and relationship challenges, and workplace violence. Ninety-seven percent of large companies offer their employees access to an EAP, which typically includes free counseling and referrals to mental healthcare.

Despite widespread availability, EAPs are woefully underutilized. Stigma is a main barrier to usage, as employees fear judgment or even penalty for accessing mental health services through their employer. Today, just 4% of workers use EAP services, far fewer than the number that could be benefiting from the offering. The EAP—originally designed as private, confidential services used in the shadows—still carries too strong a stigma of remediation.

Alongside EAPs, Benefits teams offer employees access to mental health benefits through their health plans. Mental disorders that are serious enough get referred from the EAP to a therapist or psychiatrist within the plan. Employer health insurance originated post–World War II as a result of federal tax breaks offered to businesses to help them attract employees despite government wage controls. Clinical healthcare accounts for the vast majority of a corporation's spend on all things mental health. Insurance covers therapy, psychiatry, inpatient psychiatric treatment, and psychopharmaceuticals. Many EAPs even sit within the health plan umbrella, administered by the same parent company.

All of which means that employees have come to regard EAPs and mental healthcare benefits as programs for people who are already in pretty rough shape. Employees are grateful to have access to these services—services Aggie Dunn could have only dreamed of—but they tend to interpret any employer offerings labeled "mental health" as a euphemism for mental illness. As a result, despite immensely creative, committed efforts and increasingly diverse investments, it can be difficult for Benefits teams to change the employee perception that their function manages remediation, not thriving.

Learning and Development: Upskilling the Able

The history of Learning and Development, like that of Benefits, begins with the Industrial Revolution. Prior to then, workers learned their trades either on the job or in one-on-one apprenticeships. But with industrialization, factories needed to keep up with such an unprecedented pace of production that they began to offer trainings to larger groups, with classrooms often located right off the factory floor itself.

The need to onboard large numbers of people quickly and efficiently dovetailed with the principles of "Scientific Management" then coming into vogue. The chief proponent of Scientific Management was the mechanical engineer Frederick Taylor. Machines had already greatly increased the efficiency of production; the next logical step, Taylor argued, was to increase the efficiency of the humans operating the machines. Through empirical study, best practices could be developed to reduce wasted effort and maximize productivity. Taylor's ideas gradually morphed into some of the functions owned by modern HR's Learning and Development team, or L&D. L&D is responsible for employee training, upskilling, learning, and professional growth in

service of performance and productivity. A vice president of L&D—
sometimes also called a VP of Talent, or Talent and Development—
usually reports to the CHRO and is a peer to the VP of Benefits.

Given Taylor's professional background, it's unsurprising, though
unfortunate, that his methods were mechanical in nature. He
prioritized the findings of industrial engineering, business process
management, and logistics over those of psychological science. In
treating people like a type of machine, Taylor ignored the deeply
human aspects of work. Despite its shortcomings, his system has
remained influential for decades, with lasting consequences.

Many modern corporate trainings today continue to ignore how
human beings actually learn and change. Here are a couple of common
issues with corporate instructional design:

1. Using long, one-off sessions instead of multiple shorter sessions
   repeated over time. Taylor's contemporary, psychologist
   Hermann Ebbinghaus, had already demonstrated in their day
   that without repetition we forget almost everything we are
   taught in a single go—up to 90% by the end of the month. The
   majority of business trainings occur as lengthy workshops. That
   might work for a machine, which can upload large quantities of
   data at once. It doesn't work for us.
2. Taking a one-size-fits-all approach. No two learners are the
   same, in terms of their strengths, their levels of motivation, and
   their fund of knowledge. Mass trainings that treat each learner
   as an identical cog will bore some, go over the heads of others,
   and fail to inspire the majority who are not yet ready to learn.

Harvard Business School professor Michael Beer has coined the
phrase "The Great Training Robbery" to describe the enormous
amount of corporate spend wasted on trainings that don't work. Up
to 90% of corporate learning initiatives suffer from these and other

design flaws, which minimize their effectiveness. Corporations in G20 countries spend roughly $400 billion on these programs annually.

Call that $360 billion up in flames.

The Challenges of a Disjointed Approach to Employee Growth

On the face of it, these two approaches—one originally paternalistic, one productivity-focused—have little in common. And it's still true in many modern HR departments that these functions exist as partially or fully siloed subunits, one focused on employee health, the other on performance.

The historical reasons for this two-sided approach, however, have long ceased to be relevant to our work. In the whitewater, our emotional well-being and professional development needs are intimately intertwined. As we battle extraordinary uncertainty, the skills required to manage stress are the same skills that enable sustainable career growth. The modern professional cannot succeed in leadership without emotional regulation, for example, any more than they can conquer anxiety without addressing career turbulence. And yet so many of today's most pressing workforce issues—like burnout, loneliness, and belonging—sit squarely at the margins of two separate functions.

Forward-leaning Benefits and Talent executives, including so many whom we are privileged to partner with and learn from in our research, work hard to bridge this gap through frequent communication and collaboration. They report to CHROs who likewise understand this dynamic and model collaboration at the top.

At many enterprise companies, however, the siloing of Benefits and L&D remains a significant challenge to a holistic approach to thriving. In 2017, Gabriella researched this gap across a selection of the largest companies in America. Her goal was to understand how each department thought about the overlap of their work with the other's.

The answers were hard to come by, because so often these functional counterparts knew little about each other's team. For example, one long-tenured Benefits leader at a major retailer felt that employee resilience fell under her team's purview, except that she had seen an email recently about a resilience course offered by L&D. Who, exactly, in L&D, she didn't know; she couldn't name anyone in L&D other than its senior-most executive. This type of dynamic was not uncommon. Even when prompted with names and titles of counterparts, peers often didn't recognize them.

Occasionally such division can even produce territoriality. Territoriality often occurs in siloed organizations when two functions each believe they are the rightful owner of the same work. Stress management programming, a form of resilience training, offers a helpful case study: Today all EAPs include some form of stress counseling. In addition, some Benefits teams invest in stand-alone stress management or resilience training solutions. This makes sense because people with mental health conditions struggle to cope with stress and often have lower resilience. We also know that building resilience is good for productivity and retention, and that managers and leaders disproportionately influence the well-being of their teams. For these reasons, it makes equal sense for leadership to receive extra training in this area—a type of managerial training that would sit with L&D.

Shortly before the pandemic, the L&D team at a Fortune 100 company brought their CHRO a proposal for a resilience training for leaders. When the Benefits team found out, they reminded the CHRO that they had already implemented a resilience program to lower stress. Adding another program could confuse people. Rather than bring everyone to the table, the CHRO let the idea go, the result being that leaders didn't get access to the more robust program. In retrospect there would have been no better time to work on building leadership's capacity to help their teams weather adversity.

A silver lining of COVID-19 that we observed was increased collaboration across the aisles of HR. The pandemic loosed a tidal wave of psychological needs both for workers and their families, sending HR teams around the world scrambling to help, often sacrificing their weekends in service of their workforce. For the first time we found ourselves on video calls with both the VP of Benefits and the VP of L&D at the same time. Down in the COVID-19 foxhole, holding the line against emotional chaos, their teams had found in each other sorely needed allies. This chaos was the purview of L&D, because it was affecting the performance of every employee; but it was also the purview of Benefits, because it carried deep psychological risks.

New challenges to collaboration surfaced in this climate. Benefits teams and Talent teams have different metrics of success, which map to their organizational responsibilities. Benefits teams are expected to tightly manage healthcare spend, and often employ actuaries for this reason. From their perspective, a thriving-related program is effective if it decreases the number of people who need to see therapists or psychiatrists (in other words: avoid negative ten). L&D departments, by contrast, don't even have access to healthcare billing records, let alone track them. The metrics that matter most to L&D include productivity, innovation, and employee retention (in other words: increase to positive ten).

Ideally, this divergence would produce a creative tension that would yield a more holistic design. One can imagine the VP of Benefits and the VP of L&D putting their heads together to codesign and cosponsor solutions that would achieve the aims of both teams. Thriving offerings *can*, in fact, improve both healthcare spending and performance metrics, but only if they are designed to do so from the start.

Unfortunately, in our experience, in practice it's often faster and simpler for the two teams to resolve their divergence by picking one or the other function to take the lead on. Whichever "side of the house" ends up funding a given program then naturally dominates its design and metrics of success. When we privilege one type of outcome over the other—call it surviving versus thriving—the program's focus narrows accordingly, along with the benefits to the organization.

The Proactive Organization

Both EAPs and mass factory trainings represent post hoc responses to already urgent needs. This reactive posture is part of their legacy. As we saw in chapter 3, however, far and away the most effective type of health intervention is primary prevention: preventing individuals from developing diseases in the first place. Primary prevention works best and costs the least—as long as we have the courage to act now based on likely future outcomes. Said differently, functions devoted to employee thriving must, like individual workers, embrace prospection. With market cycles constantly churning, we need our corporate leaders to always be thinking several steps ahead about human capital, understanding how the changes to come will affect their workforce, identifying the skills that will mitigate turbulence, and training their people up.

In the realm of physical health, Benefits teams lead the way in future-minded thinking. They work to ensure that health plans cover all government-recommended preventive care services, like immunizations, for example. They look to experts and chief medical officers for guidance on the latest trends in prevention and health promotion. They advocate for offerings like gym memberships to help employees avoid heart disease, or smoking cessation coaching to prevent lung cancer. In so doing, they lengthen employees' lives, and lower healthcare costs for both individuals and the corporations—a true win-win-win.

In the realm of psychological thriving, the primary prevention approach is usually thinner and harder to come by. Why should that be the case?

The answer is multifaceted. We've already seen part of it. The holistic perspective needed to enable a proactive stance is challenged by the structural split between managing costs of illness (Benefits) and managing metrics of growth (L&D). There's no equivalent of L&D for physical health, a separate HR division whose exclusive focus would be on helping employees go from not sick to extremely physically fit (zero to ten). In the realm of psychological thriving, dividing remediation and growth can shortchange both processes and make it difficult to target the core skills that unite them.

A second hurdle to implementing primary prevention springs from deeper-seated beliefs about human psychology. There are still a handful of influential corporate leaders who do not see employees' psychological well-being as their responsibility. Perhaps they rose up in the ranks of corporations that lacked a culture of employee support. Even if on some level they recognize that thriving workers perform better, they might not see a reason to change things. The implication being: *I didn't have that, and I turned out just fine.* Some point to low EAP utilization numbers—an artifact of stigma and, in some cases, low-quality services—as evidence that employees don't want help.

Third, there is the considerable challenge of proving the return on investment in prevention programs for psychological well-being. Any HR program will require a budget, and large-ticket items like resilience coaching or innovation trainings ultimately land on the desk of the chief financial officer or her deputies. CFOs speak the language of efficiency. *Buy this cloud service, save more than you pay us in server costs.* Or: *Contract with this customer revenue management offering, gain back 25% of the daily working hours of your salesforce.*

Thriving is not an efficiency sale; it's an effectiveness sale. Efficient solutions yield the same outcome more rapidly, with minimal waste.

Effective solutions get us to the *best* outcomes. Skills like rapid rapport and prospection prevent bad outcomes, while improving performance and retention. Demonstrating the chain of causality requires statistical regression models, familiarity with common psychometric measures, and a decent grasp of the epidemiology of mental illness. It looks nothing like the standard business case. It's complex, and for that reason easily dismissed as too tenuous to merit investment.

Thriving also takes time. Corporate cultures myopic about short-term gains will not be enthusiastic about paying for thriving. Short-termism is an enemy of workplace flourishing—and therefore also the enemy of performance, productivity, and sustainable success. On the other hand, the long-term gains in productivity from employee thriving will repay the investment many times over.

One of the great ironies, of course, is that businesses already spend a ton of money on programs that are neither efficient nor effective—yet somehow get funded anyway. Remember that $360 billion up in flames? How did any of that make it past the CFO?

This level of investment suggests that most corporations believe they should be doing *something*. That's the good news. But the key players involved in approving major investments—including procurement, finance, legal, and even many in HR—usually don't have the expertise to determine which offerings will move the needle. It's not easy to sort through what's evidence-based as opposed to what just sounds good on paper. The natural inclination for a nonexpert is to fund the cheapest option with the longest list of features. In the absence of the ability to weight the performance and well-being impact of one offering over another, bells and whistles often stand in for value.

All of which connects to the fourth and final hurdle to the proactive approach to employee thriving, which is apprehension about translating the available behavioral science research into practice. Do we really know enough, this argument goes, to have a sense of which psychological skills will be most vital for success—not just today, but going forward? And to lower the risk of psychological illness? Is the science precise enough to guide investment?

We believe that the answer to these questions, as outlined in the first nine chapters of this book, is a resounding yes. We have three decades of data documenting the relationship of improved psychological well-being to lowered risks of myriad mental and physical illnesses and detailing the interventions that work. On the applied science side, our industry is on its third or fourth generation of novel, evidence-based interventions, platforms, tools, and services to support employee growth and well-being. And we have learned a lot along the way. We have now summarized in these pages the five key psychological skills our research shows workers will need in order to succeed in our increasingly volatile, global, automated industries. Organizations may not be able to tackle all these challenges at once. But we have all the evidence we need to get started.

All of these barriers—the complexity of the business case, the divide between remediation and growth, the discomfort in translating behavioral science into practice—understandably make it challenging for corporations to take a primary prevention approach to employee well-being. But these hurdles are surmountable.

What, then, does the alternative look like?

We can learn, first, from those leading corporations that set their sights squarely on thriving itself. Such corporations work to bridge the gap between Benefits and L&D through collaborations at the highest levels of leadership. Hilton is one example. Hilton's senior L&D and Benefits leaders partner to think holistically about the support their people need most, working backwards from the common desired outcome of employee thriving. The result? The company is consistently rated one of the best places to work globally, regularly beating out higher-margin businesses for these accolades. Hilton's success demonstrates that it's not about spending more on your employee experience—no need for perks like on-site putting greens or dry cleaning—it's about spending *smarter*. In the words of Hilton CHRO Laura Fuentes, "To me, it boils down to creating not a work experience or an employee experience but a human experience that makes people feel like they are seen, they are welcome, they are heard, they will be taken care of, and they can take care of their families and loved ones, and that they belong to something greater than themselves." A vision that bold necessitates collaboration across the aisles.

Michael Ross, former CHRO at Visa, advisor to BetterUp, and lecturer at Stanford Graduate School of Business, highlights the need to infuse this holistic approach to building thriving deep into the meshwork of HR—from tools to processes to metrics. Without that, he says, "You're left with words on a page." For example, a core belief for the proactive organization is that employees cannot achieve their professional potential if they are not thriving, nor can the organization realize maximal returns. It follows, then, that any strategic planning targeting workforce performance and potential should include not only L&D and Talent but also Benefits. "By taking a more holistic view of their employees' well-being needs, from mental health support to performance coaching," Ross says, "modern HR functions can work together to help employees maximize their performance and potential and create a culture in which their employees can truly thrive."

In other organizations, it may not be enough to leverage existing structures and processes, in which case an even more radical approach may be called for. This approach would structurally unify those responsible for worker thriving, including large parts of Benefits and L&D, into a single unit we'll call the Employee Thriving Team (ETT). The ETT would be responsible for the physical and emotional health, personal growth, and professional growth of each individual employee. Diverse stakeholders from investors to customers to senior leadership would rely on the ETT to keep the company's most valuable asset—its people—on its edge, ready to meet the unforeseen challenges to come. This team's leading indicators of success would include measures like PERMA, organizational mattering, resilience, innovation, and prospection. Its major investments would be reviewed and approved by decision-makers fluent in the behavioral sciences, with a focus on primary prevention. Continued funding for any program would be contingent upon measurable improvement in the ETT's most important metrics: employee retention, performance, and healthcare costs. This significant structural transformation would also necessitate careful thinking about which functions that today live under the umbrellas of Benefits and L&D would need to be carved out in order to preserve this team's focus.

Such a substantial rewiring of HR—either by way of restructuring or through close and frequent collaboration between L&D and Benefits—requires the buy-in of not only the CHRO but also the CEO and even the board of directors. These leaders need to share a common vision of workforce readiness that honors employee thriving and agility as the company's strongest bulwark against the accelerating uncertainty of the future.

Perhaps someday our children will enter the workforce already armed with the skills described in this book. So many of the capabilities discussed here—resilience, cognitive agility, emotional regulation, creative self-efficacy, advanced social skills—are in fact most effectively acquired at a younger age. How we think, why we make the choices we make, how we change, what cognitive abilities we need to live a healthy, meaningful life: These are not optional topics for our generation. They are the keys to our survival and success. In the final stages of the Industrial Revolution, our forebears marshalled major educational reforms to help prepare students for new forms of work.

Today passionate, forward-thinking educators, administrators, and legislators around the globe are striving to introduce thriving topics into the classroom at all levels, all while managing their own burden of emotional labor and whitewater nausea. They need our support—as parents, and as community members invested in helping the next generation show up with a full tank of resilience, ready to go.

Conclusion

These days we're often asked by CEOs and CHROs how the pandemic has reshaped our thinking. How did COVID-19 change work? What do those changes mean for success in this new era? What psychological capabilities will we all need in order to navigate a post–COVID-19 world?

Answering these pressing questions requires a figure-ground reversal. The pandemic represents an extreme version of whitewater, but it is not different in kind from the revolution that was already in play. COVID-19's widespread impact on our economy has only been possible because of the economy's preexisting nature: global, contingent, uncertain.

As a point of comparison, consider the Great Influenza Pandemic of 1918–1920, which killed forty million worldwide, or 2% of the world's population at the time. (The equivalent today would be 160 million deaths, more than ten times the largest estimates from the first two years of COVID-19.) Despite the Spanish flu's unthinkably massive death toll, its economic impact was relatively modest, with an associated drop in GDP of 6–8%. Economic challenges were primarily local, because a truly global economy had yet to take hold. The impact of the Spanish flu took the shape of its contemporaneous world of work.

Our world looks different, and the impact of COVID-19 has likewise taken its shape, hastening the turbulence already in effect. We thought the world was changing fast before; COVID-19 showed us just how much more quickly change could come. The McKinsey Global Institute estimates that the pandemic will accelerate occupational transitions by as much as 25%. (To arrive at this number, they modeled changes in job turnover for eight hundred occupations that would result from three key trends set in motion by the pandemic: the accelerated adoption of artificial intelligence, growth in e-commerce and delivery, and changes in workplace locations and travel.) We were already tap-dancing at high speed; now the music is playing 25% faster.

We're moving 25% faster toward job loss, job change, and role change. Our existing skills, already short on shelf life, will expire 25% more quickly, particularly for those workers in lower wage brackets. We have seen the high human cost of those changes. In the year after job displacement, death rates increase by 50–100%. Suicide, depression, substance abuse, and anxiety all rise dramatically with unemployment.

All of that, across the population, 25% faster.

Hundreds of millions of global workers have personally experienced this accelerating uncertainty in just the last few years. Sadness, fear, lethargy, lack of focus, constant worry—sound familiar? Symptoms of anxiety and depression are up by as much as 400% since the start of the pandemic, particularly among young adults, communities of color, essential workers, and mothers. Substance abuse and suicidal thinking have shot up too. Some of this was driven by the first waves of job loss and job transition—indeed, rates of anxiety and depression are significantly higher in those who lost jobs during the pandemic. But even for those whose jobs and roles are as yet unchanged, increased emotional turmoil radiates from the surrounding climate of social isolation, uncertainty, and constant change.

We need not, we must not, fall victim.

We now have an exceptional historic advantage that offers a new path forward. Unlike the workers of the Industrial Revolution, who also struggled with substance abuse and anxiety in the wake of a huge labor transformation; unlike the *Homo sapiens* whose transition to agriculture heralded the first major mismatch between our daily toil and the type of work we evolved to do; we have, today, a rich and ever-growing body of evidence to help us help ourselves.

Perhaps the most humane and transformative product of tens of thousands of years of our modern brain's existence is knowledge of how to adapt, psychologically, to inhumane conditions of our own creation. Technological innovation has made life move faster and last longer. It has created vast wealth. But it has not made us thrive. The behavioral sciences provide a lifeline in chaos. They open the door to more enjoyable, fulfilled lives.

We know what skills it will take to thrive in the decades of work to come. We will need, first and foremost, an exceptional degree of psychological resilience to allow us to bounce back, unharmed, from these extreme challenges to our well-being. Core to that capability is the cognitive agility to identify and flex into new opportunities as individuals and as organizations. We will need a deep connection to our essential why—a strong and steady sense of mattering to fuel the hard work of adapting both at work and at home. We will need one another—as colleagues, as leaders, as friends—to help us succeed in the increasingly complex, interdependent modern workforce. We also need our relationships to protect us from the ills of social isolation. We no longer have our ancient, tight-knit communities of hunter-gatherers to rely on for support. We can, nevertheless, build the skills that we need to rapidly connect even in this extraordinary turbulence.

In addition, the whitewater world, for all its psychological challenges, offers us the opportunity to develop two uniquely human superpowers: prospection and creativity. The repetitive, cog-like nature of work in the Industrial Revolution *de*humanized workers. Our current transformation, by stark contrast, demands that we reconnect with our most human, creative capabilities in order to thrive. Prospection is the meta-skill for our era. The more sophisticated, accurate, and expansive our skills of foresight, the greater will be our self-determination in an era of constant change. Individuals, teams, and organizations that excel at prospection will win in the whitewater every time—if they can foresee, and then creatively respond. Creativity is no longer the special province of artists or elite tinkerers. All workers must be creatives today, observing novel trends and finding innovative responses. Organizations that cultivate creativity at all levels will see outsized returns. Those that do not will fall behind.

Each of us, as individuals, can build the PRISM powers: **P**rospection; **R**esilience and agility; **I**nnovation and creativity; **S**ocial connection by way of rapid rapport; and **M**attering. They are within reach for every reader of this book, through self-guided work, through work with coaches and trainers, or through practice with peers and friends. Each individual who undertakes the journey toward a Tomorrowmind will have made our efforts to write this book worthwhile.

From this new vantage point, we can also accelerate thriving much more dramatically through organizational change. We spend, globally, about $400 billion on worker training each year, largely honing skills that will expire in short order. American employers spend an additional $15,000 per employee per year for those employees struggling with mental illness. Reconfiguring our organizations to stop splitting workers' professional and psychological needs and instead focus proactively and holistically on the enduring human capabilities outlined in this book will radically diminish these costs, and produce outsized returns in the form of sustainable performance and innovation.

In the final decade of his life, Abraham Maslow, pioneer of humanistic psychology, turned his attention to the workplace. In his 1965 work, *Maslow on Management*, he explained this pivot as follows:

> I gave up long ago the possibility of improving the world or the whole human species via human psychotherapy. This is impracticable. As a matter of fact it is impossible quantitatively . . . Then I turned for utopian purposes to education as a way of reaching the whole human species . . . Only recently has it dawned on me that as important as education and perhaps even more important is the work life of the individual since everybody works. If the lessons of psychology, of individual psychotherapy, of social psychology, etc., can be applied to man's economic life, then my hope is that this too can be given an enlightened direction, thereby tending to influence principle in all human beings.

Sixty years later, on the backs of hundreds of thousands of research studies spanning psychology, psychiatry, organizational behavior, behavioral economics, neuroscience, and more, we have at hand the science we need to realize Maslow's vision. Thriving in the whitewater is not only possible, it is within reach for individual employees and organizations alike. We need but grab hold of the tools that exist and put in the work to develop our Tomorrowmind.

Change is coming faster every day. How will you respond?

Appendix
Whole Person Model Assessment

BetterUp is a virtual platform that facilitates individual growth and development by providing users with professional coaching, content resources that match a user's needs, and other learning and development experiences. The Whole Person Model (WPM) assessment is BetterUp's proprietary measure of the full range of personal and professional development for working adults. BetterUp developed the WPM assessment to holistically and comprehensively measure the mindsets, behaviors, and outcomes that are central to both personal well-being and success at work. It fills two primary needs: a) providing a comprehensive measure of well-being and leadership constructs with strong psychometric properties, and b) providing an actionable and development-focused reporting. The WPM assessment was developed for use in personal and professional development. It was not developed to be used in selection decisions.

The remainder of this appendix provides details on the development and validation process for the assessment. A full technical report can be requested through BetterUp's website.

The development of the WPM began in 2018 with an in-depth review of the academic literature within the fields of organizational, developmental, and positive psychology. After a thorough review of published research, specifically targeting literature focused on goal setting, well-being, and leadership, we identified and categorized both proximal and distal indicators of personal and professional growth. As a part of the literature review, the BetterUp Labs psychometrics team identified common and widely used measures of WPM constructs which, in turn, provided guidance for drafting an initial pool of items across a broad range of categories. Feedback from BetterUp's psychologists, scientific advisors, and business leaders helped further refine the initial item pool. The overall structure of the WPM assessment was validated on samples representative of professional workers across a variety of industries at both the individual contributor and manager level.

To develop items and scales that measure each component of the WPM, members of BetterUp Labs followed best practices as outlined in the *Standards* (American Educational Research Association, 2014). The first step in designing the WPM was to iteratively identify constructs to include, drop, or modify in the model. A literature review was conducted, and discussions were held with key stakeholders and subject matter experts. Overall, specific constructs were chosen using the wealth of professional expertise of the initial validation team, the empirical analyses of the existing data collected by BetterUp from 2016 to 2018, and by evaluating stakeholder interviews. A hypothesized model was developed by a team of nine industrial/organizational psychologists, including BetterUp Labs team members, contractors, and university faculty. BetterUp developed the WPM to establish baselines, provide feedback, and track development during coaching engagements. The initially hypothesized structure of the WPM included higher-order factors for Inspiring behaviors (core leadership behaviors) and Thriving states (personal well-being). Mindsets and outcomes are directly and distally related to core behaviors that are targets of change. Thriving and Inspiring factors were hypothesized to be composed of three or four broader dimensions, each consisting of two to three narrower subdimensions. After finalizing the hypothesized structure of the Thriving and Inspiring components, BetterUp psychologists wrote operational definitions for all constructs.

From the hypothesized WPM assessment structure, items were written to measure the relevant Mindsets, Thriving and Inspiring behaviors, and Outcomes. Specific attention was paid to creating alternate forms measuring leadership behaviors depending on whether the respondent was an individual contributor or people manager. All items were compiled, reviewed, and revised by two separate team members. A post-review discussion was then held to resolve issues and remove items as needed. A final set of 345 items was created and administered to a representative validation sample. Additionally, existing psychometric scales previously validated were coadministered in the validation sample to evaluate discriminant and convergent validity evidence of the WPM.

To confirm the structure of the WPM, 1,030 qualified workers were recruited for participation. All participants eligible for inclusion in the validation study had previously completed other studies with BetterUp, which allowed access to additional assessment scores. Overall, our sample was 57% male, had an average of thirty-nine years of age, had an average job tenure of six years, and worked an average of forty-two hours per week. Similar numbers of people leaders (N = 485) and individual contributors (N = 545) were recruited to be able to appropriately evaluate two assessment forms of leadership behaviors. Participants were directed to the appropriate version of the leadership assessment based on their current role.

Item analysis was initially conducted to identify and remove poorly performing items from the full set of 345 items. This was determined by evaluating means, standard deviations, skewness, kurtosis, inter-item correlations, item-total correlations, and internal consistency of scales composed of the item(s) in question. Items were considered poorly performing if their means were too high, standard deviations were too low, skewness and kurtosis values were too high, or inter-item/item-total correlations were too low (in both relative and absolute terms). Overall, we tested whether the items within each scale correlated highly enough that a total score was appropriate for each item set.

These analyses led to a reduction in the number of items administered across the domains of WPM: Mindsets, Thriving Behaviors, Inspiring Behaviors, and Outcomes. Mindsets and Outcomes scales are based on well-validated and extensively studied constructs (e.g., self-efficacy, locus of control, stress, burnout). Therefore, factor analysis was not used to test the factor structure of Mindset and Outcome measures. Item analysis was used to reduce the items on each subscale within Mindsets and Outcomes, whereas hierarchical factor analysis was used to reduce item sets from Thriving and Inspiring domains. All scales demonstrated high internal consistency.

A hierarchical factor analysis was performed to confirm the structural model and recover the measurement model of Thriving and Inspiring domains. The structural model consisted of several subdimensions loading onto broader dimensions, which were then loaded onto either higher order Thriving or Inspiring factors. To assess the factor structure of the WPM, a series of confirmatory factor analyses (CFA) were fit using maximum likelihood estimation procedures in *MPlus 8.0*. The original sample of 1,030 participants was divided in half to create two samples to cross-validate our model. This was intended to avoid overfitting the model to one set of participants if model modifications were necessary. The final structure of the Thriving domain demonstrated excellent fit based on commonly used SEM cutoffs (see Hu & Bentler, 1999)—$\chi^2(480) = 864.25$, $p > .05$, CFI = .95, RMSEA = .04, SRMR = .06—and demonstrated nearly identical fit in the holdout sample: $\chi^2(480) = 873.45$, $p > .05$, CFI =

.95, RMSEA = .04, SRMR = .05. For the Inspiring domain, validation and holdout samples were created. The initial validation and holdout sample contained half of the total available individual contributors (N = 273) and half people leaders (N = 243). The people leaders sample was the primary validation sample for iterative model testing and the individual contributor validation sample was used to provide additional information when model modifications were necessary. As a result of having two forms of Inspiring items with minor wording adjustments for individual contributors and people managers, we further divided the Inspiring sample. In total we had four independent samples for Inspiring. The final structure of Inspiring for people leaders yielded acceptable fit for people leaders: $\chi^2(242)$ = 441.841, p > .05, CFI = .92, $RMSEA$ = .06, $SRMR$ = .06. Model fit on the people leaders holdout sample was acceptable: $\chi^2(242)$ = 454.95, p > .05, CFI = .90, $RMSEA$ = .06, $SRMR$ = .06. The same pattern held for the individual contributor validation sample: $\chi^2(242)$ = 432.746, p > .05, CFI = .93, $RMSEA$ = .05, $SRMR$ = .06. The model fit on the individual contributor holdout sample also showed acceptable fit: $\chi^2(242)$ = 426.70, p > .05, CFI = .89, $RMSEA$ = .07, $SRMR$ = .07. In fitting all four samples, a Heywood case was identified (i.e., λ > 1.0 and negative residual variance on one dimension). The Heywood case was treated by constraining the residual variance of the dimension to be positive, and the model was then rerun in all four samples. This treatment did not influence the fit statistics.

Existing scales previously validated in the well-being and leadership literature were used to evaluate discriminant and convergent validity. The WPM assessment demonstrated the expected pattern of correlations with these measures. Several multivariate analyses of variance (MANOVAs) were conducted to detect differences across managerial status, gender, and ethnicity on the components of WPM. Although there were a small number of statistically significant differences across demographic groups, the magnitude of these differences was small and accounted for very little of the variance. Additionally, our one-month and three-month test-retest analyses found WPM 2.0 to be stable over time in the validation sample that had not received professional coaching.

Additional information on the WPM and its validation process can be requested from the BetterUp Labs team through the BetterUp website.

Acknowledgments

We wish to acknowledge the significant contributions of many friends, family members, and colleagues to this book.

Thank you to Alexi Robichaux and Eduardo Medina, founders of BetterUp, for their visionary work creating the company that brought us together. Thank you to our colleagues at BetterUp, particularly the BetterUp Labs family, for their many rich contributions to the ideas and insights we have humbly attempted to collect here for the benefit of a broader audience.

Thank you to Alexi Robichaux, Naomi Arbit, Andrew Reece, Roy Baumeister, Rebecca Goldstein, Sonja Lyubomirsky, John Seely Brown, Christine Carter, Philip Streit, Barry Schwartz, Kurt Grey, Diana Tamir, Ayelet Ruscio, Betty Sue Flowers, Yisroel Brumer, David Yaden, Jackie Gaffney, Austin Eubanks, Elena Auer, Sebastian Marin, Nkosi Jones, Michael Ross, Karen Lai, Shevaun Lee, Tom Van Gilder, Evan Sinar, Derek Hutchinson, Alexis Jeannotte, Allison Yost, Erin Eatough, Shonna Waters, Adam Rosenzweig, and Sarah Sugarman for their contributions to this work.

Thank you to Chris Parris-Lamb and Stephanie Hitchcock for believing in the project, and for painstakingly shepherding the manuscript from one stage to the next.

Thank you to Jesse Kellerman and Mandy Seligman for their unwavering support. And finally, a special thank-you from Gabriella to Oscar, Masha, Teddy, Henry, and Abram. We hope to leave this world of work a little better in time for your arrival.

Notes

INTRODUCTION

2 **"I've always embraced change"**: Graeme Payne, conversation with Gabriella Rosen Kellerman, November 11, 2021.

2 **the region surrounding Christchurch**: "Regional Gross Domestic Product: Year Ended March 2019," New Zealand Government, accessed February 28, 2022, https://www.stats.govt.nz/information-releases/regional-gross -domestic-product-year-ended-march-2019; "Exploring Our Economy Series, Volume 1: Exploring the Christchurch Industries," ChristchurchNZ, https://www.christchurchnz.com/media/vnqfyya1/volume-1_explore-our -industries.pdf; "Situation and Outlook for Primary Industries June 2021," New Zealand Ministry for Primary Industries, https://www.mpi.govt.nz /dmsdocument/45451-Situation-and-Outlook-for-Primary-Industries-SOPI -June-2021.

2 **luggable at their desk**: Graeme Payne, *The New Era of Cybersecurity Breaches* (USA: CyberSecurity4Executives, 2019), 1–2.

4 **the first CISO—pronounced *SEE-so*—in history**: Payne, *The New Era of Cybersecurity Breaches*, 5.

4 **a loss of $1 *trillion* in 2020 alone**: Payne, *The New Era of Cybersecurity Breaches*, 6, 167–68; Tonya Riley, "The Cybersecurity 202: Global Losses from Cybercrime Skyrocketed to Nearly $1 Trillion in 2020, New Report Finds," *Washington Post*, December 7, 2020, https://www.washingtonpost.com /politics/2020/12/07/cybersecurity-202-global-losses-cybercrime-skyrocketed -nearly-1-trillion-2020/.

5 **"Equifax handles twelve hundred times that amount of data every day"**: Payne, *The New Era of Cybersecurity Breaches*, 35.

5 **bank account information of a stranger**: Neil Ford, "Credit Reporting Company Equifax Suffers Old-Fashioned Data Breach," IT Governance, https://www.itgovernanceusa.com/blog/credit-reporting-company-equifax -suffers-old-fashioned-data-breach.

6 **called the most expensive data breach in history**: John McCrank and Jim Finkle, "Equifax Breach Could Be Most Costly in Corporate History," Reuters, March 2, 2018.

7 **"against the backdrop of all the facts"**: Payne, *The New Era of Cybersecurity Breaches*, 129.

8 **"viewed by prospective employers?"**: Payne, *The New Era of Cybersecurity Breaches*, 113, 175.

9 **struggles with burnout**: Kristy Threlkeld, "Employee Burnout Report," Indeed.com, March 11, 2021, https://www.indeed.com/lead/preventing-employee-burnout-report; "Employee burnout is ubiquitous, alarming—and still underreported," McKinsey & Company, April 16, 2021, https://www.mckinsey.com/featured-insights/coronavirus-leading-through-the-crisis/charting-the-path-to-the-next-normal/employee-burnout-is-ubiquitous-alarming-and-still-underreported.

9 **impacting their personal relationships**: "Workplace Stress Continues to Mount," Korn Ferry, https://www.kornferry.com/insights/this-week-in-leadership/workplace-stress-motivation.

9 **thousands of unnecessary deaths**: J. Goh, J. Pfeffer, and S.A. Zenios, "The Relationship between Workplace Stressors and Mortality and Health Costs in the United States," *Management Science* 62, no. 2 (March 2015): 608–28.

10 **forms of work**: For a compelling overview of the toll of workplace stress today, see Jeffrey Pfeffer, *Dying for a Paycheck* (New York: Harper Business, 2018).

10 **As many as 80%**: James Manyika, Susan Lund, Michael Chui, Jacques Bughin, Jonathan Woetzel, Parul Batra, Ryan Ko, and Saurabh Sanghvi, "Jobs Lost, Jobs Gained: What the Future of Work Will Mean for Jobs, Skills, and Wages," McKinsey Global Institute, November 28, 2017, https://www.mckinsey.com/featured-insights/future-of-work/jobs-lost-jobs-gained-what-the-future-of-work-will-mean-for-jobs-skills-and-wages.

10 **In the year after job displacement**: Daniel Sullivan and Till von Wachter, "Job Displacement and Mortality: An Analysis Using Administrative Data," *Quarterly Journal of Economics* 124, no. 3 (August 2009): 1265–1306.

10 **unnaturally fast rate of turnover in our working groups**: "Economic News Release," Bureau of Labor and Statistics, https://www.bls.gov/news.release/tenure.t01.htm.

11 **An estimated 25–30% of the US workforce**: Estimate by Global Workplace Analytics, "Work at Home After Covid-19," https://globalworkplaceanalytics.com/work-at-home-after-Covid-19Covid-19-our-forecast.

11 **120,000 excess deaths per year in the US, and up to one million in China**: Pfeffer, *Dying for a Paycheck*.

CHAPTER ONE: OUR BRAINS AT WORK

19 **intervals of one or more millennia**: Felipe Fernandez Arnesto, "Before the Farmers: Culture and Climate, from the Emergence of *Homo sapiens* to about Ten Thousand Years Ago," in *The Cambridge World History, Volume 1: Introducing World History (to 10,000 BCE)*, ed. David Christian (Cambridge: Cambridge University Press, 2017), 316; Patrick Manning, "Migration in Human

History," in *The Cambridge World History, Volume 1: Introducing World History (to 10,000 BCE)*, ed. David Christian (Cambridge: Cambridge University Press, 2017), 281.

19 **shorter forearms and lower legs**: John F. Hoffecker, "Migration and Innovation in Paleolithic Europe," in *The Cambridge World History, Volume 1: Introducing World History (to 10,000 BCE)*, ed. David Christian (Cambridge: Cambridge University Press, 2017), 400.

19 **Something like seventy thousand years ago**: 100,000–35,000 years ago seems to be the most accurate range. Simon Neubauer, Jean-Jacques Hublin, and Philipp Gunz, "The Evolution of Modern Human Brain Shape," *Science Advances* 4, no. 1 (January 24, 2018). Historian Yuval Noah Harari pegged this at seventy thousand years, relying on evidence beyond brain size in Harari, *Sapiens: A Brief History of Humankind* (New York: Harper, 2015).

19 **These regions contribute to**: Neubauer et al., "The Evolution of Modern Human Brain Shape."

20 **create friction and then fire**: John F. Hoffecker and Ian T. Hoffecker, "Technological Complexity and the Global Dispersal of Modern Humans," *Evolutionary Anthropology* 26, no. 6 (2017): 285–99. Neanderthals were known primarily to transfer fire, rather than create it de novo. A.C. Sorensen, E. Claud, and M.A. Soressi, "Neandertal Fire-Making Technology Inferred from Microwear Analysis," *Scientific Reports* 8, no. 1 (July 2018): 10065; and Neubauer et al., "The Evolution of Modern Human Brain Shape."

20 **Complex syntactic language**: We did also need new hardware beyond the neural to allow for this language. As of about fifty thousand years ago, *Homo sapiens* developed a pharynx that sits at a right angle compared to the mouth, where other hominids did not. The vocalizations this enables come at the cost of the risk of choking to death. Chris Ehret, "Early Humans: Tools, Language, and Culture," in *The Cambridge World History, Volume 1: Introducing World History (to 10,000 BCE)*, ed. David Christian (Cambridge: Cambridge University Press, 2017), 344.

20 **for the exchange of abstractions**: Harari, *Sapiens*, 59.

20 **transcend the here and now**: John F. Hoffecker and Ian T. Hoffecker, "The Structural and Functional Complexity of Hunter-Gatherer Technology," *Journal of Archaeological Method and Theory* 25, no. 1 (March 2018).

21 **three to five hours**: Marshall Sahlins, "Hunter-Gatherers: Insights from a Golden Affluent Age," *Pacific Ecologist* (Winter 2009), https://pacificecologist.org/archive/18/pe18-hunter-gatherers.pdf.

22 **pottery to cooling units**: John T. Hoffecker, "Migration and Innovation in Paleolithic Europe," in *The Cambridge World History, Volume 1: Introducing World History (to 10,000 BCE)*, ed. David Christian (Cambridge: Cambridge University Press, 2017), 406–10.

22 **archaeologists struggle to explain**: Samuel Bowles and Jung-Kyoo Choi, "Coevolution of Farming and Private Property During the Early Holocene,"

Proceedings of the National Academy of Sciences of the United States of America, 110, no. 22 (July 2012): 8830–35.

23 **those that could be domesticated**: See Matthew Ridley's *How Innovation Works and Why It Flourishes in Freedom* (New York: Harper, 2021) for his discussion of agriculture, but also for his documentation of innovation, not from single genius but from multiple contributors.

23 **way of working**: Alan H. Simmons, "Early Agriculture in Southwest Asia," in *The Cambridge World History, Volume 2: A World with Agriculture 12,000 BCE to 500 CE*, ed. Graeme Barker and Candice Goucher (Cambridge: Cambridge University Press, 2017), 217.

23 **ways nature could foil them**: Tom Dillehay, "Nanchoc Valley, Peru," in *The Cambridge World History, Volume 2: A World with Agriculture 12,000 BCE to 500 CE*, ed. Graeme Barker and Candice Goucher (Cambridge: Cambridge University Press, 2017), 552.

24 **extremely powerful parietal and frontal lobes**: Simon Neubauer, Jean-Jacques Hublin, and Philipp Gunz, "The Evolution of Modern Human Brain Shape," *Science Advances* 4, no. 1 (January 24, 2018).

24 **our prospective thinking is devoted to planning**: Roy F. Baumeister, Wilhelm Hofmann, Amy Summerville, Philip T. Reiss, Kathleen D. Vohs, "Everyday Thoughts in Time: Experience Sampling Studies of Mental Time Travel," *Personality and Social Psychology Bulletin* 46, no. 12 (March 25, 2020): 1631–48.

24 **disease spread readily**: Katherine J. Latham, "Human Health and the Neolithic Revolution: An Overview of Impacts of the Agricultural Transition on Oral Health, Epidemiology, and the Human Body," *Nebraska Anthropologist* (2013): 187.

24 **Prolonged worry over distant and nebulous events**: Dan W. Grupe and Jack B. Nitschke, "Uncertainty and Anticipation in Anxiety: An Integrated Neurobiological and Psychological Perspective," *Nature Reviews Neuroscience* 14, no. 7 (June 2013): 488–501; see also Alison A. Macintosh, Ron Pinhasi, and Jay T. Stock, "Early Life Conditions and Physiological Stress Following the Transition to Farming in Central/Southeast Europe: Skeletal Growth Impairment and 6,000 Years of Gradual Recovery," *PLOS ONE* 11, no. 2 (February 2016): e0148468; and Spencer Wells, *Pandora's Seed: The Unforeseen Cost of Civilization* (New York: Random House, 2010).

26 **lifetime of kneeling at the grinding stone**: Xinyi Lui, Zhijun Zhao, and Guoxiang Liu, "Xinglonggou, China," in *The Cambridge World History, Volume 2: A World with Agriculture 12,000 BCE to 500 CE*, ed. Graeme Barker and Candice Goucher (Cambridge: Cambridge University Press, 2017), 342. Specialization occasionally took more exotic forms. Farming communities traded for rare crafts like mirrors or exotic jadeite axes, which would have been produced by craftspeople who may well have enjoyed their work. See Amy Bogaard, "Communities," in *The Cambridge World History, Volume 2: A*

World with Agriculture 12,000 BCE to 500 CE, ed. Graeme Barker and Candice Goucher (Cambridge: Cambridge University Press, 2017), 153.

26 **forced labor, including some ten million children**: Kate Hodal, "One in 200 People Is a Slave. Why?" *The Guardian,* February 25, 2019, https://www .theguardian.com/news/2019/feb/25/modern-slavery-trafficking-persons-one -in-200.

26 **By 100 CE, just one to two million foragers remained, compared with 250 million farmers**: Harari, *Sapiens*, 142.

27 **eighty-nine witnesses**: Marjorie Bloy, "Michael Thomas Sadler (1780– 1835)," A Web of English History, http://www.historyhome.co.uk/people /sadlerbg.htm.

27 **Here is Crabtree being interviewed by Sadler**: This represents excerpts of Matthew Crabtree's testimony. "The Sadler Report on Child Labor," https:// www.academia.edu/35166832/The_Sadler_Report_Report_on_Child_Labor.

29 **made them worse**: Paul Josephson, "The History of World Technology, 1750–Present," in *The Cambridge World History, Volume 7: Production, Destruction, and Connection, 1750–Present: Structure, Spaces, and Boundary Making*, ed. J. R. McNeill and Kenneth Pomeranz (Cambridge: Cambridge University Press, 2015), 136–63.

30 **fill spots on the assembly line**: James Manyika, Susan Lund, Michael Chui, Jacques Bughin, Jonathan Woetzel, Parul Batra, Ryan Ko, and Saurabh Sanghvi, "Jobs Lost, Jobs Gained: What the Future of Work Will Mean for Jobs, Skills, and Wages," McKinsey Global Institute, November 28, 2017, https://www.mckinsey.com/featured-insights/future-of-work/jobs-lost-jobs -gained-what-the-future-of-work-will-mean-for-jobs-skills-and-wages.

30 **Friendly societies have been called**: Bernard Semmel, "*The Friendly Societies in England, 1815–1875.* By P. H. J. H. Gosden (Manchester: Manchester University Press, 1961). Published in the United States (New York: Barnes and Noble, 1961), pp. 262. $6.50," in *Journal of Economic History* 22, no. 2 (1962): 271–72.

30 **ensure fair wages for all**: "Fenwick Weavers' Society Foundation Charter, 1761," National Library of Scotland, https://www.nls.uk/learning-zone /politics-and-society/labour-history/fenwick-weavers.

31 **160 million children globally**: "Child Labour: Global Estimates 2020, Trends and the Road Forward," International Labour Organization, UNICEF, 2020, https://www.ilo.org/global/topics/child-labour/lang–en/index.htm.

31 **over the ensuing decades**: Edward Shorter, *A History of Psychiatry* (Hoboken, NJ: Wiley, 1998), 129–30.

31 **at Queen Square Hospital in London**: Ruth E. Taylor, "Death of Neurasthenia and Its Psychological Reincarnation: A Study of Neurasthenia at the National Hospital for the Relief and Cure of the Paralysed and Epileptic, Queen Square, London, 1870–1932," *British Journal of Psychiatry* 179, no. 6 (December 2001): figure 1. Neurasthenia was even more common among wealthier individuals. Recently Jonathan Malesic has suggested that burnout

is the closest modern equivalent to neurasthenia. Jonathan Malesic, *The End of Burnout* (Berkeley, CA: University of California Press, 2022).

31 **alarmingly high prevalence of neurasthenia**: Sidney I. Schwab, "Neurasthenia among Garment Workers," *American Economic Review* 1, no. 2 (April 1911): 265–70.

32 **The modern inhabitants of former heavily industrialized areas show**: Martin Obschonka, Michael Stuetzer, Peter J. Rentfrow, Leigh Shaw-Taylor, Max Satchell, Rainer K. Silbereisen, Jeff Potter, and Samuel D. Gosling, "In the Shadow of Coal: How Large-Scale Industries Contributed to Present-Day Regional Differences in Personality and Well-Being," *Journal of Personality and Social Psychology* 115, no. 5 (November 2018): 903–27.

32 **Obschonka and team then successfully replicated**: Martin Obschonka et al., "In the Shadow of Coal."

32 **particularly for the urban working class**: The need to restrict alcohol consumption was not new and was first documented in Hammurabi's Code itself. See David J. Hanson, "Historical Evolution of Alcohol Consumption in Society," *Alcohol: Science, Policy and Public Health*, May 2013. See also Peter Anderson and Ben Baumberg, *Alcohol in Europe: A Public Health Perspective*, A Report for the European Commission, June 2006, https://ec.europa.eu/health /archive/ph_determinants/life_style/alcohol/documents/alcohol_europe_en.pdf.

33 **"may readily be imagined"**: Friedrich Engels, "Work Is the Curse of the Drinking Classes," in *The Conditions of the Working Class in England*, https:// www.laphamsquarterly.org/intoxication/work-curse-drinking-classes.

33 **to all employees fighting addiction**: William White and David Sharar, "The Evolution of Employee Assistance: A Brief History and Trend Analysis," *EAP Digest* 3, no. 4 (2003): 16–24.

33 **this peculiar confluence of motives**: Niels Ju Nielsen, "Industrial Paternalism in the 19th Century. Old or New?" *Ethnologia Europaea* 30, no. 1 (January 2000): 59–74.

CHAPTER TWO: THE TWIN TRIALS

35 **General Motors Detroit-Hamtramck Assembly plant**: Jamie L. LaReau, "Here's Where GM Layoffs Stand After Stunning Blow to Factory Workers," *Detroit Free Press*, May 6, 2019; Jamie L. LaReau, "General Motors to Close Detroit, Ohio, Canada Plants," *Detroit Free Press*, November 26, 2018.

35 **flipping them for a small profit**: Jamie L. LaReau, "Massive Garage in Livonia Saving People Thousands on Car Repairs," *Detroit Free Press*, April 20, 2019.

35 **the promised rewards**: John Gallagher, "GM's Hamtramck Plant Closing Reopens Old Controversy in Detroit," *Detroit Free Press*, November 26, 2018.

36 **electrical engineer by training**: "Mary T. Barra," General Motors, https:// www.gm.com/company/leadership.detail.html/Pages/news/bios/gm/Mary -Barra.

36 **Her 2013 appointment to CEO**: Sara Murray, "GM's Promotion of Barra to CEO a Breakthrough for Women," *Wall Street Journal*, December 10, 2013.

36 **"We need to make sure we have the right skill set"**: LaReau, "General Motors to Close."

36 **"As William Faulkner once said"**: Gallagher, "GM's Hamtramck Plant Closing Reopens Old Controversy in Detroit."

37 **"from ground zero"**: LaReau, "Here's Where GM Layoffs Stand After Stunning Blow to Factory Workers."

37 **"so they won't panic"**: John Seely Brown, "The Future of Work: Navigating the Whitewater," *Pacific Standard*, https://psmag.com/economics/the-future -of-work-navigating-the-whitewater.

38 **cognitive skills**: David Epstein's *Range* offers a particularly masterful look at how essential generalist thinking is to innovation and success. David Epstein, *Range* (New York: Riverhead Books, 2019).

39 **nearly 20–25% of the US labor force will be displaced**: Karen Harris, Austin Kimson, and Andrew Schwedel, "Labor 2030: The Collision of Demographics, Automation, and Inequality," Bain and Company, February 2018, https://www.bain.com/insights/labor-2030-the-collision-of-demographics -automation-and-inequality/.

39 **The World Economic Forum estimates**: "The Future of Jobs Report 2020," World Economic Forum, October 2020, https://www3.weforum.org/docs/WEF _Future_of_Jobs_2020.pdf.

39 **According to the McKinsey Global Institute's models**: Manyika et al., "Jobs Lost, Jobs Gained: What the Future of Work Will Mean for Jobs, Skills, and Wages," McKinsey Global Institute, November 28, 2017.

39 **Inventor Ray Kurzweil**: Ray Kurzweil, "The Law of Accelerating Returns," https://www.kurzweilai.net/the-law-of-accelerating-returns; and Ray Kurzweil, *The Singularity Is Near: When Humans Transcend Biology* (New York: Viking, 2005).

39 **"Rather we will witness"**: Kurzweil, "The Law of Accelerating Returns." See also Kurzweil, *The Singularity Is Near.*

40 **more like every ten years**: Yuval Noah Harari, on the panel "Putting Jobs Out of Work," World Economic Forum Annual Meeting 2018, https://www .youtube.com/watch?v=bU78taHasS0.

40 **By 2040, more than half of the new cars on the market will be electric**: Peter Valdes Dapena, "By 2040, More Than Half of New Cars Will Be Electric," CNN, May 15, 2019, https://www.cnn.com/2019/05/15/business /electric-car-outlook-bloomberg.

40 **Soft skills have recently been rebranded**: Manyika et al., "Jobs Lost, Jobs Gained: What the Future of Work Will Mean for Jobs, Skills, and Wages."

41 **triggered by the end of the Cold War**: "Who First Originated the Term VUCA (Volatility, Uncertainty, Complexity and Ambiguity)?" U.S. Army Heritage and Education Center, https://usawc.libanswers.com/faq/84869.

42 **in our world of work**: See "vuca" in Google Trends, https://trends.google
.com/trends/explore?date=all&q=vuca.

42 **About a decade ahead of VUCA**: Horst W. J. Rittel and Melvin M. Webber,
"Dilemmas in a General Theory of Planning," *Policy Sciences* 4, no. 2 (June
1973): 155–69.

42 **all examples of wicked problems**: Jon Kolko, *Wicked Problems: Problems
Worth Solving* excerpted in *Stanford Social Innovation Review*, March 6, 2012.

42 **"face constant change or unprecedented problems"**: John C. Camillus,
"Strategy as a Wicked Problem," *Harvard Business Review*, May 2008, https://
hbr.org/2008/05/strategy-as-a-wicked-problem.

43 **offering nine thousand jobs**: Jamie L. LaReau, "GM-UAW Deal Calls for
9,000 Jobs, $9,000 Ratification Bonus, e-Truck at Detroit-Hamtramck,"
Detroit Free Press, October 16, 2019.

43 **number had dropped to 2,200**: Robin Murdoch, "General Motors
Announces $2.2B Investment in Hamtramck Plant," Fox 2 Detroit News,
January 27, 2020, https://www.fox2detroit.com/news/general-motors
-announces-2-2b-investment-in-hamtramck-plant; Andrew J. Hawkins,
"GM Rebrands Its Detroit-Hamtramck Plant as 'Factory Zero' for Electric and
Autonomous Vehicles," *The Verge*, October 16, 2020, https://www.theverge
.com/2020/10/16/21519358/gm-factory-zero-detroit-hamtramck-electric
-autonomous-vehicles.

43 **what any of this will mean for them**: Kalea Hall, "GM's Detroit-
Hamtramck Assembly Poised to Begin Electric Transformation," *Detroit News*,
February 19, 2020.

43 **wasted no time in applying elsewhere**: LaReau, "Here's Where GM Layoffs
Stand."

44 **Volatility describes**: Google's English Dictionary, powered by Oxford Languages,
accessed February 28, 2022.

44 **Employment instability, for example**: Pfeffer, *Dying for a Paycheck.*

44 **our physical and emotional health tank**: Daniel Sullivan and Till von
Wachter, "Job Displacement and Mortality: An Analysis Using Administrative
Data," *The Quarterly Journal of Economics* 124, no. 3 (August 2009): 1265–
1306; S.V. Kasl and S. Cobb, "Blood Pressure Changes in Men Undergoing
Job Loss: A Preliminary Report," *Psychosomatic Medicine* 32, no. 1 (January
1970): 19–38; Robert Wood Johnson Foundation, "How Does Employment—
or Unemployment—Affect Health?" Health Policy Snapshot series, March 12,
2013; Wolfram Kawohl and Carlos Nordt, "COVID-19, Unemployment, and
Suicide," *The Lancet Psychiatry* 7, no. 5 (May 2020): 389–90; Karsten I. Paul
and Klaus Moser, "Unemployment Impairs Mental Health: Meta-Analyses,"
Journal of Vocational Behavior 74, no. 3 (June 2009): 264–82; Allison Milner,
A. Page, and Anthony D. LaMontagne, "Cause and Effect in Studies on
Unemployment, Mental Health and Suicide: A Meta-Analytic and Conceptual
Review," *Psychological Medicine* 44, no. 5 (July 2013): 1–9.

45 **Remote work**: Sandi Mann and Lynn Holdsworth, "The Psychological Impact of Teleworking: Stress, Emotions and Health," *New Technology, Work and Employment* 18, no. 3 (October 2003): 196–211.

45 **cigarettes per day**: Vivek Murthy, "Work and the Loneliness Epidemic," *Harvard Business Review*, September 26, 2017, https://hbr.org/2017/09/work-and-the-loneliness-epidemic.

CHAPTER THREE: OUR HISTORICAL ADVANTAGE

47 **"darker, meaner half"**: Abraham H. Maslow, *Motivation and Personality* (New York: Harper & Row, 1954), 354.

48 **And so the Joint Chiefs of Staff appointed**: Gerald Ramaho, "Salute Our Troops: Ret. Army Colonel Survived 9/11, Serves Post-traumatic Stress Victims," *3 News*, May 17, 2019; "Jill W. Chambers," Syracuse University, https://ivmf.syracuse.edu/team-member/jill-w-chambers/; Skip Vaughn, "Chambers Helping Alleviate Post-traumatic Stress," *Redstone Arsenal: Federal Center of Excellence*, January 19, 2022, https://www.theredstonerocket.com/eedition/page_764c7bb4-6b31-58f4-8c1b-136c285cdc9d.html; "Jill Chambers," *Women of the Military* (podcast), June 27, 2022, https://women-of-the-military.simplecast.com/episodes/jill-chambers-YqeUcc3w.

48 **it still has no cure**: It's difficult to estimate the total historical spend on PTSD treatment and research. One 2014 report estimated that the US government spends $3 billion per year on treatment alone. IOM (Institute of Medicine), *Treatment for Posttraumatic Stress Disorder in Military and Veteran Populations: Final Assessment* (Washington, DC: The National Academies Press, June 2014).

49 **cope with setbacks**: Some have recently pointed out that the idea of post-traumatic growth may lead those experiencing trauma to feel pressured to view terrible events in a positive light. It's an important consideration, particularly for clinicians. David Robson, "The Complicated Truth of Post-traumatic Growth," *Worklife BBC*, March 13, 2022, https://www.bbc.com/worklife/article/20220311-the-complicated-truth-of-post-traumatic-growth.

50 **breathtaking consolidation of power**: It is noteworthy that the parallel evolution of these wisdom traditions coincided with the rise of tyranny and slavery. The essence of well-being comes into stark clarity when we suffer most.

51 **the pathologies of individual consciousness**: Although psychoanalysis is often described as a pseudoscience, some of its founders had more empirical aspirations. Among the many theories explaining why Freud and Jung, fathers of psychoanalysis, parted ways is the idea that Jung took a more empirical approach to their studies. P. E. Stepansky, "The Empiricist as Rebel: Jung, Freud, and the Burdens of Discipleship," *Journal of the History of the Behavioral Sciences* 12, no. 3 (July 1976): 216–39.

51 **behaviorism**: Harvey Carr and John B. Watson, "Orientation in the White Rat," *Journal of Comparative Neurology & Psychology* 18, no. 1 (January 1908): 27–44, https://doi.org/10.1002/cne.920180103; John Broadus Watson, "Kinaesthetic and Organic Sensations: Their Role in the Reactions of the White Rat to the Maze," *The Psychological Review: Monograph Supplements* 8, no. 2 (1907): i–101, https://doi.org/10.1037/h0093040.

51 **lithium for bipolar disorder**: Shorter, *A History of Psychiatry*, chapter 6.

52 **mental illness would one day be curable**: M. E. P. Seligman and M. Csikszentmihalyi, "Positive Psychology: An Introduction," *American Psychologist* 55, no. 1 (January 2000): 5–14.

52 **sedatives regularly**: Shorter, *A History of Psychiatry*, 319.

52 **use a psychiatric drug today**: Thomas J. Moore and Donald R. Mattison, "Adult Utilization of Psychiatric Drugs and Differences by Sex, Age, and Race," *JAMA Internal Medicine* 177, no. 2 (February 2017): 274–75; https://jamanetwork.com/journals/jamainternalmedicine/fullarticle/2592697; Sarah G. Miller, "1 in 6 Americans Takes a Psychiatric Drug," *Scientific American*, December 13, 2016, https://www.scientificamerican.com/article/1-in-6-americans-takes-a-psychiatric-drug/; David E. Bloom et al., *The Global Economic Burden of Noncommunicable Diseases* (Geneva: World Economic Forum, September 2011).

53 **Timothy Leary**: Harvard Department of Psychology, https://psychology.fas.harvard.edu/people/timothy-leary.

53 **the scientific method itself with suspicion**: Donald E. Polkinghorne, "Research Methodology in Humanistic Psychology," *The Humanistic Psychologist* 20, no. 2–3 (1992): 218–42.

53 **"planned product of a scientific society"**: Carl R. Rogers, "The Place of the Person in the New World of the Behavioral Sciences," *Personnel and Guidance Journal* 39, no. 6 (February 1961).

54 **research grants each year**: "FY 2019 Budget—Congressional Justification," National Institute of Mental Health, https://www.nimh.nih.gov/about/budget/fy-2019-budget-congressional-justification.shtml.

54 **prescription for a psychiatric drug in 2013**: Moore and Mattison, "Adult Utilization of Psychiatric Drugs and Differences by Sex, Age, and Race," 274–75; Bloom et al., *Global Economic Burden of Noncommunicable Diseases*.

54 **not a single truly novel psychiatric medication**: Steven E. Hyman, "Psychiatric Drug Development: Diagnosing a Crisis," *Cerebrum* 2013 (March–April 2013): 5.

54 **"do not exist for psychiatric disorders"**: Steven E. Hyman, "Revolution Stalled," *Science Translational Medicine* 4, no. 155 (October 10, 2012): 155cm11.

55 **Tom Insel, who was head of the NIMH**: Thomas Insel, "Transforming Diagnosis," NIMH Director's Blog Post, National Institute of Mental Health, April 29, 2013, http://psychrights.org/2013/130429NIMHTransforming

Diagnosis.htm. More recently Insel published his own, fuller account of his learnings in Thomas Insel, *Healing: Our Path From Mental Illness to Mental Health* (New York: Penguin, 2022).

57 **As Csikszentmihalyi wrote in 2000**: Seligman and Csikszentmihalyi, "Positive Psychology: An Introduction," 5–14.

59 **analyzed 347 different studies**: Alan Carr, Katie Cullen, Cora Keeney, Ciaran Canning, Olwyn Mooney, Ellen Chinseallaigh, and Annie O'Dowd, "Effectiveness of Positive Psychology Interventions: A Systematic Review and Meta-Analysis, *Journal of Positive Psychology* 16, no. 6 (2021): 749–69.

60 **performance at work**: Martin E. P. Seligman, Andrew R. Allen, Loryana L. Vie, Tiffany E. Ho, Lawrence M. Scheier, Rhonda Cornum, and Paul B. Lester, "PTSD: Catastrophizing in Combat as Risk and Protection," *Clinical Psychological Science* 7, no. 3 (January 28, 2019): 516–29, https://doi .org/10.1177/2167702618813532; Peter D. Harms, Mitchel N. Herian, Dina V. Krasikova, Adam J. Vanhove, and Paul B. Lester, "The Comprehensive Soldier and Family Fitness Evaluation. Report #4: Evaluation of Resilience Training and Mental and Behavioral Health Outcomes," University of Nebraska, Lincoln, 2013, http://digitalcommons.unl.edu/pdharms/10; Paul B. Lester, Peter D. Harms, Mitchel N. Herian, Dina V. Krasikova, and Sarah J. Beal, "The Comprehensive Soldier Fitness Program Evaluation. Report #3: Longitudinal Analysis of the Impact of Master Resilience Training on Self-Reported Resilience and Physical Health," University of Nebraska, Lincoln, 2011; Paul B. Lester, Emily P. Stewart, Loryana L. Vie, Douglas G. Bonett, Martin E. P. Seligman, and Ed Diener, "Happy Soldiers Are the Highest Performers," *Journal of Happiness Studies* 23, no. 2 (August 25, 2021).

60 **manifesto in the *New York Times***: Milton Friedman, "A Friedman Doctrine—The Social Responsibility of Business Is to Increase Its Profits," *New York Times*, September 13, 1970, https://www.nytimes.com/1970/09/13 /archives/a-friedman-doctrine-the-social-responsibility-of-business-is-to.html.

60 **when the inevitable occurs**: "Greed Is Good. Except When It's Bad," *New York Times DealBook,* September 13, 2020.

CHAPTER FOUR: THE BUILDING BLOCKS OF RESILIENCE

61 **As Major General Bob Scales**: Major General Robert H. Scales, "Clausewitz and World War IV," *Armed Forces Journal*, July 1, 2006.

62 **"Imagine how the psychological, behavioral, and emotional strength"**: Scales, "Clausewitz and World War IV."

62 **320% more year-over-year growth**: Alexis Jeannotte, Erin Eatough, and Gabriella Kellerman, "Resilience in an Age of Uncertainty," BetterUp 2020, https://grow.betterup.com/resources/resilience-in-an-age-of-uncertainty.

62 **resilience can refer to**: For a review of the literature and analysis of resilience constructs, see the appendix of Luca Giustiniano, Stewart R. Clegg, Miguel

Pina e Cunha, and Arménio Rego, ed.; *Elgar Introduction to Theories of Organizational Resilience* (Cheltenham, UK: Edward Elgar Publishing, 2018).

63 **coined by essayist Nassim Nicholas Taleb**: Nassim Nicholas Taleb, *Antifragile* (New York: Random House, 2012).

65 **hijacked by an emotional flood**: Daniel Goleman, *Emotional Intelligence* (New York: Bantam, 1996).

66 **Within just three months of coaching**: This and other similar statistics in this book come from BetterUp data comparing pre- and post-coaching scores on BetterUp's Whole Person Model (WPM) assessment. For more on the WPM, see the appendix on 227. Thank you to Derek Hutchinson and Sebastian Marin for their help with the appendix.

69 **even in the face of *inescapable* bad events**: Seligman, *Flourish*, 129.

70 **Thinking optimistically is good for both mind and body** : Seligman, *Flourish*, chapter 9.

70 **Since the sample population worked**: Paul B. Lester, Ed Diener, and Martin Seligman, "Top Performers Have a Superpower: Happiness," *MIT Sloan Management Review*, February 16, 2022.

71 **More than thirty studies**: Paula M. Loveday, Geoff P. Lovell, and Christian M. Jones, "The Best Possible Selves Intervention: A Review of the Literature to Evaluate Efficacy and Guide Future Research," *Journal of Happiness Studies* 19 (February 2018): 607–28.

72 **a booking agent for local bands**: LaReau, "Here's Where GM Layoffs Stand After Stunning Blow to Factory Workers"; LaReau, "General Motors to Close Detroit, Ohio, Canada Plants."

73 **in just three months of coaching**: This and other similar statistics in this book come from BetterUp data comparing pre- and post-coaching scores on BetterUp's Whole Person Model (WPM) assessment. For more on the WPM, see the appendix on 227.

73 **Catastrophizers are low on optimism**: Seligman et al., "PTSD: Catastrophizing in Combat as Risk and Protection," 516–29.

75 **perceived inadequacy**: Kristin D. Neff, "The Development and Validation of a Scale to Measure Self-Compassion," *Self and Identity* 2, no. 3 (2003): 223–50.

76 **experienced throughout history**: Optimism, self-compassion, and self-efficacy also hang together. As one example, Neff and colleagues demonstrated that a three-week self-compassion training boosts not only self-compassion but also optimism and self-efficacy. Elke Smeets, Kristin Neff, Hugo Alberts, and Madelon Peters, "Meeting Suffering with Kindness: Effects of a Brief Self-Compassion Intervention for Female College Students," *Journal of Clinical Psychology* 70, no. 9 (September 2014): 794–807.

76 **struggling with PTSD**: Teresa M. Au, Shannon Sauer-Zavala, Matthew W. King, Nicola Petrocchi, David H. Barlow, and Brett T. Litz, "Compassion-Based Therapy for Trauma-Related Shame and Posttraumatic Stress: Initial Evaluation Using a Multiple Baseline Design," *Behavior Therapy* 48, no. 2

(March 2017): 207–21; Elaine Beaumont, Mark Durkin, Sue McAndrew, and Colin R. Martin, "Using Compassion Focused Therapy as an Adjunct to Trauma-Focused CBT for Fire Service Personnel Suffering with Trauma-Related Symptoms," *The Cognitive Behaviour Therapist* 9 (January 2016): 34.

77 **greater challenges over time**: Albert Bandura, "An Agentic Perspective on Positive Psychology," in Shane J. Lopez, ed., *Positive Psychology: Exploring the Best in People, Volume 1, Discovering Human Strengths* (Westport, CT: Praeger, 2008), 167–96.

77 **the following story**: Shaya is a composite of several individuals.

79 **results come quick**: Alexis M. Jeannotte, Derek M. Hutchinson, Gabriella Rosen Kellerman, "The Time to Change for Mental Health and Well-Being via Virtual Professional Coaching: Longitudinal Observational Study," *Journal of Medical Internet Research* 23, no. 7 (May 2021): e27774.

80 **higher year-over-year growth**: Jeannotte et al., "Resilience in an Age of Uncertainty."

80 **more cognitively agile**: Jeannotte et al., "Resilience in an Age of Uncertainty."

80 **their leadership competencies**: Jeannotte et al., "Resilience in an Age of Uncertainty."

CHAPTER FIVE: THE MEANING RUSH

83 **"almost any how"**: Friedrich Nietzsche, "Epigrams and Arrows" in *Twilight of the Idols* (Indianapolis: Hackett, 1997), 6.

84 **"close to being meaningless"**: Abraham Maslow, *Maslow on Management* (Hoboken, NJ: Wiley, 1998), 58.

84 **fundamental to education, work, and counseling**: Neil Postman and Charles Weingartner, "Meaning Making" *in Teaching as a Subversive Activity* (New York: Delacorte Press, 1969), 82–97.

85 **"define their corporate missions"**: Reid Hoffman, foreword to Fred Kofman, *The Meaning Revolution* (Sydney, Australia: Currency, 2018), xv.

85 **"Refresh the world. Make a difference"**: "Purpose," Coca-Cola, accessed March 15, 2022, www.coca-colacompany.com/company/purpose-and-vision.

85 **Young advised**: Will Richards, "Neil Young Encourages Spotify Employees to Quit over Joe Rogan Scandal," *Rolling Stone UK*, February 8, 2022, https://www.rollingstone.co.uk/music/news/neil-young-encourages-spotify-employees-to-quit-over-joe-rogan-scandal-10954/.

86 **Psychologist Michael Steger**: Frank Martela and Michael F. Steger, "The Three Meanings of Meaning in Life: Distinguishing Coherence, Purpose, and Significance," *Journal of Positive Psychology* 11, no. 5 (2016): 531–45.

86 **depending on their orientation**: Amy Wrzesniewski, Clark McCauley, Paul Rozin, Barry Schwartz, "Jobs, Careers, and Callings: People's Relations to Their Work," *Journal of Research in Personality* 31, no. 1 (March 1997): 21–33.

87 **industries, tenures, and incomes**: Andrew Reece, Gabriella Kellerman, and Alexi Robichaux, "Meaning and Purpose at Work," BetterUp 2018, https://www.betterup.com/en-us/resources/reports/meaning-and-purpose-report.

88 **on their mortgage**: "Mortgage Burden Exceeds Historic Levels in 10 of the Largest US Markets," Zillow Press Release, September 6, 2018, http://zillow.mediaroom.com/2018-09-06-Mortgage-Burden-Exceeds-Historic-Levels-in-10-of-the-Largest-U-S-Markets.

88 **"the level of effort people could give"**: Aubrey Daniels, "Discretionary Effort," Aubrey Daniels International, https://www.aubreydaniels.com/discretionary-effort.

89 **positive impact on our overall well-being**: Scott Barry Kaufman, *Transcend* (New York: TarcherPerigee, 2020), 160.

89 **known as self-determination theory**: R. M. Ryan and E. L. Deci, "Self-Determination Theory and the Facilitation of Intrinsic Motivation, Social Development, and Well-Being," *The American Psychologist* 55, no. 1 (2000): 68–78, https://pubmed.ncbi.nlm.nih.gov/11392867/.

90 **find more purposeful work**: David Graeber, *Bullshit Jobs* (New York: Simon & Schuster, 2018). See also N.B., "Bullshit Jobs and the Yoke of Managerial Feudalism," *The Economist*, June 29, 2018, https://www.economist.com/open-future/2018/06/29/bullshit-jobs-and-the-yoke-of-managerial-feudalism.

91 **their work is knowledge work**: Ethan S. Bernstein, "The Transparency Paradox: A Role for Privacy in Organizational Learning and Operational Control," *Administrative Science Quarterly* 57, no. 2 (June 2012): 181–216.

92 **drivers of workplace meaning**: Marjolein Lips-Wiersma and Sarah Wright, "Measuring the Meaning of Meaningful Work: Development and Validation of the Comprehensive Meaningful Work Scale (CMWS)," *Group & Organization Management* 37, no. 5 (2012): 655–85.

94 **purpose and satisfaction**: Anton Sytine, "The Role of Savoring Positive Experiences When Faced with Challenge and Hindrance Demands: A Longitudinal Study," Clemson University, dissertation presented May 2019, https://tigerprints.clemson.edu/cgi/viewcontent.cgi?article=3383&context=all_dissertations.

95 **"its persistence and its flourishing, *matters*"**: Rebecca Goldstein, "The Mattering Instinct," *Edge*, March 16, 2016, https://www.edge.org/conversation/rebecca_newberger_goldstein-the-mattering-instinct.

96 **Without it, we falter**: For an excellent review of the literature on purpose and well-being, as well as an insightful look at how Maslow foretold many of these findings, see the "Purpose" chapter in Kaufman's *Transcend*.

97 **Marty and colleagues in PERMA**: "PERMA Theory of Well-Being and PERMA Workshops," Positive Psychology Center at the University of Pennsylvania, https://ppc.sas.upenn.edu/learn-more/perma-theory-well-being-and-perma-workshops.

97 **"psychological loss of one's purpose"**: Kai-Fu Lee, *AI Superpowers* (Harper Business, 2018), 21.

97 **"a crisis of meaning, not employment"**: Yuval Noah Harari, spoken during "Putting Jobs Out of Work," World Economic Forum Annual Meeting 2018, https://www.youtube.com/watch?v=bU78taHasS0.

97 **a few years or less**: "Economic News Release," Bureau of Labor and Statistics, accessed February 28, 2022, https://www.bls.gov/news.release/tenure.t01.htm.

97 **Psychometric scales are necessary to measure**: Validating a new scale requires a significant amount of theoretical and quantitative work. Our aspirations for this instrument were (a) that it measure what we want it to measure, and (b) that it correlates with key outcomes of interest such as job satisfaction and intent to stay with an organization.

98 **You can use it to evaluate your own sense**: The scale is available for personal growth and research purposes, not for commercial use. Andrew Reece, David Yaden, Gabriella Kellerman, Alexi Robichaux, Rebecca Goldstein, Barry Schwartz, Martin Seligman, and Roy Baumeister, "Mattering Is an Indicator of Organizational Health and Employee Success," *Journal of Positive Psychology* 16, no. 2 (2021): 228–48.

101 **"meaningful and purposeful"**: Victor E. Frankl, *Man's Search for Meaning* (Boston: Beacon Press, 1992), 33.

CHAPTER SIX: RAPID RAPPORT

104 **offered more substantial forms of help**: John M. Darley and C. Daniel Batson, "From Jerusalem to Jericho: A Study of Situational and Dispositional Variables in Helping Behavior," *Journal of Personality and Social Psychology* 27, no. 1 (1973): 100–08.

105 **never enough time to get it done**: Cassie Mogilner, Zoë Chance, and Michael I. Norton, "Giving Time Gives You Time," *Psychological Science* 23, no. 10 (October 1, 2012): 1233–38.

105 **eat lunch at their desks**: "Just One in Five Employees Take Actual Lunch Break," Talent Solutions Right Management, October 16, 2012. This has no doubt changed due to the pandemic, but we have not located data updating these numbers.

105 **show their patients compassion**: Helen Reiss, John M. Kelley, Robert W. Bailey, Emily J. Dunn, and Margot Phillips, "Empathy Training for Resident Physicians," *Journal of General Internal Medicine* 27, no. 10 (October 2012): 1280–86.

105 **Or multitasking**: David E. Meyer, Jeffrey E. Evans, Erick Lauber, and Joshua Rubinstein, "Activation of Brain Mechanisms for Executive Mental Processes in Cognitive Task Switching," *Journal of Cognitive Neuroscience* 9 (1997).

105 **texting or talking on the phone**: National Highway Traffic Safety Administration, "Traffic Safety Facts Research Notes 2016: Distracted Driving," (Department of Transportation, Washington, DC: NHTSA, 2015).

106 **Nick Humphrey was first to hypothesize**: N. K. Humphrey, "The Social Function of Intellect" in *Growing Points in Ethology*, eds. P. P. G. Bateson and R. A. Hinde (Cambridge, UK: Cambridge University Press, 1976), 303–17.

106 **our amygdala, and more**: Robert M. Sapolsky, *Behave* (New York: Penguin, 2017), 51, 243.

106 **30% of Americans worked remotely**: "State of Remote Work 2019," Owl Labs, https://resources.owllabs.com/state-of-remote-work/2019.

106 **some days per week**: Erik Brynjolfsson, John Horton, Christos A. Makridis, Alex Mas, Adam Ozimek, Daniel Rock, and Hong-Yi TuYe, "How Many Americans Work Remotely," Stanford Digital Economy Lab, March 22, 2022, digitaleconomy.stanford.edu/publications/how-many-americans-work -remotely/.

106 **four years before starting over**: "Employee Tenure in 2020," Bureau of Labor Statistics, September 22, 2020, https://www.bls.gov/news.release/pdf /tenure.pdf.

108 **if we have meaningful social support**: Julianne Holt-Lunstad, Timothy B. Smith, and J. Bradley Layton, "Social Relationships and Mortality Risk: A Meta-Analytic Review," *PLOS Medicine* 7, no. 7 (July 27, 2010). This study and a number of others covered in this chapter are discussed in the wonderful book *Compassionomics*, by Stephen Trzeciak and Anthony Mazzarelli (Pensacola, FL: Struder Group, 2019), which reviews the literature on compassion in the practice of healthcare.

108 **risk of early death**: Julianne Holt-Lunstad, Timothy B. Smith, Mark Bake, Tyler Harris, and David Stephenson, "Loneliness and Social Isolation as Risk Factors for Mortality: A Meta-Analytic Review," *Perspectives on Psychological Science* 10, no. 2 (March 2015).

109 **without experiencing them ourselves**: Originally the definitions "sympathy" and "empathy" were switched, with empathy connoting the more distanced, intellectual experience of another's pain. Over time, empathy has come to mean what sympathy used to mean—deeply feeling another's pain as one's own. We adopt this more common usage to avoid confusion. See Susan Lanzoni, "A Short History of Empathy," *The Atlantic*, October 15, 2015.

109 **feeling of love**: Barbara L. Frederickson, *Love 2.0* (New York: Plume, 2013).

111 **and more sustained attention**: Sylvain Laborde, Emma Mosley, and Julian F. Thayer, "Heart Rate Variability and Cardiac Vagal Tone in Psychophysiological Research—Recommendations for Experiment Planning, Data Analysis, and Data Reporting," *Frontiers of Psychology* 8 (February 2017): 213.

111 **loved, loving, and safe**: Oxytocin has also been implicated in out-group dynamics, contributing to the Us-Them challenge outlined later in the chapter. See Robert Sapolsky, *Behave*.

111 **more severe discomfort**: Chapters 3 and 4 of Trzeciak and Mazzarelli's *Compassionomics* nicely summarize the full literature on the psychological and physiological benefits of compassion.

112 **compassion versus out of obligation**: Sapolsky, *Behave*, 523.

112 **our mind's eye**: With thanks to Shawn Achor for pointing us to this study. Simone Schnall, Kent D. Harber, Jeanine K. Stefanucci, and Dennis R. Proffitt, "Social Support and the Perception of Geographical Slant," *Journal of Experimental Social Psychology* 44, no. 5 (September 1, 2008).

113 **are more likely to quit**: Shawn Achor, Gabriella Rosen Kellerman, Andrew Reece, and Alexi Robichaux, "The Loneliest Workers, According to Research," *Harvard Business Review*, March 19, 2018.

113 **who don't have a best friend**: Tom Rath and Jim Harter, "Your Friends and Your Social Well-Being," *Gallup Business Journal*, August 2010; Barbara A. Winstead, Valerian J. Derlega, Melinda J. Montgomery, and Constance Pilkington, "The Quality of Friendships at Work and Job Satisfaction," *Journal of Social and Personal Relationships* 12, no. 2 (May 1, 1995).

113 **teams with weaker relationships**: See, for example, Brock Bastian, Jolanda Jetten, Hannibal A. Thai, and Niklas K. Steffens, "Shared Adversity Increases Team Creativity Through Fostering Supportive Interaction," *Frontiers in Psychology* (November 23, 2018), https://doi.org/10.3389/fpsyg.2018.02309.

113 **sophistication of Tasmanian tools deteriorates**: Jared Diamond, *Guns, Germs, and Steel: The Fate of Human Societies* (New York: W. W. Norton, 1997).

114 **We recruited two thousand American workers**: You may have noticed that our lab often uses sample sizes of about two thousand workers. This number has worked well for us because of the robust statistical power it generates. Some studies call for fewer participants, some more. You may have also noticed that we tend to focus on full-time employees rather than part-time workers. The vast majority of global workers today are full-time employees (OECD, "Part-time Employment Rate [Indicator]," 2022, https://doi.org/10.1787/f2ad596c-en). This is also the segment we have studied most extensively in our research.

115 **for their teams as for themselves**: Evan Carr, Andrew Reece, Gabriella Rosen Kellerman, Alexi Robichaux, "The Value of Belonging at Work," *Harvard Business Review*, December 16, 2019.

116 **"healing process"**: Kenneth B. Schwartz, "A Patient's Story," *Boston Globe Magazine*, July 16, 1995.

117 **major medical errors**: For a robust discussion of the patient health benefits of physician compassion, see Trzeciak and Mazzarelli's *Compassionomics*, chapter 6, "Compassion Is Vital for Health Care Quality."

117 **not because we don't care about outcomes**: Becky Bright, "Doctors' Interpersonal Skills Are Valued More Than Training," *Wall Street Journal*, September 28, 2004.

117 **"an extreme form of customer satisfaction"**: Donald C. Barnes and Alexandra Krallman, "Customer Delight: A Review and Agenda for Research," *Journal of Marketing Theory and Practice* 27, no. 2 (2019): 174–95.

118 **$1,750 per person per day**: See pricing at https://www.disneyinstitute.com /disneys-approach-quality-service/course-details/, accessed March 1, 2022.

118 **with a company's future earnings**: Often but not always. See for example Jan Eklof, Olga Podkorytova, and Aleksandra Malova, "Linking Customer Satisfaction with Financial Performance: An Empirical Study of Scandinavian Banks," *Total Quality Management & Business Excellence* 31 (2020): 15–16, 1684–1702; and Timothy Keiningham, Sunil Gupta, Lerzan Aksoy, and Alexander Buoye, "The High Price of Customer Satisfaction," *MIT Sloan Management Review* 55, no. 3 (Spring 2014).

118 **even substance abuse**: Da-Yee Jeung, Changsoo Kim, and Sei-Jin Chang, "Emotional Labor and Burnout: A Review of the Literature," *Yonsei Medical Journal* 59, no. 2 (March 2018): 187–93.

118 **even in the face of vitriol**: Gary Stix, "Emotional Labor Is a Store Clerk Confronting a Maskless Customer," *Scientific American*, https://www .scientificamerican.com/article/emotional-labor-is-a-store-clerk-confronting -a-maskless-customer/.

118 **increases risk for burnout**: Da-Yee Jeung et al., "Emotional Labor and Burnout," 187–93.

118 **service industry burnout is of national importance**: Rumki Majumdar and Daniel Bachman, "Changing the Lens: GDP from the Industry Viewpoint," Deloitte Insights, July 2019, https://www2.deloitte.com/us/en/insights /economy/spotlight/economics-insights-analysis-07-2019.

119 **they lack the time to treat**: Helen Reiss, "Empathy Training for Resident Physicians," 1280–86.

119 **during the pandemic itself**: "State of Remote Work 2019," https://resources .owllabs.com/state-of-remote-work/2019; Brodie Boland, Aaron De Smet, Rob Palter, and Aditya Sanghvi, "Reimagining the Office and Work Life after Covid-19," McKinsey and Company, June 8, 2020, https://www.mckinsey .com/business-functions/organization/our-insights/reimagining-the-office-and -work-life-after-Covid-19; Brynjolfsson et al., "How Many Americans Work Remotely," digitaleconomy.stanford.edu/publications/how-many-americans -work-remotely/.

120 **40% of development teams collocated**: Scott Wambler, "Software Development at Scale," Ambysoft, http://www.ambysoft.com/surveys/state OfITUnion2014Q2.html.

120 **high social media use substantially increased**: Liu Yi Lin, Jaime E. Sidani, Ariel Shensa, Ana Radovic, Elizabeth Miller, Jason B. Colditz, Beth L. Hoffman, Leila M. Giles, and Brian A. Primack, "Association between Social Media Use and Depression among U.S. Young Adults," *Depress Anxiety* 33, no. 4 (April 2016): 323–31, https://doi.org/10.1002/da.22466. Note that the jury is still out on the extent of this negative effect, however, with some studies finding more modest relationships. The work of Christopher Ferguson has been most influential in debunking some of the findings overstating the negative psychological impact of social media. See, for

example, Christopher J. Ferguson, "Does the Internet Make the World Worse? Depression, Aggression, and Polarization in the Social Media Age," *Bulletin of Science, Technology & Society* 41, no. 4 (December 2021): 116–35, https://doi .org/10.1177/02704676211064567.

120 **the less connected we feel:** Brian A. Primack, Ariel Shensa, Jaime E. Sidani, Erin O. Whaite, Liu Yi Lin, Daniel Rosen, Jason B. Colditz, Ana Radovic, and Elizabeth Miller, "Social Media Use and Perceived Social Isolation among Young Adults in the U.S.," *American Journal of Preventative Medicine* 53, no. 1 (July 1, 2017): 1–8.

120 **we can hope to achieve in conversation:** Andrew K. Przybylski and Netta Weinstein, "Can You Connect with Me Now? How the Presence of Mobile Communication Influences Face-to-Face Conversation Quality," *Journal of Social and Personal Relationships* 30, no. 3 (July 19, 2012).

120 **improves subjective well-being:** Hunt Allcott, Luca Braghieri, Sarah Eichmeyer, and Matthew Gentzkow, "The Welfare Effects of Social Media," *American Economic Review* 110, no. 3 (March 2020); Melissa G. Hunt, Rachel Marx, Courtney Lipson, and Jordyn Young, "No More FOMO: Limiting Social Media Decreases Loneliness and Depression," *Journal of Social and Clinical Psychology* 37, no. 10 (November 2018): 751–68.

121 **perspective of a close loved one:** Sapolsky, *Behave*, 133, 395, 533.

121 **"doing so for a Them takes work":** Sapolsky, *Behave*, 533.

CHAPTER SEVEN: RAPID RAPPORT II

124 **title of the article sums up:** Cassie Mogilner, Zoë Chance, and Michael I. Norton, "Giving Time Gives You Time," *Psychological Science* 23, no. 10 (October 1, 2012): 1233–38.

125 **did not say these things:** Linda A. Fogarty, Barbara A. Curbow, John R. Wingard, Karen McDonnell, and Mark R. Somerfield, "Can 40 seconds of Compassion Reduce Patient Anxiety?" *Journal of Clinical Oncology* 17, no. 1 (January 1999) as quoted in Trzeciak and Mazzarelli's *Compassionomics*, 250–53.

125 *less than one minute*: Trzeciak and Mazzarelli, *Compassionomics*, 250–64.

126 **for each additional statement:** Rachel Weiss, Eric Vittinghoff, Margaret C. Fang, Jenica E. W. Cimino, Kristen Adams Chasteen, Robert M. Arnold, Andrew D. Auerbach, and Wendy G. Anderson, "Associations of Physician Empathy with Patient Anxiety and Ratings of Communications in Hospital Admission Encounters," *Journal of Hospital Medicine* 12, no. 10 (October 2017): 805–10.

126 **three hours at work each day:** Joe Rampton, "Wasted Employee Time Adds Up: Here's How to Fix It," *Entrepreneur*, July 13, 2018.

130 **their medication regimen:** Tabor E. Flickinger, Somnath Saha, Debra Roter, P. Todd Korthius, Victoria Sharp, Jonathan Cohn, Susan Eggly, Richard D. Moore, and Mary Catherine Beach, "Clinician Empathy Is Associated with

Differences in Patient-Clinician Communication Behaviors and Higher Medication Self-Efficacy in HIV Care," *Patient Education and Counseling* 99, no. 2 (February 2016) as cited in Trzeciak and Mazzarelli's *Compassionomics*, 131.

130 **they felt less alone and more secure**: Andrew Reece, Evan Carr, Roy Baumeister, and Gabriella Rosen Kellerman, "Outcasts and Saboteurs: Intervention Strategies to Reduce the Negative Effects of Social Exclusion on Team Outcomes," *PLOS ONE* 16, no. 5 (May 2021): e0249851.

131 **individual-level traits**: Sapolsky, *Behave*, 420.

131 **"that of Mason/non-Mason"**: Sapolsky, *Behave*, 409.

131 **Sam Gaertner and John Dovidio**: Samuel L. Gaertner, John F. Dovidio, Phyllis A. Anastasio, Betty A. Bachman, and Mary C. Rust, "The Common Ingroup Identity Model," *European Review of Social Psychology*, 4 (1993): 1–26.

131 **in a merger, for example**: Samuel L. Gaertner and John F. Dovidio, "A Common Ingroup Identity: A Categorization-based Approach for Reducing Intergroup Bias," in Todd D. Nelson, ed., *Handbook of Prejudice, Stereotyping, and Discrimination* (London: Psychology Press, 2009), 489–505.

132 **negotiation strategies use recategorization**: Works generated by the Harvard Negotiation Project have been particularly influential in this approach, though they do not use the word *recategorization*. See, for example, *Beyond Reason: Using Emotions as You Negotiate*, by Roger Fisher and Daniel Shapiro (New York: Penguin, 2006).

134 **Communications experts distinguish**: Michael Purdy, "What Is Listening?" in *Listening in Everyday Life: A Personal and Professional Approach*, eds. Michael Purdy and Deborah Borisoff (Lanham, MD: University Press of America, 1997): 1–20.

135 **has better effects**: Katherine Unger Baillie, "Two Types of Empathy Elicit Different Health Effects, Penn Psychologist Shows," *Penn Today*, May 24, 2017, https://penntoday.upenn.edu/news/two-types-empathy-elicit-different -health-effects-penn-psychologist-shows.

CHAPTER EIGHT: PROSPECTION

139 **"we've ever done for the web"**: Caroline McCarthy, "Facebook F8: One Graph to Rule Them All," *CNET*, April 21, 2010, https://www.cnet.com /news/facebook-f8-one-graph-to-rule-them-all/.

139 **preserve access to the information indefinitely**: Christina Warren, "Facebook Open Graph: What It Means for Privacy," *Mashable*, April 21, 2010, https://mashable.com/2010/04/21/open-graph-privacy/.

140 **more, or fewer, international friends?**: Maurice H. Yearwood, Amy Cuddy, Nishtha Lamba, Wu Youyou, Ilmo van der Lowe, Paul K. Piff, Charles Gronin, Pete Fleming, Emiliana Simon-Thomas, Dacher Keltner, and Aleksandr Spectre, "On Wealth and Diversity of Friendships: High Social Class People around the World Have Fewer International Friends," *Personality*

and Individual Differences 87 (December 2015): 224–29. Kogan published this piece under a pseudonym, Aleksandr Spectre.

140 **just under three hundred thousand people**: Maurice H. Yearwood et al., "On Wealth and Diversity of Friendships: High Social Class People around the World Have Fewer International Friends," 224–29.

141 **even once its commercial potential became clear**: Issie Lapowsky, "The Man Who Saw the Dangers of Cambridge Analytica Years Ago," *Wired*, June 19, 2018, https://www.wired.com/story/the-man-who-saw-the-dangers -of-cambridge-analytica/.

141 **often unwittingly**: "Statement from the University of Cambridge about Dr. Aleksandr Kogan," University of Cambridge, March 23, 2018, https:// www.cam.ac.uk/notices/news/statement-from-the-university-of-cambridge -about-dr-aleksandr-kogan.

141 **data for eighty-seven million Facebook users**: Cecilia Kang and Sheera Frenkel, "Facebook Says Cambridge Analytica Harvested Data of Up to 87 Million Users," *New York Times*, April 4, 2018.

141 **in the United States**: Tom Cheshire, "Behind the Scenes at Donald Trump's Digital War Room," *Sky News*, October 22, 2016, https://news.sky.com/story /behind-the-scenes-at-donald-trumps-uk-digital-war-room-10626155.

141 **eventually fined Facebook $5 billion**: "FTC Imposes $5 Billion Penalty and Sweeping New Privacy Restrictions on Facebook," Federal Trade Commission, July 24, 2019, https://www.ftc.gov/news-events/news/press-releases/2019/07 /ftc-imposes-5-billion-penalty-sweeping-new-privacy-restrictions-facebook.

143 **we define prospection as**: See Introduction by Peter Railton to Martin E. P. Seligman, Peter Railton, Roy F. Baumeister, and Chandra Sripada, *Homo Prospectus* (New York: Oxford University Press, 2016); Dan Gilbert and Tim Wilson, "Prospection: Experiencing the Future," *Science* 317, no. 5843 (September 7, 2007): 1351–54; Randy L. Buckner and Daniel C. Carroll, "Self-Projection and the Brain," *Trends in Cognitive Sciences* 11, no. 2 (February 2007): 49–57.

143 **envision and plan for the future**: Seligman et al., *Homo Prospectus*.

144 **Prospective ability also correlates**: Andrew Reece et al., "The Future-Minded Leader," BetterUp Annual Report, 2022, https://grow.betterup .com/resources/future-minded-leader. See also Austin Eubanks, Andrew Reece, Alex Liebscher, Ayelet Meron Ruscio, Roy Baumeister, and Martin Seligman, "Pragmatic Prospection Is Linked with Positive Life and Workplace Outcomes," PsyArXiv Preprints, May 17, 2022, https://doi.org/10.31234 /osf.io/af9hj.

145 **teams whose leaders score higher in prospection**: Andrew Reece et al., "The Future-Minded Leader," https://grow.betterup.com/resources/future -minded-leader.

145 **33% less likely to quit**: For more on the personal and professional benefits of prospection, see Austin Eubanks et al., "Pragmatic Prospection Is Linked with Positive Life and Workplace Outcomes," PsyArXiv Preprints, May 17, 2022, https://doi.org/10.31234/osf.io/af9hj.

146 **6,600 emergency calls went nowhere**: "April 2014 Multistate 911 Outage: Cause and Impact," FCC, *Public Safety Docket No 14-72*, October 2014.

147 **our mental downtime**: Randy L. Buckner, Jessica R. Andrews-Hanna, and Daniel L. Schacter, "The Brain's Default Network: Anatomy, Function, and Relevance to Disease," *Annals of the New York Academy of Sciences* 1124 (March 2008): 1–38.

148 **not stasis but vibrant activity**: Marcus E. Raichle and Abraham Z. Snyder, "A Default Mode of Brain Function: A Brief History of an Evolving Idea," *NeuroImage* 37, no. 4 (October 2007): 1083–90; discussion 1097–99.

148 **as when we daydream**: Jessica R. Andrews-Hanna, Jay S. Reidler, Christine Huang, and Randy L. Buckner, "Evidence for the Default Network's Role in Spontaneous Cognition," *Journal of Neurophysiology* 104, no. 1 (May 2010): 322–35; Kalina Christoff, Alan M. Gordon, Jonathan Smallwood, Rachelle Smith, and Jonathan W. Schooler, "Experience Sampling during fMRI Reveals Default Network and Executive System Contributions to Mind Wandering," *Proceedings of the National Academy of Sciences of the United States of America* 106, no. 21 (May 26, 2009): 8719–24; Malia F. Mason, Michael I. Norton, John D. Van Horn, Daniel M. Wegner, Scott Grafton, and C. Neil Macrae, "Wandering Minds: The Default Network and Stimulus-Independent Thought," *Science* 315, no. 5810 (January 19, 207): 393–5.

148 **"patterns, generalizations, interpretations, and insights"**: Chandra Sripada, chapter 4 in Seligman et al., *Homo Prospectus*.

149 **shifts away from daydreaming**: Xiao-Fei Yang, Julia Bossmann, Birte Schiffhauer, Matthew Jordan, and Mary Helen Immordino-Yang, "Intrinsic Default Mode Network Connectivity Predicts Spontaneous Verbal Descriptions of Autobiographical Memories during Social Processing," *Frontiers in Psychology* 3 (2012): 592; Kun Wang, Chunsui Yu, Lijuan Xu, Wen Qin, Kuncheng Li, Lin Xu, and Tianzi Jaing, "Offline Memory Reprocessing: Involvement of the Brain's Default Network in Spontaneous Thought Processes," *PLOS ONE* 4 (March 2009): e4867.

150 **To address his conundrum**: Roy F. Baumeister, Kathleen D. Vohs, and Gabriele Oettingen, "Pragmatic Prospection: How and Why People Think about the Future," *Review of General Psychology* 20, no. 1 (March 2016): 3–16.

152 **to address this difficulty**: Ann Marie Roepke, Lizbeth Benson, Eli Tsukayama, and David Bryce Yaden, "Prospective Writing: Randomized Controlled Trial of an Intervention for Facilitating Growth after Adversity," *Journal of Positive Psychology* 13, no. 6 (2018): 627–42, https://doi.org/0.1080/17439760.2017.1365161.

153 **work backwards toward plans for preparation**: J. Peter Scoblic, "Learning from the Future: How to Make Robust Strategy in Times of Deep Uncertainty," *Harvard Business Review*, July–August 2020, 38–47.

159 **this correction happened without dampening**: Austin Eubanks, Andrew Reece, Alex Liebscher, and Roy Baumeister, "Enforcing Pragmatic Future-

Mindedness Cures the Innovator's Bias," PsyArXiv Preprints, May 16, 2022, https://psyarxiv.com/59ma8/.

159 **the beginnings of a new, specific intervention**: A single series of studies does not establish a new cognitive bias, but it does start to outline a potential stumbling block for all of us as prospectors, as well as a novel way around it.

160 **Vice President of Design Margaret Stewart**: Margaret Stewart, "Breadth and Depth: Why I'm Optimistic about Facebook's Responsible Innovation Efforts," Facebook, June 17, 2021, https://tech.fb.com/responsible-innovation/.

161 **"we are building responsibly"**: Ina Fried, "Scoop: Facebook Hire Aims to Infuse Ethics into Product Design," *Axios*, Feb 27, 2020.

CHAPTER NINE: WHEN WE ARE ALL CREATIVES

163 **The arrival of AI**: "A Conversation with Kai-Fu Lee," *Edge*, March 26, 2018, https://www.edge.org/conversation/kai_fu_lee-we-are-here-to-create.

165 **what it had been in April 2019**: "Covid-19 Pandemic: Observations on the Ongoing Recovery of the Aviation Industry," US Government Accountability Office, October 21, 2021, https://www.gao.gov/products/gao-22-104429.

167 **The airline had invested**: Zach Schonbrun, "For Some Flight Attendants, Shtick Comes with the Safety Spiel," *New York Times*, May 23, 2016, https://www.nytimes.com/2016/05/24/business/elvis-airlines-flight-attendants-passengers.html.

168 **"express your creativity"**: Hannah Sampson, "Southwest's Plan to Conquer the Airline Industry, One Joke at a Time," *Washington Post*, October 16, 2019, https://www.washingtonpost.com/travel/2019/10/16/southwests-plan-conquer-airline-industry-one-joke-time/.

169 **Useful and desirable for an audience**: D. K. Simonton, "Defining Creativity: Don't We Also Need to Define What Is Not Creative?" *Journal of Creative Behavior* 52, no. 1 (March 2018): 80–90.

170 **innovation will be a critical work skill**: "The Future of Jobs Report 2020," https://www3.weforum.org/docs/WEF_Future_of_Jobs_2020.pdf; Manyika et al., "Jobs Lost, Jobs Gained: What the Future of Work Will Mean for Jobs, Skills, and Wages."

170 **News outposts today use bots**: Luke Dormehl, "Bye Humans! The *Washington Post* Is Using a Robot to Report on the Rio Olympics," *Digital Trends*, August 8, 2016, https://www.digitaltrends.com/cool-tech/ai-olympic-writer/.

170 **AI-generated blogs . . . to replace human content**: The proliferation of these firms has been remarkably rapid in the last few years, in part thanks to the talents of GPT-3. Writesonic, INK, Jasper, Copymatic, Frase, Rytr, Copy.ai, AI Writer, and Hyperwrite are examples, as of this writing.

172 **fantasizing about the future**: Oshin Vartanian, "Neuroscience of Creativity" in *The Cambridge Handbook of Creativity*, James Kaufman and Robert Sternberg, eds. (Cambridge: Cambridge University Press, 2019), 156.

172 **creative problem to be solved**: Vartanian, "Neuroscience of Creativity," 157.

173 **Daniel Kahneman in his book**: Daniel Kahneman, *Thinking, Fast and Slow* (New York: Farrar, Straus and Giroux, 2013).

173 **creation can feel mysterious or romantic**: For a superb review of the literature on conscious vs. unconscious creativity, see Roy Baumeister, Brandon J. Schmeichel, and C. Nathan DeWall, "Creativity and Consciousness: Evidence from Psychology Experiments" in *The Philosophy of Creativity: New Essays*, Elliot Samuel Paul and Scott Barry Kaufman, eds. (New York: Oxford University Press, 2014), 185–98.

173–74 **"Consciousness puts them together"**: Roy Baumeister et al., "Creativity and Consciousness: Evidence from Psychology Experiments" in *The Philosophy of Creativity: New Essays*, 185–98.

174 **to a lesser degree than, for example, one's mood**: Research coming out of the laboratory of our colleague Dr. Sonja Lyubomirsky has been particularly promising in demonstrating that introversion and extraversion can be changed. For example, Seth Margolis and Sonja Lyubomirsky, "Experimental Manipulation of Extraverted and Introverted Behavior and Its Effects on Well-Being," *Journal of Experimental Psychology: General* 149, no. 4 (2020): 719–31.

175 **"the core of the creative personality"**: Victoria C. Oleynick et al., "Openness/Intellect: The Core of the Creative Personality" in Gregory J. Feist, Ronnie Reiter-Palmon, and James C. Kaufman, eds., *The Cambridge Handbook of Creativity and Personality Research* (Cambridge: Cambridge University Press, 2017), 9–27.

175 **people with high degrees of openness**: Roger E. Beaty, Scott Barry Kaufman, Mathias Benedek, Rex E. Jung, Yoed N. Kenett, Emanuel Jauk, Aljoscha C. Neubauer, and Paul J. Silvia, "Personality and Complex Brain Networks: The Role of Openness to Experience in Default Network Efficiency," *Human Brain Mapping* 37, no. 2 (February 2016): 773–79.

175 **Dopamine is one of the neurotransmitters**: Linh C. Dang, James P. O'Neill and William J. Jagust, "Dopamine Supports Coupling of Attention-Related Networks," *Journal of Neuroscience* 32, no. 28 (July 11, 2012): 9582–87, https://doi.org/10.1523/JNEUROSCI.0909-12.2012.

175 **significant genetic variation in numbers of dopamine receptors**: The dopamine receptor DRD4 has been shown to be involved in creative fluency and originality. Genetic variation of the dopamine receptor known as DRD2 has also been implicated in creative potential. Greater densities of DRD2 in the part of the brain known as the thalamus has been shown to predict creative fluency. Finally, a gene, DAT, connected to the transportation of dopamine, has been implicated in the originality of ideas. See Baptiste Barbot and Henry Eff, "The Genetic Basis of Creativity" in *The Cambridge Handbook of Creativity*, James Kaufman and Robert Sternberg, eds. (Cambridge: Cambridge

University Press, 2019), 135–39; Colin G. DeYoung, Dante Cicchetti, Fred A. Rogosch, Jeremy R. Gray, Maria Eastman, and Elena L. Grigorenko, "Sources of Cognitive Exploration: Genetic Variation in the Prefrontal Dopamine System Predicts Openness/Intellect," *Journal of Research in Personality* 45, no. 4 (August 2011): 364–71.

176 **dopamine, in new ideas**: Tanja Sophie Schweizer, "The Psychology of Novelty-Seeking, Creativity, and Innovation: Neurocognitive Aspects within a Work-Psychological Perspective," *Creativity and Innovation Management* 15, no. 2 (June 2006): 164–72.

176 *nothing to do with genetics*: R. A. Power and M. Pluess, "Heritability Estimates of the Big Five Personality Traits Based on Common Genetic Variants," *Translational Psychiatry* 5, no. 7 (July 14, 2015): e604; see also Baptiste Barbot and Henry Eff, "The Genetic Basis of Creativity," in *The Cambridge Handbook of Creativity*, 132–47.

176 **cognitive agility**: Josh Allen, "Conceptualizing Learning Agility and Investigating its Nomological Network," *FIU Electronic Theses and Dissertations* (2016), 2575. https://digitalcommons.fiu.edu/etd/2575.

176 **to focus where we need to**: Mathias Benedek and Emanuel Jauk, "Creative and Cognitive Control" in *The Cambridge Handbook of Creativity*, James Kaufman and Robert Sternberg, eds. (Cambridge: Cambridge University Press, 2019), 200–23.

176 **positive moods stimulate creativity**: Matthijs Baas, "In the Mood for Creativity" in *The Cambridge Handbook of Creativity*, James Kaufman and Robert Sternberg, eds. (Cambridge: Cambridge University Press, 2019), 265.

176 **emotional regulation**: Zorana Ivcevic and Jessica Hoffman, "Emotions and Creativity" in *The Cambridge Handbook of Creativity*, James Kaufman and Robert Sternberg, eds. (Cambridge: Cambridge University Press, 2019), 283.

177 **creative self-efficacy for students**: Robert J. Sternberg, "Enhancing People's Creativity" in *The Cambridge Handbook of Creativity*, James Kaufman and Robert Sternberg, eds. (Cambridge: Cambridge University Press, 2019), 132–47.

177 **18% more creative**: Alexis Jeannotte, Erin Eatough, and Gabriella Kellerman, "Resilience in an Age of Uncertainty," BetterUp 2020, https://grow.betterup.com/resources/resilience-in-an-age-of-uncertainty.

178 **diminish, rather than increase, creative output**: Theresa Amabile, "How to Kill Creativity," *Harvard Business Review*, September 1998, https://hbr.org/1998/09/how-to-kill-creativity.

178 **strongest predictors of well-being and performance**: R. M. Ryan and E. L. Deci, "Self-Determination Theory and the Facilitation of Intrinsic Motivation, Social Development, and Well-Being," *The American Psychologist* 55, no. 1 (January 1, 2000): 68–78.

179 **with an apple falling on Newton's head**: James Gleick, *Isaac Newton* (New York: Pantheon, 2003).

182 **Whitney failed . . . before finally succeeding**: Christopher Roser, *"Faster, Better, Cheaper" in the History of Manufacturing* (New York: Productivity Press, 2016); "The Factory," Eli Whitney Museum and Workshop, www.eliwhitney .org/museum/about-eli-whitney/factory.

182 **ten thousand years to complete**: Frank Arute et al., "Quantum Supremacy Using a Programmable Superconducting Processor," *Nature* 574 (October 23, 2019): 505–10.

183 **"That was the curious incident"**: Arthur Conan Doyle, *Silver Blaze* (Memoirs of Sherlock Holmes Book 1), 1892.

185 **doing $45 billion in revenue in 2020**: Todd Bishop, "Amazon Web Services Posts Record $13.5B in *Profits* for 2020 in Andy Jassy's AWS Swan Song," *Geek Wire*, February 2, 2021, https://www.geekwire.com/2021/amazon-web -services-posts-record-13-5b-profits-2020-andy-jassys-aws-swan-song/. See also Brandon Butler, "The Myth about How Amazon's Web Service Started Just Won't Die," *Network World*, March 2, 2015.

185 **$28 billion**: "Salesforce Signs Definitive Agreement to Acquire Slack," Salesforce Press Release, December 1, 2020, https://investor.salesforce.com /press-releases/press-release-details/2020/Salesforce-Signs-Definitive -Agreement-to-Acquire-Slack.

185 **radically different from what the rest of us see today**: Megan L. Meyer, Hal E. Hershfield, Adam G. Waytz, Judith N. Mildner, and Diana I. Tamir, "Creative Expertise Is Associated with Transcending the Here and Now," *Journal of Personality and Social Psychology* 116, no. 4 (April 2019): 483–94, https://doi.org/10.1037/pspa0000148.

185 **"this final product of my brain"**: Nicolai Tesla, "My Inventions I: My Early Life," 1919, https://teslauniverse.com/nikola-tesla/articles/my-inventions-i -my-early-life.

185 **Among Tesla's distal brain children**: Tesla Science Center, https:// teslasciencecenter.org/nikola-tesla-inventions/.

186 **cryptographer David Chaum**: David Chaum, "Blind Signatures for Untraceable Payments," *Advances in Cryptology Proceedings of Crypto* 82 (1983): 199–203.

186 **acquire PayPal in 2002**: "Timeline of Paypal," Wikipedia, https://en .wikipedia.org/wiki/Timeline_of_PayPal; "PayPal," Wikipedia, https:// en.wikipedia.org/wiki/PayPal.

186 **PayPal usage now outstripped its initial use case**: Brian O'Connell, "History of PayPal: Timeline and Facts," *The Street*, August 26, 2019.

186 **$25 billion**: "PayPal Holdings Revenue 2013–2022," MacroTrends.net, accessed May 2, 2022, https://www.macrotrends.net/stocks/charts/PYPL /paypal-holdings/revenue.

187 **The buyer is not yet ready**: This distrust is the topic of academic and commercial research. Matthew Hutson, "People Don't Trust Driverless Cars. Researchers Are Trying to Change That," *Science*, December 14, 2017, https://

www.science.org/content/article/people-don-t-trust-driverless-cars-researchers
-are-trying-change.

187 **Truly driverless operation**: See, for example, "Autopilot and Full Self-
Driving Capability," Tesla.com, https://www.tesla.com/support/autopilot.
"Full autonomy" is not yet commercially available to Tesla drivers, but this
page explains how and when it will become so and offers "autopilot" as a less
autonomous alternative to "fully self-driving."

187 **the creative pair**: Joshua Wolf Shenk, *Powers of Two: Finding the Essence of
Innovation in Creative Pairs* (Boston: Houghton Mifflin Harcourt, 2014).

188 **all emerged through collective elaboration**: Walter Isaacson, *The Innovators:
How a Group of Hackers, Geniuses and Geeks Created the Digital Revolution* (New
York: Simon & Schuster, 2015). See also Steven Johnson's *Where Good Ideas
Come From,* chapter 3 (New York: Riverhead Books, 2010) on the importance
of intellectual connectivity.

188 **when skill and knowledge sets complement each other**: Simon Rodan
and Charles Galunic, "More than Network Structure: How Knowledge
Heterogeneity Influences Managerial Performance and Innovation," *Strategic
Management Journal* 25, no. 6 (June 2004): 541–62.

188 **a team with a broad set of experiences**: Stuart A. Kauffman, "Approaches
to the Origin of Life on Earth," *Life* 1, no. 1 (December 2011): 34–48. We
also recommend Steven Johnson's *Where Good Ideas Come From* for a brilliant
exposition of the history of innovation as the recombination of neighboring
ideas.

188 **exhibited by successful creative teams**: Roni Reiter-Palmon, Kevin
S. Mitchell, and Ryan Royston, "Improving Creativity in Organizational
Settings" in *The Cambridge Handbook of Creativity*, James Kaufman and Robert
Sternberg, eds. (Cambridge: Cambridge University Press, 2019), 519.

188 **more effective evaluation of creative ideas**: Reiter-Palmon, Mitchell, and
Royston, "Improving Creativity," 519.

188–89 **third key feature**: Reiter-Palmon, Mitchell, and Royston, "Improving
Creativity," 519.

189 **higher psychological safety produces better team learning**: Amy
Edmondson, "Psychological Safety and Learning Behavior in Work Teams,"
Administrative Science Quarterly 44, no. 2 (June 1999): 350–83; Amy C.
Edmondson and Zhike Lei, "Psychological Safety: The History, Renaissance,
and Future of an Interpersonal Construct," *Annual Review of Organizational
Psychology and Organizational Behavior* 1, no. 1 (March 2014): 23–43.

190 **Definitions of success**: Michael D. Mumford, Robert W. Martin, Samantha
Elliott, and Tristan McIntosh, "Leading for Creativity" in *The Cambridge
Handbook of Creativity*, James Kaufman and Robert Sternberg, eds. (Cambridge:
Cambridge University Press, 2019), 552.

190 **we often focus on . . . prospection**: Rebecca L. McMillan, Scott Barry Kaufman, and Jerome L. Singer, "Ode to Positive Constructive Daydreaming," *Frontiers in Psychology* 4 (September 2013): 626.

192 **not conscious**: We have intentionally skirted the depths of the controversy over the term "unconscious" here, and use it simply to mean *nonconscious*. For a fuller, evidence-based exposition of the difference between conscious and unconscious states, and what we do and don't know about them today, we recommend Jonathan Schooler, Michael Mrazek, Benjamin Baird, and Piotr Winkielman, "Minding the Mind: The Value of Distinguishing among Unconscious, Conscious, and Metaconscious Processes," *APA Handbook of Personality and Social Psychology* 1 (2015), 179–202.

193 **tunnel vision that can result**: Robert J. Sternberg, "Enhancing People's Creativity" in *The Cambridge Handbook of Creativity*, James Kaufman and Robert Sternberg, eds. (Cambridge: Cambridge University Press, 2019), 132–47.

194 **produce more creative work**: R. J. Sternberg and W. M. Williams, "Teaching for Creativity: Two Dozen Tips" in R. D. Small and A. P. Thomas, eds., *Plain Talk about Education* (Covington, LA: Center for Development and Learning, 2001), 153–65; Ginamarie Scott, Lyle E. Leritz and Michael D. Mumford, "The Effectiveness of Creativity Training: A Quantitative Review," *Creativity Research Journal* 16, no. 4 (2004): 361–88.

194 **the web can be a friend, not a foe**: See Johnson, *Where Good Ideas Come From*.

195 **follow it with downtime**: Benedek and Jauk, "Creative and Cognitive Control" in *The Cambridge Handbook of Creativity*, 212.

195 **Of all four conditions**: Benjamin Baird, Jonathan Smallwood, Michael Mrazek, Julia W. Y. Kam, Michael S. Franklin, and Jonathan Schooler, "Inspired by Distraction: Mind-Wandering Facilitates Creative Incubation," *Psychological Science* 23, no. 10 (August 2012): 1117–22.

196 **it will undermine creative mind-wandering**: Jonathan W. Schooler, Michael Mrazek, Michael Franklin, Claire Zedelius, James Broadway, Benjamin Mooneyham, and Benjamin Baird, "The Middle Way: Finding the Balance between Mindfulness and Mind-Wandering" in Brian H. Ross, ed., *The Psychology of Learning and Motivation*, vol. 60 (Cambridge, MA: Academic Press, 2014), 1–33.

196 **creativity interventions in schools**: Robert J. Sternberg, "Enhancing People's Creativity" in *The Cambridge Handbook of Creativity*, James Kaufman and Robert Sternberg, eds., (Cambridge: Cambridge University Press, 2019), 132–47; see also R. J. Sternberg, "Teaching for Creativity," in *Nurturing Creativity in the Classroom*, eds. Ronald A. Beghetto and James C. Kaufman (Cambridge, UK: Cambridge University Press, 2010), 394–414.

199 **leverage for improving the creativity of teams**: Kamal Birdi, "A Lighthouse in the Desert? Evaluating the Effects of Creativity Training on Employee Innovation," *Journal of Creative Behavior* 41, no. 4 (December 2007).

199 **"The principal limitation on what creative people can accomplish"**: Paula Tierney and Steven M. Farmer, "Creative Self-Efficacy Development

and Creative Performance Over Time," *Journal of Applied Psychology* 96, no. 2 (March 2011): 277–93.

200 **Honor the thinking**: Reiter-Palmon, Mitchell, and Royston, "Improving Creativity," 524–5.

200 **Managers must not dampen**: Reiter-Palmon, Mitchell, and Royston, "Improving Creativity," 535.

200 **access to a broader set of ideas**: Michael Arena, *Adaptive Space* (New York: McGraw-Hill, 2018).

201 **Firm-level creative "hygiene"**: Davide Ravasi and Majken Schultz, "Responding to Organizational Identity Threats: Exploring the Role of Organizational Culture," *Academy of Management Journal* 49, no. 3 (June 2006): 433–58.

203 **creativity is a core leadership skill**: "New Year, New Leadership: 5 Skills Needed to Succeed in 2021," *Adobe Experience Blog*, Adobe, January 28, 2021, https://business.adobe.com/blog/perspectives/new-year-new-leadership-5-skills -needed-to-succeed-in-2021.

CHAPTER TEN: FUTURE-PROOFING THE WORKFORCE

205 **ailing father and infant son**: The details of Aggie Dunn's life are drawn from several sources, which contain slightly conflicting information on dates. See Nikki Mandell, *The Corporation as Family* (Chapel Hill: UNC Press, 2002); Frank Miller and Mary Ann Coghill, "Sex and the Personnel Manager," *Industrial and Labor Relations Review* 18, no. 1 (1964): 32–44; Dale A. Masi, "The History of Employee Assistance Programs in the US," Employee Assistance Research Foundation, 2020, https://www.eapassn.org/Portals/11 /Docs/EAP%20History/The_History_of_EAPs_in_the_US.pdf.

206 **"and they understood me"**: Nikki Mandell, *The Corporation as Family* (Chapel Hill: UNC Press, 2002).

206 **in her honor**: Robert C. Alberts, "The Good Provider, HJ Heinz and His 57 Varieties," *The Western Pennsylvania Historical Magazine* 56, no. 4 (1973); "Today in History: November 24, 1924," *Holland Sentinel,* November 24, 2014.

208 **benefiting from the offering**: "How Can We Promote Our EAP to Increase Its Usage," Mental Health America, accessed May 10, 2022, https:// mhanational.org/how-can-we-promote-our-eap-increase-its-usage.

211 **minimize their effectiveness**: Roberta Holland, "Companies Waste Billions of Dollars on Ineffective Corporate Training," *Forbes*, July 25, 2016, https:// www.forbes.com/sites/hbsworkingknowledge/2016/07/25/companies-waste -billions-of-dollars-on-ineffective-corporate-training.

211 **Corporations in G20 countries**: Philipp Kolo, Rainer Strack, Philippe Cavat, Roselinde Torres, and Vikram Bhalla, "Corporate Universities: An Engine for Human Capital," Boston Consulting Group, July 18, 2013, https://www.bcg

.com/publications/2013/people-organization-corporate-universities-engine
-human-capital.

212 **owner of the same work**: "Good HR, Bad HR: Silo Mentalities and
Communities of Practice," *Human Resource Management International Digest* 26,
no. 2 (March 2018): 38–40.

212 **stress counseling**: "SHRM's Guide to Employee Assistance Programs,"
Society for Human Resource Management, https://www.shrm.org
/resourcesandtools/hr-topics/employee-relations/pages/eap-buyers-guide.aspx.

218 **"belong to something greater than themselves"**: "We've All Heard of IQ
and EQ. But What Is Your CQ—Your 'Crisis Quotient?' " Strategic CHRO
Interview with Laura Fuentes, ExCo Leadership + Performance, May 31, 2022,
https://www.excoleadership.com/articles/weve-all-heard-of-iq-and-eq-but
-what-is-your-cq-your-crisis-quotient/.

219 **our forebears marshalled major educational reforms**: In 1910, in the last
stages of the Industrial Revolution, just 9% of Americans had a high school
diploma, a percentage that equates to about eight million people at that time.
Most teenagers worked. They had to support their families, and there weren't
enough high schools to go around. The shortage cut both ways: Growth in
retail, corporate, and service sectors was fueling labor demands for white-
collar workers. But there weren't enough of them available, either, because of
the lack of high schools. Change began locally. In 1925, local governments
raised over 75% of the funding for primary and secondary education, with the
rest coming from state, county, and federal budgets. Legislation helped speed
things along: tuition laws, compelling towns without high schools to pay for
their residents to learn elsewhere; compulsory education laws; and child labor
laws. In just thirty years, the number of Americans graduating secondary
school grew by more than 800%. By 1940, more than 50% of Americans—
roughly 66 million people—had a high school diploma. See Thomas D.
Snyder, "120 Years of American Education: A Statistical Portrait," U.S.
Department of Education, Office of Educational Research and Improvement,
National Center for Education Statistics, Washington, D.C., January 19, 1993;
"US High School Graduation Rates," Safe and Civil Schools, https://www
.safeandcivilschools.com/research/graduation_rates.php.

CONCLUSION

221 **associated drop in GDP of 6–8%**: Robert J. Barro, José F. Ursúa, and Joanna
Weng, "The Coronavirus and the Great Influenza Pandemic: Lessons from
the 'Spanish Flu' for the Coronavirus's Potential Effects on Mortality and
Economic Activity," NBER Working Paper No. 26866, March 2020, revised
April 2020, https://www.nber.org/system/files/working_papers/w26866/w
26866.pdf.

221 **contemporaneous world of work**: Other, older pandemics may well have
had a more significant impact on labor transformations. For example, the
Black Death is believed to have created such a significant labor shortage that

it empowered workers to ask for better conditions. Christine Johnson, "How the Black Death Made Life Better," Washington University Department of History, June 18, 2021, https://history.wustl.edu/news/how-black-death -made-life-better.

222 **three key trends:** "The Future of Work after Covid-19," McKinsey Global Institute, February 18, 2021.

222 **death rates increase by 50–100%:** Daniel Sullivan and Till von Wachter, "Job Displacement and Mortality: An Analysis Using Administrative Data," *The Quarterly Journal of Economics* 124, no. 3 (August 2009): 1265–1306.

222 **Suicide, depression, substance abuse, and anxiety:** Wolfram Kawohl and Carlos Nordt, "COVID-19, Unemployment, and Suicide," *The Lancet Psychiatry*, 7, no. 5 (May 1, 2020): 389–90; Karsten Paul and Klaus Moser, "Unemployment Impairs Mental Health: Meta-Analyses," *Journal of Vocational Behavior* 74, no. 3 (June 2009): 264–82; Allison Milner, A. Page, and Anthony D. LaMontagne, "Cause and Effect in Studies on Unemployment, Mental Health and Suicide: A Meta-Analytic and Conceptual Review," *Psychological Medicine* 44, no. 5: 909–17.

222 **essential workers, and mothers:** Nirmita Panchal, Rabah Kamal, Cynthia Cox, and Rachel Garfield, "The Implications of COVID-19 for Mental Health and Substance Use," Kaiser Family Foundation, February 10, 2021, https:// www.kff.org/coronavirus-Covid-19/issue-brief/the-implications-of-Covid-19 -for-mental-health-and-substance-use/.

224 **We spend, globally:** Philipp Kolo, R. Strack, Philippe Cavat, R. Torres, and Vikram Bhalla, "Corporate Universities: An Engine for Human Capital," Boston Consulting Group, July 18, 2013.

224 **$15,000 per employee per year for those employees struggling with mental illness:** "New Mental Health Cost Calculator Shows Why Investing in Mental Health is Good for Business," National Safety Council, May 13, 2021, https://www.nsc.org/newsroom/new-mental-health-cost-calculator -demonstrates-why; Angelica LaVito, "Anxiety Is Expensive: Employee Mental Health Costs Rise Twice as Fast as All Other Medical Expenses," CNBC, September 27, 2018.

225 **"tending to influence principle in all human beings":** Abraham Maslow, *Maslow on Management* (Hoboken, NJ: Wiley, 1998), 21. Originally titled *Eupsychian Management: A Journal.*

Index

About the Authors

GABRIELLA ROSEN KELLERMAN, MD, has served as chief product officer and chief innovation officer at BetterUp, founding CEO of LifeLink, former executive at Castlight Health, and an advisor to healthcare, coaching, and behavior-change technology companies. Trained in psychiatry and fMRI research, she holds an MD with honors from Mount Sinai School of Medicine and a BA summa cum laude from Harvard University. Her work has been published and featured in *The Atlantic*, *Harvard Business Review*, *Inc.*, *Forbes*, *JAMA*, and many more. *Tomorrowmind* is her first book.

MARTIN SELIGMAN, PhD, is a professor at the University of Pennsylvania, director of the Positive Psychology Center, and former president of the American Psychological Association. He received his BA in philosophy from Princeton University and his PhD in psychology from the University of Pennsylvania and holds ten honorary doctorates. He was named the most influential psychologist in the world by Academic Influence. Along with writing for numerous scholarly publications and appearing in the *New York Times*, *Time*, *Newsweek*, and many others, he is also the author and coauthor of more than thirty books, including *Flourish*, *Authentic Happiness*, and *Tomorrowmind*.